PEOPLE OF PARADOX

PEOPLE
OF PARADOX

*An Inquiry
Concerning the Origins of
American Civilization*

❧ · ❧

by Michael Kammen

VINTAGE BOOKS
A Division of Random House
New York

FIRST VINTAGE BOOKS EDITION, September 1973

Copyright © 1972 by Michael Kammen

All rights reserved under International and
Pan-American Copyright Conventions.
Published in the United States by Random House, Inc.,
New York, and simultaneously in Canada by
Random House of Canada Limited, Toronto.
Originally published by Alfred A. Knopf, Inc., in 1972.

Grateful acknowledgment is extended to Lionel Trilling for permission to quote from *The Liberal Imagination: Essays on Literature and Society*, Doubleday Anchor edition, 1950; to Cambridge University Press for a quotation from Clayton Robert's *The Growth of Responsible Government in Stuart England*, 1966; to W. W. Norton & Co., Inc., for a quotation from Erik Erikson's *Childhood and Society*, 2nd edition, 1963, Copyright 1950, © 1963 by W. W. Norton & Company, Inc.; to Charles Scribner's Sons for a quotation from Jacques Maritain's *Reflections on America*, 1958; to The Clarendon Press, Oxford, for a quotation from Laurence Stone's *The Crisis of the Aristocracy*, 1965; to Little, Brown and Company for permission to reprint the poem "England Experts" by Ogden Nash from *Verses from 1929*, Copyright 1936 by the Curtis Publishing Co.; to Appleton-Century-Crofts, Educational Division, Meredith Corporation, for a quotation from Carl Becker's "Everyman His Own Historian," Copyright 1935 by F. S. Crofts; to Charles Scribner's Sons for a quotation from George Santayana's *Character and Opinion in the United States*, 1920; to Alfred A. Knopf, Inc., for a quotation from Carl Becker's "Freedom and Responsibility in the American Way of Life," 1945; and to Holt, Rinehart and Winston, Inc., for permission to reprint "The Gift Outright" by Robert Frost from *The Poetry of Robert Frost*, edited by Edward Connery Lathes, Copyright 1942 by Robert Frost, Copyright © 1970 by Lesley Frost Ballantine.

Library of Congress Cataloging in Publication Data

Kammen, Michael G
    People of paradox.

    Reprint of the 1st ed. published by Knopf, New York.
    Includes bibliographical references.
        1. United States—Civilization—To 1783.
    2. National characteristics, American.   I. Title.
[E162.K2   1973]   917.3'03   73–6646
ISBN 0–394–71933–6

Manufactured in the United States of America

for Carol

Only in obedience I send you some of my paradoxes; I love you & myself & them too well to
send them willingly for they carry with them a
confession of their lightnesse & my shame. But
indeed they were made rather to deceave tyme
than her daughter truth.

—JOHN DONNE

CONTENTS

vii

PART THREE:
THE IMPLICATIONS OF BIFORMITY

ILLUSTRATIONS

PREFACE

WHEN AN AUTHOR completes a slender volume concerning a large and complex subject—a book of "significant trifles" was the phrase Galsworthy used—he is often tempted to write a wordy prologue in order to justify, qualify, or apologize for his efforts. Although I have tried to resist that temptation, I do feel compelled to remark upon the genesis, thrust, and structure of *People of Paradox;* for it came to be written partly by choice and partly by chance.

For quite some while now, and particularly during the past twenty-five years, many books about American culture and character have been published. Some of them are extremely perceptive and interesting; others naïve or foolish; and most of them tend to confirm Jacques Barzun's observation that "of all the books that no one can write, those about nations and national character are the most impossible." In reading the accumulated literature, I found again and again a pervasively static quality: examinations of things as they once were at a particular moment in time, or as they "now" are. Why, I wondered, were these efforts not more concerned with the ongoing dynamics of America's past, with the emergence of cultural tendencies in their historical context?

If the search for American civilization is indeed like a quest for the Arabian phoenix—it is said to exist, but no one knows where—then perhaps previous attempts have been based upon precarious premises. Perhaps what we require is an inquiry into the formative centuries of our past, when American history was really English history *d'outre-mer*, with our eyes open to the formation of a style, temper, and set of habits recognizably ancestral to and determinative of our own. One of the great virtues of examining the colonial period intensively, as the novelist John P. Marquand once mentioned, is that it enables us to see "the genius of America not dilute but in a saturate solution."

So I determined to make such an inquiry, and began looking at processes, products, and perceptions of change in the seventeenth- and eighteenth-century colonies. The more I looked, of course, the more I found (academic researchers being notorious for finding what they set out to locate). But eventually I also felt a little like the black Labrador puppy in a recent news note: "Mr. James Bercot was training his seven-month-old pup to retrieve by throwing a small cloth dummy into Puget Sound for the dog to fetch. On one toss, the dog dashed into the water and brought back an eight-foot octopus, a native denizen of the Sound but far from its usual deep-water habitat." Well, I too may have retrieved an octopus. To say the least, I have found more than I bargained for or expected when I first took the plunge. I would like to think also that my historical octopus, however unwieldy and elusive, is a native denizen of these shores, though hitherto obscure because wary and often well concealed.

The octopus image is actually an appropriate one for yet another, more important reason. A genus of cephalopod mollusks, the octopus has a look of complexity about it. Anything with eight undulating arms can hardly avoid it; so, too, with the chapters that follow. American historical writing, despite its richness and diversity, has often been simplistic and reductive in its explanatory efforts. Consequently, I have stressed complexity and multiplicity, although not, I hope, at the expense of clarity. Moreover, I do not regard *People of Paradox* as a study in social pathology. Rather, I have tried to unravel some tangled origins of a complex culture: the nature of its complexity, how it came to be that way, and some of the attendant dilemmas. American civilization has offered great opportunities; but it has also proffered importunities equally large. There is both grandeur and pettiness in the so-called American experience. Hence its interpreter must somehow be unambiguous about ambiguities, must see several sides of many questions without being ultimately indecisive in his conclusions.

This book has considerable traffic with ambiguities: with the simultaneity of enthusiasm and melancholy, Pollyanna and Cassandra, fatalistic optimism in the American style. Charles Dickens caught something of its essence in *Martin Chuzzlewit:*

> "You have come to visit our country, Sir, at a season of great commercial depression," said the major.
>
> "At an alarming crisis," said the colonel.
>
> "At a period of unprecedented stagnation," said Mr. Jefferson Brick.
>
> "I'm sorry to hear that," returned Martin. "It's not likely to last, I hope?"
>
> Martin knew nothing about America, or he would have known perfectly well that if its individual citizens, to a man, are to be believed, it always is depressed, and always is stagnated, and always is at an alarming crisis, and never was otherwise; though as a body they are ready to make oath upon the Evangelists at any hour of the day or night, that it is the most thriving and prosperous of all countries on the habitable globe.

I will be told, I suspect, that mine is a Manichean vision. Perhaps; but it might be more accurate to call it syncretistic. By that I mean to suggest the attempted reconciliation or union—by Americans historically, not by me alone—of different or opposing principles, practices, and parties. More on syncretism in Part Two.

What about the strategy and structure of this book? Both have posed difficulties which I still have not resolved to my own satisfaction. Prokofiev's *Peter and the Wolf* (1936) and Benjamin Britten's *The Young Person's Guide to the Orchestra* (1945) were written with the same end in view: to explicate and demonstrate the nature and function of symphonic music and instruments. Yet I find the former composition as delight-ful, sophisticated, and subtle as I find the latter repetitive, re-ductive, and mechanical. In *Peter and the Wolf*, each instru-ment has not only its own voice, but its own tune as well; so that in short order various leitmotifs evoke certain cerebral and emotional responses from the attentive listener. I have tried to profit from Prokofiev's example, and hope the reader will watch for the introduction, interaction, and configuration of certain discrete voices and themes. Perhaps he will thereby achieve with felicity what I took five years to grasp by serendipity.

More specifically, the structure of this book is sufficiently intricate for a brief guide to be in order. In the first chapter I try to locate my inquiry in the larger context of American historical writing: where I stand with respect to predecessors. In Chapters 2 and 3 I scrutinize colonial origins through two quite different filters—partially to achieve new perspectives, but also in order to provide the reader with conceptual tools he must have in order to comprehend Part Two (Chapters 4–6). Chapters 2 and 3 thus can stand as autonomous essays; but they are also essential for an understanding of the general problem posed in Chapter 4. Chapters 5 and 6 then present detailed specifications and explications of that problem, first in early modern England, then in colonial America. Chapter 7 takes a critical "moment" in our history, the Revolution, and views it in terms of the phenomenon discussed in Chapter 4, historical developments demonstrated in Chapter 6, and the explanatory apparatus offered earlier in Chapters 2 and 3. In brief, the structure of *People* is neither neatly chronological nor thoroughly thematic; but rather, an interweaving of both. Some readers may find it helpful to read Chapter 4 first, for it is ultimately the axle upon which the whole endeavor goes forward.

The pages that follow attempt to identify and isolate a cluster of major strands, place them in the broadest possible historical context, trace their emergence and development, and suggest some of their consequences for the grace of living in this land. Although *People* is primarily concerned with the seventeenth and eighteenth centuries, it has seemed worthwhile to indicate, at least briefly, the relationship of my themes to nineteenth- and twentieth-century realities. In some respects my knowledge of colonial times has helped me to understand the American style today; while in other areas the contemporary scene has enabled me to perceive tendencies in the colonies I might otherwise have missed. In short, through the years that I have lived with *People of Paradox* there has been what I must call a simultaneity of realization. I have tried to work forward from the determinants of culture, as well as backward from the expressions of culture. Consequently, historical knowledge, intuition, and experience have reinforced one another in ways I can no longer sort out. Therein, perhaps, lies the single-mindedness—and the whiggishness—of my themes, as well as my attempt to discuss the nineteenth and twentieth centuries in the final two chapters. In so doing I have tried to obviate the dilemma defined by the late William Faulkner: "the writer in America . . . is a little like the old court jester. He's supposed to speak his vicious paradoxes with some sense in them, but he isn't part of whatever fabric it is that makes a nation."

Ultimately my intention is explicitly this: to highlight the figure in the carpet. I view early American history as one would an oriental carpet with a busy and intricate design. A remarkable amount of recent work has made the warp and woof of that carpet much clearer than ever before; but the pattern, the inherent figure, has remained elusive. Some scholars may object that that last contention is overstated (even that there is no single figure), and that it demeans the work of industrious and intelligent colleagues. I hope not. For this book owes much to predecessors and contemporaries. I would like to think that I have somehow ravished their work without deflowering it. In any case, *People of Paradox* is meant to be exploratory, to be heuristic in stimulating interest as a means of furthering investigation. With Mr. Justice Holmes, I think that "there is nothing like a paradox to take the scum off your mind." And so, I would like to believe that my perception of the figure in the carpet is personal without being eccentric, creative without being cranky, and comprehensive while remaining comprehensible. *Dixi.*

THIS BOOK WAS CONCEIVED AND COMPLETED in Ithaca, New York, a place Miss Frances Perkins once called "the most centrally isolated spot on the eastern seaboard." Colleagues at Cornell University have provided help in many different ways; and I appreciate their encouragement as well as their diversity. My friends in the Research Club of Cornell gave me a responsive hearing in December 1970; and my students have listened with patience and responded with percipience over the years. In particular, Alvan R. Brick, Terry Dash, Douglas Greenberg, and Merete Staubo provided information and insight. Professors Sanford Budick of the English Department, John Reps and Michael Hugo-Brunt of the Department of City and Regional Planning answered many queries thoughtfully and patiently.

The Humanities Center of The Johns Hopkins University, the John Anson Kittredge Educational Fund (whose Board of Control is chaired by Walter Muir Whitehill), and the American Council of Learned Societies provided me in 1968–9 with fifteen months in which to read and think and begin to write under ideal circumstances. I am deeply obliged to those institutions, and to Professor Jack P. Greene for an invaluable year of conversation in Baltimore. Everett and Kinney Thiele provided a convenient and comfortable place to live that year. Significantly, when my wife and I settled in we found upon the bedroom wall an art nouveau poster proclaiming HALLE-LUJAH THE PILL! in tall white letters; but on the night table nearby a delightful squat brass stork from the Orient—a fertility token.

Sections of the book benefited from two stimulating colloquia concerned with the comparative history of colonization, one held at the University of Michigan in October 1968 and the other at Johns Hopkins University in May 1969. In March 1969, I presented some major themes of *People of Paradox* to colleagues at the Columbia University Faculty Seminar in

Early American History and Culture. Their friendly but penetrating suggestions came at a crucial moment for me, and I
am properly appreciative.

I am most grateful to a cluster of good friends who read
and candidly criticized the manuscript at several stages:
Michael J. Colacurcio, David M. Davidson, John Demos, Philip
J. Greven, Jr., Clive Holmes, Joseph F. Kett, Walter LaFeber,
F. J. Levy, Kenneth A. Lockridge, Mary Beth Norton, Fred
Somkin, and Mack Walker. With a volume of this sort, it is
particularly necessary to invoke the traditional caveat that they
are in no way responsible for the flaws of judgment and research which inevitably remain.

Sandy Huttleston and Roberta Ludgate prepared the final
typescript with good cheer. And two beloved ladies have helped
in more ways than I can now recollect or repay: my wife Carol
and my editor, Jane N. Garrett. Timidly I may say to them of
this book, as John Dryden did to his patron, the Earl of
Mulgrave: "some things in it have passed your approbation,
and many your amendment."

August 1971   MICHAEL KAMMEN

PART ONE

The Unrecorded Hum
of Implication

❧ · ☙

To accomplish this worke the whole maine
of my Industrie hath been imploid . . . with a
firme setled study of the truth . . . I right willingly acknowledge that I may erre much. Who
shooting all day long doth alwaies hit the mark?
There may be mistakings in regard of my unskil-
fulnes, for who is so skilfull that strugling with
Time in the foggie darke sea of Antiquity, may
not run upon rocks? It may be that I have been
misled by the credit of authors and others whom
I tooke to be most true, and worthy of credit. . . .
Others may be more skilfull and more exactly observe the particularities of the places where they
are conversant; if they, or any other, whosoever,
will advertise mee wherein I am mistaken, I will
amend it with manifold thankes . . . if it proceed
from good meaning, and not from a spirit of contradiction and quarrelling, which doe not befit
such as are well bred, and affect the truth.

WILLIAM CAMDEN, *Britannia* (1637)

PROLEGOMENON

> "Owl kept his head and told us that the opposite of an Introduction, my dear Pooh, was a Contradiction."
>
> A. A. MILNE, *The World of Pooh*

IN 1790, AT THE CLOSE of the colonial period and the beginning of the so-called Federal era, Mr. Noah Webster remarked that "our national character is not yet formed." He was wrong, I think; and I am sanguine about saying so because Frederick Jackson Turner and Henry Adams (who were both wise as well as professorial) believed that the fundamental components of American nationality had in fact been recognizably fashioned by the beginning of the nineteenth century. I am less sanguine, however, about the phrase "national character" because it implies for most people some singular ethos or mystique. Catching hold of such an ethos firmly by the tail is difficult enough with smaller societies such as Samoa, Sumatra, or Liechtenstein; with a large and heterogeneous people, it is well nigh impossible.

Therefore I prefer to talk about national *style*. Perhaps I am deceiving myself, if not others, by using an euphemism; but I really do believe that there are differences between style, which can be perceived, and character, which cannot. By style I simply mean the ways we clothe ourselves in certain social roles and emotional robes, the ways we respond to problems, relate to others, and recognize the realities within ourselves; the accommodations and compromises we make. Taken alto-

3

gether, an accumulation of "stylistic modes" just might lead toward an ontological approach to American history—a quest for its very being, its historic drive and destiny.

It is worth a try, I think, because only in a country where it is so unclear what is American do people worry so much about the threat of things "un-American." Most of us tend to assume, in some vague or vainglorious fashion, that our civilization is unique. But most of us also become uncomfortable when challenged to defend that assumption. My own view is that all national societies are unique, in some degree or in various ways, but that the United States may *also* be unique because of the very intensity and complexity of its uniqueness. Now that must sound like a bit of gibberish, so let me illustrate what I mean. Australia, like the United States, has been a nation of immigrants; but not of such extremely diverse immigrants in their national origins. Canada, like the United States, is a democracy; but it was not inevitably democratic from the outset (New France never enjoyed representative government) and achieved democracy rather late in its development. Brazil has extensive natural resources; but they have not been so readily accessible or usable as those of the United States. China has long had a remarkable sense of self and chosen-ness, like the United States; but has been much more exclusivist in its outlook, with attendant implications.

One way to begin to locate the genesis and genetics of our vaunted "genius," or uniqueness, as a civilization might be to think about the process of cultural transmission from the Old World to the New, for that process involved both attrition and accretion. What ultimately matters, I think, is the particular juxtaposition or interaction of attrition and accretion. That's fairly abstract; let me try to be more specific again.

Suppose we select four or five social institutions—such as the city, the family, the school, indentured servitude, and the religious sect—and ask what kinds of influences shaped the particular forms those institutions would take in colonial America. We find that the European original or prototype of the institution is determinative, as well as the particular environment encountered in North America, not to mention the impact of changes within that environment during the years of colonization and development. But even those factors are insufficient. We must also include the influx of ideas about these social institutions from changing European societies, and the altered attitudes of colonists toward traditional (and not always adaptable) institutions. Then we can consider what functions each institution performed in Europe, and ask whether those functions changed in a colonial setting (and if so, why). We can also ask which Europeans and Africans consciously sought to transplant their institutions intact, which regarded those institutions as defective (hoping to mold new ones), and which had little or no choice in the matter?

We begin, thereby, to view the pattern of institutional development in terms of what the biologist calls epigenesis—"the formation of an organic germ as a new product"—a theory that the germ is brought into existence by successive accretions and not merely developed in the process of reproduction. We can add yet another dimension of complexity, moreover, if we insist upon the importance of chronological variables. Just as heat, light, and mass are important variables to the physicist, chronological continuity is of crucial importance to the historian. The family had existed as a social institution for a very long time prior to English colonization, but Quakerism as a sect had not. Consequently, the sanctions and traditions of each would be affected differently in the wilderness.

Not surprisingly, we also find the course of institutional history flowing differently in diverse regions. In certain situations an altered consciousness caused men to change their social systems; in others, unplanned changes in their societies forced men to adjust their mind-sets; in still others, there must have been a near-coincidence of realization and rationalization. In New England, institutions were *relatively* stable and viable at the outset, but became less so with the passage of generations. In the southern and middle colonies, by contrast, institutions started out weak or nonexistent, but gradually grew in strength until, after a century, many were doing their jobs quite adequately. The impact of this contrast upon historians has been to give colonial New England the reputation of regression, and other regions the appearance of ascension.

Ever since the halcyon days of the "imperial school" of American historians, half a century ago, we have been accustomed to think about the colonies as "reflections" of British culture, as extensions of the English polity and society overseas. We have been conditioned against the whiggish fallacy of regarding the early settlements as progenitors of our own time and place, as seedlings of the mighty oak of democracy. Like little George Washington "barking" that poor cherry tree, historians Charles M. Andrews and George Louis Beer took the ax to George Bancroft's providential tree of uninterrupted growth. Well, provincial America—to muddle our metaphors —may have been more nearly a reflection of British culture than a garden for optimistic transcendentalists in search of roots; but I would prefer yet a third alternative to the oft-used images of roots and reflections. My preference, albeit less elegant, is for *refraction*, meaning to break the course of something, and turn it away from its direct line of continuity; "especially to deflect at a certain angle at the point of passage from one medium into another of different density." That, to me, is surely what must have happened to British culture in North America: refraction rather than reflection.

There is yet another notion about the historic relation between Europe and America that may be in need of revision. I am thinking of the provocative assumption, first offered by Professor Hartz in 1955, that because the United States never underwent a feudal phase it could not develop viable traditions of the right (or by subsequent reaction, the left). My uneasiness with Hartz's remarkable book, *The Liberal Tradition in America*, derives not so much from his nineteenth- and twentieth-century extrapolations, but from his implicit picture of the colonies. For America did not simply spring from the head of Zeus, fully grown. Although the colonies did not undergo medieval feudalism, it does not necessarily follow that they burst forth from swaddling clothes into modernity either.

I have an uncomfortable feeling about those historians for whom American history commences in the *annus mirabilis* 1776, or 1787, or 1815. Theirs is an "immaculate conception" approach, oblivious to a century and a half of prior fertilization, germination, gestation—the metaphor is infinitely flexible, and stretches us back once again to epigenesis. My own view is that the colonial period had many medieval characteristics, both figurative and literal, and hence much to be discarded and diffused before emerging into the bright glare of modernity. It might be instructive, therefore, to compare colonial America as the origins of a major civilization, with the beginnings of, say, Medieval Europe or Renaissance Italy. Doing so is a tricky business, of course, because in the latter two cases we are concerned with temporal differentiations in history: how one society or era develops sequentially or vertically in time from another. With the colonial origins of American civilization we must deal with a spatial differentiation as well: how groups of men separate themselves horizontally from their contemporaneous cultures.

So long as we remain sensitive to these nuances of difference, it is profitable to cast spotlights upon *The Making of the Middle Ages*, by R. W. Southern, and *The Italian Renaissance in Its Historical Background*, by Denys Hay, both splendid books, in order to illuminate more fully our own center stage. What stimuli seem to have been conducive to the rise of new civilizations, and what conditions seem to accompany their emergence? I observe that western Europe in the early Middle Ages "was not at home with its past, had not identified itself with its past" yet; that it was gripped by a spirit of religious fervor; that it underwent, especially in the tenth century, a disintegration of authority and confusion concerning critical questions of legitimacy; that it was characterized by a pursuit of knowledge beyond the ancient boundaries of Latin tradition; that higher learning was nevertheless something of a luxury, monopolized by a priestly class; and that

> the social arrangements of the eleventh and twelfth centuries were bedevilled by disputes about titles to

lands and dignities [and] had the capacity to cause endless exasperation and confusion. As a consequence of this, the primary function of the medieval ruler was that of organizing justice and pronouncing judgment. . . . Men acquiesced in government because, whether themselves litigious or not—and most men were—they were involved in a web of conflicting claims and counter-claims which could have no end until they had been pressed as far as money and strength would allow.[1]

All of these phenomena also happen to have been central to the life of seventeenth-century America. Equally striking is the fact that Medieval Europe and the English colonies both began as covenanted societies in which most men were bound by clusters of formal obligations: oaths, covenants, bonds, and indentures. When these formal obligations began to disintegrate, or became less pervasive, new eras opened, ones more loosely structured and permissive.

Looking at the background of the Italian Renaissance, one finds still other parallels to the genesis of North American civilization: that the origins of a civilization have much to do with its own growth in self-consciousness; that the pluralism and diversity of the Italian city-states could nonetheless produce a common civilization ("a dominant diversity, modified by certain cohesive pressures"); that law played a very large and special part in the life of the communities; and that the emergence of cultural unity in Italy by the early sixteenth century brought with it a more generalized sense of commonality.[2]

Let my purpose not be misunderstood here, for I do not wish to be a naïve literalist. I merely mean to suggest that there may be certain structural and historical attributes common to the emergence of early modern civilizations, at least in the western tradition, and that the cosmology of the English colonists shared almost as much in common with medieval Chris

1. R. W. Southern: *The Making of the Middle Ages* (New Haven, 1953), 36, 68, 80–1, 92, 108, 145–6, 192–3.
2. Denys Hay: *The Italian Renaissance in Its Historical Background* (Cambridge, 1961), 26, 47, 56–7, 67–8, 173–4, 178.

tendom as it anticipated the realm of "King Andrew" the Democrat.[3] Unquestionably, any comparative glance at the beginnings of Medieval Europe, Renaissance Europe, and America, however superficial, should also awaken us to profound distinctions. The *idea* of Europe, for example, emerged historically well after Medieval Europe had become a recognized reality in the political, religious, and economic realms. Whereas the idea of America, as El Dorado and Paradise, surfaced before the fact of America, prior to colonization, and thereby conditioned the form the "facts" would take, and even what people would make of them.[4] Sir Thomas More's *Utopia*, for example, preceded by more than a century the utopian schemes of Puritan Boston or Pilgrim Plymouth. There is a sense in which Americans, from the outset, could not fully control their own destiny because they had a mythology before they even had a country. Moreover, latecomers in the eighteenth and nineteenth centuries would then have to accommodate their expectations to a reality already out of kilter with earlier assumptions.

Finally, yet another contrast occurs: sixteenth- and seventeenth-century Europeans, such as Sir Thomas More, or Lope de Vega, or William Penn, might well indulge in social fantasies about the prospects of new life in the newer world. But colonials who lived the reality could not normally afford the luxury of fabulous pipe dreams. They had to cope and hope, rather than dream and scheme. Hence, perhaps, the apparent indifference of many Americans to utopian thought and social planning. He who carves out a kingdom, at considerable cost in sweat, and tears, and time, is not readily given to visions of social alternatives. The ubiquitous abundance of success may

3. See Luis Weckmann: "The Middle Ages in the Conquest of America," *Speculum*, XXVI (1951), 130–41; Charles Verlinden: *The Beginnings of Modern Colonization* (Ithaca, 1970); Samuel P. Huntington: *Political Order in Changing Societies* (New Haven, 1968), 96–9, 105.

4. Cf. Denys Hay: *Europe. The Emergence of an Idea* (Edinburgh, 1957), and Louis B. Wright: *The Dream of Prosperity in Colonial America* (New York, 1965).

well have conditioned the common air we all breathe more than the absence of feudalism. I would prefer, at any rate, to argue from positive rather than negative evidence.

I am not myself fully convinced of the "medieval character" of colonial America, and therefore perhaps not entirely convincing on this issue. It is an elusive insight, and one of limited utility. But its utility is twofold if it lays to rest once and for all the Lockean notion that "in the beginning all the world was America," or that we always have been what we are today; and if it suggests as well how very much has changed since the days of Captain John Smith and Governor John Winthrop. Consider these two versions of the same "document": one from the *Bay Psalm Book* of 1640, the first book printed in North America; the other from a region of the modern mind, a demonstration of its distemper.

> The Lord to mee a shepheard is, want therefore shall not I.
> Hee in the folds of tender-grasse, doth cause mee downe to lie
> To waters calme mee gently leads. Restore my soule doth hee:
> he doth in paths of righteousness: for his names sake leade mee.
> Yea though in valley of deaths shade I walk, none ill I'le feare:
> because thou art with mee, thy rod, and staffe my comfort are.
> For mee a table thou has spread, in presence of my foes:
> thou dost annoynt my head with oyle, my cup it overflowes.
> Goodnes & mercy surely shall all my dayes follow mee:
> and in the Lords house I shall dwell so long as dayes shall bee.

But then

> The Lord is my external, internal, integrated mechanism. I shall not be deprived of gratifications for my visceral generic hungers or my need dispositions. He

motivates me to orient myself toward a nonsocial object effectiveness significance. He positions me in a nondecisional situation. He maximizes my adjustment.

You may chuckle, and say that's a facile juxtaposition; I would suggest that it is highly symptomatic of the profundity of change between then and now. So long as our assessment of continuities and discontinuities in American history tends to concentrate upon politics and public institutions, we will overlook many of the major alterations and innovations, for there is indeed a certain underlying consistency to the ways men compete for power and distribute it. If, on the other hand, we think about the uses and abuses of human energies in America— what we create and what we destroy—our emphasis may alter. For we have shifted from being a conquest culture to being a consumer culture, from a culture of exploitation to a culture of exhibition, from a culture of self-sufficiency to a culture of self-indulgence, from a culture that would maximize its labor to one that would maximize its leisure, from provincial powerlessness to paralyzed omnipotence.

Changes in the ways we think about labor and leisure bring into view yet another major measure of difference. I don't think we will fully understand early American minds until we realize that their conception of time was different from our own. Their notions of work and war, of leisure and communication, indeed of life and love were unlike ours because they did not measure or conceive of time quite as we do. Their sense of long-range time—the ephemeral nature of this world, and eternity of the next; their millennial, or chiliastic, view of history; their urgency about preparation for salvation because death might come suddenly—and their sense of immediate time set them apart as being distinctly "pre-modern." Would there be time enough after the colonists' arrival to build shelters and gather adequate food for winter? Would an apprentice or indentured servant fulfill his allotted span of time? Perhaps.

They measured distance in units of time, not in miles; and the slowness of communications meant that the pace and pulse of their lives would be reckoned by different mechanisms than our own. Living from sunup to sundown, and by the seasons, they budgeted time the way we budget money. Work and war were waged seasonally. Life was shorter but women gave over a longer span of their shorter lives to the production of new lives. Time moved more slowly in men's minds then because there were few clocks and no wristwatches; yet idleness was a greater sin because it denied social as well as personal responsibilities.

In short, we now shape time to the patterns of our lives. We work round the clock if necessary; the four to midnight shift if required; and not at all for prearranged blocks of time called "vacations." They knew no regular vacations, for the patterns of their lives were governed by imperatives of time more inexorable than any other aspect of their existence. In the last analysis, it seems to me, they were more relaxed than we about proximate time, but had a greater sense of urgency about ultimate time, their "allotted span." They hoped to get Somewhere slowly: *Festina lente*, "Make haste slowly," was the charming phrase in their almanacs and chit-chat.[5] We, by contrast, seem to be going Nowhere in a hurry.

Sometimes even the suffixes we use can be revealing. Think for a moment about the suffix "ship." We associate craftsmanship, draftsmanship, marksmanship, sportsmanship, seamanship, and apprenticeship with an older, earlier America. We associate gamesmanship, brinkmanship, and salesmanship with our own. The older "ships," so to speak, had to do with man's skills in dealing with nature or producing a quality product. The newer "ships" have to do with fooling other people, or besting them. Have we moved from an age of dexterity to an age of asperity?

The generations of Americans that made and lived through the revolutionary era, 1750 to 1840 let us say, had the most

5. For suggestive nuggets, see Arthur H. Cole: "The Tempo of Mercantile Life in Colonial America." *Business History Review*, XXXIII (1959), 277–99; James Kirke Paulding: *The Dutchman's Fireside* (1831: New Haven, 1966), 252; Keith Thomas: "Work and Leisure in Pre-Industrial Society," *Past and Present*, XXIX (1964), 50–66.

extraordinary sense of optimism about the future of America: its productivity, liberty, modernity, innocence, and expansiveness. Jefferson's generation was exultant about the prospects for American civilization. We, by contrast, have developed serious reservations about the "goodness" of American values and our own performance; so we are skeptical about spreading them; some of our citizens would even immunize the planet against our malaise. Having become self-critical and anti-imperialistic, we look nostalgically but ambivalently to our past, at once yearning and condemning. The Founding Fathers had their eyes on the future; we have ours on the past, when not absolutely averted in shame. We tend to think less about where we are going than about where we have been, about simpler times, and about opportunities missed. Having turned our Janus-heads, we show the face of Cassandra while concealing the profile of Pollyanna. There may even be a sense in which Professor J. H. Plumb's recent essay, *The Death of the Past*, is mistitled; and that what really has died is the future.

Maybe, and maybe not. I cannot be sure, and many will disagree. But those of us who are historians, custodians of the past by definition, must try to recapture what Lionel Trilling once called "the huge, unrecorded hum of implication," because the life of the future is predicated upon the implication of the past. The historian is the memory of civilization. A civilization without memory ceases to be civilized. A civilization without history ceases to have identity. Without identity there is no purpose; without purpose civilization will wither.

CHAPTER 1

THE OLD WORLD
AND THE NEW, PARI PASSU

> Some of the charm of the past consists of the quiet—
> the great distracting buzz of implication has stopped and
> we are left only with what has been fully phrased and
> precisely stated. And part of the melancholy of the past
> comes from our knowledge that the huge, unrecorded
> hum of implication was once there and left no trace—we
> feel that because it is evanescent it is especially human.
>
> LIONEL TRILLING, *The Liberal Imagination* (1950)

MOST ATTEMPTS to interpret America's history and culture have had a certain monolithic quality. Authors have been
obliged to seek the quintessence of it all through a master key
that would open many, if not every door. But when so many
different keys are serried before us, we confront ordered confusion. Which is the one we want? Has the driving force in our
history been nationalistic expansion, a sense of mission,
pietism, the absence of feudalism, or the propulsion of American democratic thought? Each explanation has its advocates.
"The emigrants who colonized the shores of America in the
beginning of the seventeenth century," wrote Alexis de Tocqueville, "somehow separated the democratic principle from all the
principles which it had to contend with in the old communities
of Europe, and transplanted it alone to the New World. It has
there been able to spread in perfect freedom, and peaceably

to determine the character of the laws by influencing the manners of the country." [1] How familiar, how logical, how attractive; yet how simplistic, too.

In recent years, students of American character and culture have "discovered" some serious methodological problems in their quest. Indeed, these conundrums have in some cases been beatified into metaphysical issues. Although they are not our proper concern here, I must remark upon one issue in particular: that of uniqueness. Individual characteristics found among Americans are surely not unique; but the total constellation of American attributes, and its effect upon thought and action, may very well be home-grown and *sui generis*. If so, that constellation is the phoenix for which we are searching.

There are traps scattered everywhere, however, for hunters of the unique and indigenous, traps left inadvertently by earlier writers with bifocal vision who were especially concerned with two periods of our past: the great age of colonization and the era of the American Revolution. Alongside the seventeenth-century settlements there had inevitably appeared a literature of promotion and justification, most of it celebrating the uniqueness of the "Strange New World, thet yit wast never young." Then, in the later eighteenth century, a generation of anxious and verbose revolutionaries needed to prove to themselves and to the world that they were different, a *new* breed of men. So historians have studied the tracts on colonization, scrutinized the oracular Founding Fathers, and agreed that a new civilization must indeed have sprung up quite early in the course of human events in America.

One of the most comprehensive and seductive variations on this theme has been elaborated over the past twenty years by Daniel Boorstin. According to him, the ideas and institutions brought to the New World by Europeans were rapidly transformed by an intractable environment and unexpected circumstances. So that Americans from the outset became what Euro-

1. *Democracy in America*, ed. Phillips Bradley (New York, 1945) I, 14.

peans were not: practical rather than theoretical, pragmatic
rather than ideological, mobile rather than stationary, dynamic
rather than static, institutionally simplified rather than complex, underpopulated rather than over, and relatively homogeneous. Professor Boorstin's vision of American cultural origins
has been so influential and pervasive that we are obliged for a
moment to examine its premises and implications in some
critical detail. His approach, however intriguing, depends upon
certain assumptions about early modern Europe, about the role
and success of ideas there, about the nature (or absence) of
ideas in America, and about the peculiar powers of New World
environments to defeat the best laid plans of mortal men.[2]

Let us consider for a moment the concept of Europe itself,
a rather meaningless geographical notion for the study of
American origins. Colonials didn't come from Europe. They
came from East Anglia, Bristol, London, Ulster, Leyden, and
Nantes. Yet students of American history tend to use "Europe"
as a comparative foil, and attribute to that continent all sorts
of general qualities and tendencies that are true hither but not
thither, in 1600 but no longer in 1650. What we must learn
from the new and precise school of local historians in England
is that a yeoman in Devonshire, say, was very different from a
yeoman in the East Midlands, and that the practice of medicine
in Yorkshire was not the same as its practice in London. Students of American culture, especially its origins, must be less
glib in generalizing about what was normative hither and yon
in early modern Europe.

Secondly, let us think for a moment about the matter of
environment. Historians of colonial America have written as
though immigrants from the Old World, which must have been
almost entirely under cultivation, civilized and urbanized,
sailed away to a "howling wilderness" where impenetrable
forests, impossible beasts, and imperceivable savages awaited.
Nonsense. In 1620, when the Pilgrims landed at Plymouth
Rock, there were extensive outlying areas of England still

2. See especially *The Americans. The Colonial Experience* (New
York, 1958); and *The Genius of American Politics* (Chicago, 1953).

awaiting "colonization": Lancashire, Yorkshire, Cumberland in the north, and Devon to the west; as well as sweeping extents of marshlands, royal forests, and commons throughout. England too had woods, and wolves, and wild boar. England too offered environmental obstacles.

And what of the obverse image? Just how thick and inscrutable was the primeval American wilderness? Thick enough, and surely mysterious to the fearful immigrant. Yet from the earliest newcomers' accounts we know that there were considerable areas of cleared land, and here and there, especially in the valleys of the larger rivers, there were "rich and fruitful spots of land, such as they call interval land, in levels and champaign ground, without trees or stones." Nor was the forest necessarily a tangled jungle. Twice each year local Indians had been accustomed to "fire the Countrey," burning out the underbrush and younger trees. Consequently, the woods were "thin of Timber in many places, like our Parkes in England." In many places a man might ride through the forest on horseback. In the uplands, as it happened, graceful columns of ancient trees rose to heights of twenty or thirty feet before spreading their broad branches. Within the wide woodland aisles, farmers would even find fodder for their herds of swine and cattle.[3]

The New World forest, then, was not so very unlike European forests. It could even be hospitable, and certainly lacked any mystical power to defeat inevitably all the utopian schemes of European dreamers. We must realize that many an ivory tower crumbled to rubble in seventeenth-century England too, brought down by domestic realities.[4] Moreover, many utopian fantasies designed for colonial undertakings were modified or abandoned because of *English* exigencies as well as American ones. William Penn's idealistic hopes and plans for his pro-

3. See Robert R. Walcott: "Husbandry in Colonial New England," *New England Quarterly*, IX (1936), 220.
4. See Alfred Cohen: "The Kingdom of God in Puritan Thought. A Study of the English Puritan Quest for the Fifth Monarchy" (unpublished Ph.D. dissertation, University of Indiana, 1961).

prietary province, for example, had to be altered during the 1680's because of his peculiar role in court politics at home. Penn's policies toward the Indians of his province were eminently practical, but were undermined over the years by greedy Europeans on the make. In short, many English designs for the Atlantic colonies were defeated at home by English circumstances, or by Englishmen abroad, rather than by the American environment *per se*.[5]

Let us turn to another sort of self-deception. Our inclination to view ourselves as practical men has too often caused us to cast the European as an inflexible ideologue. The historical record, however, reveals how very tough-minded the European has often been. We may illustrate this fact with examples taken from just one strand of European history, a strand where one might expect theoretical considerations to have prevailed over practical ones: the development of representative institutions. All the way back in the thirteenth century, when the English Parliament was given birth and life, Simon de Montfort and his party (who served as midwife in the process), were guided by events more than by principles in placing their reliance on the lesser gentry and townsfolk of the realm. In western Europe during the sixteenth century, the vital problem of the proper powers of legislative deputies was not regarded as an abstruse and theoretical question. It was viewed and handled in practical terms. Franchois Vranck, the Pensionary of Gouda, to take a typical example, developed a purely historical theory of sovereignty and ignored natural law and natural rights. Netherlanders generally were guided by "common sense and practical experience." In England, where new concepts of parliamentary representation were also developing, Queen Elizabeth was "content to sink theory in expediency"; and great numbers of parliamentary decisions were made along the most pragmatic lines imaginable.[6]

5. See Francis P. Jennings: "Miquon's Passing: Indian-European Relations in Colonial Pennsylvania, 1674 to 1755" (unpublished Ph.D. dissertation, University of Pennsylvania, 1965).

6. George L. Haskins: *The Growth of English Representative Government* (Philadelphia, 1948), 63–5; H. G. Koenigsberger: "The

One might well argue that the emergence of political institutions would force any and all societies to be practical; that the real measure of a nation's intellectual and emotional inclination comes with its development of religious and philosophical systems of thought. Here too, however, the importance of ideology in the European temper has been misread and misused. William Perkins, the great Cambridge theologian whose writings profoundly influenced early New England minds, ranked with Calvin and was translated into many European languages. Nonetheless, he was a practical rather than a speculative theologian, a Puritan popularizer in search of tangible results. Similarly, Dr. William Ames, his most eminent student, and more than any other figure the source of New England's Church polity, differed little from Perkins in thought and wrote influential texts by compactly systematizing and summarizing. John Milton, that anguished English Puritan, wrote his great theoretical works for the most practical reasons. Indeed, he was forced to by circumstance and necessity: his unpopularity as a Cambridge student, his inability to obtain a fellowship, his marriage and separation from a girl half his age, his blindness, imprisonment, ultimate poverty, and obscurity. A generation later John Locke became England's great philosopher, characteristically English because of his devotion to common sense, his mistrust of metaphysics, and his doctrine that all knowledge comes from experience.

The pragmatic American colonists, we are often told, were the children, or perhaps stepchildren, of ideological Stuart Englishmen. Nevertheless, one of the best and most recent descriptions of constitutional development in seventeenth-century England seems exactly to correspond with Professor Boorstin's conception of political processes in America, and bears no resemblance to his caricature of early modern Europe:

Powers of Deputies in Sixteenth-Century Assemblies," in *Album Helen Maud Cam* (Louvain and Paris, 1961), 239–43; Louise F. Brown: "Ideas of Representation from Elizabeth to Charles II," *Journal of Modern History*, XI (1939), 29, 31.

Seventeenth-century Englishmen possessed no blue-print for the building of responsible government. The historical process by which responsible government developed was erratic, experimental, labyrinthine, and myopic. It was marked by trial and error, by a search for expedients, by the stress of immediate political quarrels, by the exigencies of party and personal strife, by present fears and proximate hopes. Furthermore, these changes occurred gradually, step by step, with no thought beyond the immediate demand of the moment. Precedent succeeded precedent, claim followed claim, but no one consciously strove to transfer the sceptre from the King's hands to Parliament's. Instead they sought to win immediate political demands, and sought to weaken the King's control of executive power only when that control obstructed the winning of their demands.[7]

Another historian of British government has recently demonstrated how practical rather than doctrinaire the English were, over the long haul, in establishing constitutional structures overseas. They rarely attempted to export a pre-packaged model of colonial polity, but rather "temporised, hoping for a stable form of government to evolve locally." Practicality, then, is not a peculiarly American virtue; and the commitment to practicality, as Peter Gay has observed, "is after all itself an idea, an idea in fact with a long and honored history."[8]

OUR MISCONCEPTIONS about the relative roles played by ideas and environment in Europe are more than matched by misunderstandings of their respective importance in the American context. We have been taught that few European ideas or institutions survived in the New World; that original or systematic thought was stifled here; and that nearly all ideologies

7. Clayton Roberts: *The Growth of Responsible Government in Stuart England* (Cambridge, 1966), 431.
8. Frederick Madden: "Some Origins and Purposes in the Formation of British Colonial Government," in *Essays in Imperial Government Presented to Margery Perham* (Oxford, 1963), 21–2; Peter Gay: "The Enlightenment," in *The Comparative Approach to American History*, ed. C. Vann Woodward (New York, 1968), 35.

cut against the American grain. How then are we to explain and understand our attitudes toward black men, red men, and people of color generally? For our conceptions of the Negro, of savagery, of personal freedom and bondage all originated in Europe and were imported to the colonies where they took root and flourished.[9] How are we to explain the triumph of authority and order in the northern colonies if not, at least in part, as a victory of Old World customs over New World experience? If not in terms of *both* tradition *and* design? New England's legal systems, for example, derived from received precepts as well as from the social and economic needs of the colonists. The law provided an anchor to accepted tradition as well as a vessel to navigate the seas of change.[1]

To suggest that America has enjoyed the absence of ideological disputation, speculative thought, and theoretical science dishonors many distinguished provincials by simply ignoring them. Colonial New England's finest poet, for example, Edward Taylor, was a speculative as well as a practical theologian. And Dr. John Mitchell of Urbanna, Virginia, was an eminent scientist of theoretical inclinations whose work was read and respected in England.[2] Many of the first immigrants, and many subsequently, came as a means of expressing their cerebral and social protest against conditions of life and thought at home. Once an American establishment had formed and hardened, generations of domestic dissenters were spawned; so that the tradition and proclivity of nonconformity in the United States has been to devour its elders rather than its young. During the third quarter of the eighteenth century,

9. Winthrop D. Jordan: *White Over Black. American Attitudes Toward the Negro, 1550–1812* (Chapel Hill, 1968), 48 ff.; Roy Harvey Pearce: *The Savages of America. A Study of the Indian and the Idea of Civilization* (Baltimore, 1965), 82 ff.

1. George Haskins: *Law and Authority in Early Massachusetts. A Study in Tradition and Design* (New York, 1960), esp. ch. 1.

2. See Norman S. Grabo: *Edward Taylor* (New Haven, 1961), esp. 24–39; Theodore Hornberger: "The Scientific Ideas of John Mitchell," *Huntington Library Quarterly*, X (1947), 277–96. Significantly, Boorstin's *The Colonial Experience* does not discuss Taylor and has merely one fleeting mention of Mitchell.

colonials became so ideologically committed as to make resolution of the Anglo-American constitutional crisis impossible. Three-quarters of a century later, another crusade with intellectual as well as emotional underpinnings tore the union apart by producing an ideological impasse that would even outlast fragile efforts at reconstruction.

It is undeniably true that some notions carried to America by settlers were destroyed or altered by the environment they encountered and by the concatenation of events. It is equally true, however, that discarded ideas were usually replaced by new ones, and that transplanted Europeans did not simply lapse into mindlessness. We have recently been shown that for many decades the Puritans' conception of "wilderness" was not the one they brought to New England, but one rooted in the very experience of wilderness life. The first colonists had believed they were coming to Canaan, a land flowing with milk and honey. Promptly upon suffering the "greatest difficulties, and sorest labours," the promised land became the very wilderness through which a generation was obliged to wander before entering Canaan. The forests of New England acquired a moral function in the Puritan cosmology; and their agonies of primitive life served to reinforce the Puritans' view that they were God's chosen people.[3]

Historians who have been inoculated with the serum of environmentalism, from Turner to Boorstin, have reacted virulently to any suggestion that things European might long survive the trans-Atlantic voyage to North America. Yet the *peculiarly* transforming powers of ocean, forests, and plains located between 32 and 48 degrees of latitude are difficult to discover. Colonists from Spain and Portugal brought to Latin America powerful traditions of the medieval Iberian municipal community. These traditions were firmly implanted in legislation for the Indies on such matters as municipal control of

---

3. Edward Johnson: *The Wonder-Working Providence of Sions Saviour in New England* (New York, 1910), 11, 52, 106, 111, 115, 219, 234–5, 239; Alan Heimert: "Puritanism, the Wilderness and the Frontier," *New England Quarterly*, XXVI (1953), 361–82.

common lands, the corporate or guild structure of urban crafts, professions, and commerce, election of town officials by property owners, and price controls. Nevertheless, "as the external threats to survival were lifted, the disintegrative attraction of plain, mine, and forest was asserted." [4] Since the civilizations of North and South America have evolved in such profoundly dissimilar ways, it is difficult to determine just what the *unique* role of environment has been in the history of these United States.

WE ARE THEREFORE OBLIGED to seek some other, more complex explanation for the origins of American culture. Obviously environment cannot be discounted. It has meant much. So too have the kinds of people who came, the moment in time when they arrived, the assumptions they brought, and the process of change they underwent here. It is equally obvious that we must pay considerable attention to what was happening in Europe during the seventeenth and eighteenth centuries; but it is not at all obvious why. One reason has been defined and illustrated by Howard Mumford Jones as "the profound and central truth that American culture arises from the interplay of two great sets of forces—the Old World and the New. The Old World projected into the New a rich, complex, and contradictory set of habits, forces, practices, values, and presuppositions; and the New World accepted, modified, or rejected these or fused them with inventions of its own." [5]

Another reason rests in the attitudes colonists developed toward Europe, and consequently about their own place in time, space, and history. They held that an antithesis existed between the virtue of the New World and the vice of the Old. The former, as Cushing Strout has put it, "found its dark antithesis" in the latter. Yet America was much more than the obverse of Europe. Its special and historic mission was

4. Richard M. Morse: "Some Characteristics of Latin American Urban History," *American Historical Review*, LXVII (1962), 329.
5. *O Strange New World. American Culture: The Formative Years* (New York, 1964), viii, 391.

compounded of three national purposes: abstention from the system of European politics and wars; the expansion of republican institutions across the North American continent; and the sustained maintenance of an example of freedom for oppressed peoples everywhere.[6] Because ambivalence and ambiguity have complicated America's relationship with Europe, because "Europe has been to us stern father and kind mother, formidable enemy and brave ally, helpful teacher and reluctant pupil," stimulus and irritant, it is imperative that we not only probe this cluster of paradoxes, but establish as clearly as we can what western Europe during the *ancien régime* was really about.

It is this necessity of knowing seventeenth- and eighteenth-century Europe that has posed the greatest problem for students of early American culture. In our haste to make comparisons and discover points of difference and departure, we have perpetrated a strange kind of confusion. We have compared the movement and ferment in adolescent colonies whose history we know well, with a stationary and stilted Europe of our own contrivance. One noted historian characteristically put it this way: "There was more social change going on in America than in England; America was a new and highly dynamic society; English society was relatively old, and, in this period, relatively static."[7] What utterly romantic tushery! I must insist that western Europe in the seventeenth and eighteenth centuries was *not* static, that America and Europe were changing simultaneously, in many of the same directions, but at different rates of speed according to which idea, institution, or social pattern one happens to examine.

In the absence of intellectual and institutional impediments, certain types of change occurred more quickly in the colonies. Technological advantages and economic maturity, however,

6. Strout: *The American Image of the Old World* (New York, 1963), ix–x, 14–15, 18.

7. Max Savelle: "Prolegomena to a History of Liberalism in Eighteenth-Century Anglo-America," in *Is Liberalism Dead and Other Essays* (Seattle, 1967), 45.

facilitated other forms of change more rapidly in Europe. Not only was the Old World not static during the early modern period, one might even argue that European colonization flourished precisely when it did because much that was medieval was running concurrently with, and yet giving way to, the beginning of things modern. Feudal forms of tenure were being adapted to a new agriculture; an educational revolution was in process; medieval concepts of law and government were being shaken to their very foundations. Because European monarchs were constantly in search of more centralized control, power struggles resulted and produced an awkward fragility in societies of the *ancien régime*. Historians are just now coming to appreciate that ordinary individuals living then were much less restricted in activities and aspirations than we customarily believed; and that the dynamics of change and intellectual ferment were everywhere present or near the surface.[8]

It has also been part of our conventional wisdom to assume that the colonies steadily deviated during their development away from English norms. Several generations of Americans have felt that the freshets of our culture sprang, in Constance Rourke's words, "from a life peculiar to these shores; they were part of a fresh configuration."[9] My own belief is that once the earliest settlements were established, essentially by mid-seventeenth century, provincial culture in significant ways "began to line up again with English traditions."[1] A form of political

8. See Alan Everitt: "The Changing Pattern of Labouring Life," in *The Agrarian History of England and Wales*, IV, 1500–1640 (Cambridge, 1967), 454–65; G. R. Cragg: *From Puritanism to the Age of Reason. A Study of Changes in Religious Thought Within the Church of England, 1600–1700* (Cambridge, 1950); Eugene L. Asher: *The Resistance to the Maritime Classes. The Survival of Feudalism in the France of Colbert* (Berkeley, 1960); Shelby T. McCloy: *The Humanitarian Movement in Eighteenth-Century France* (Lexington, Ky., 1957).

9. *The Roots of American Culture and Other Essays* (New York, 1942), 51.

1. Edward Eggleston: *The Transit of Civilization from England to America in the Seventeenth Century* (2nd ed., Boston, 1959), 191. See also John M. Murrin: "Anglicizing an American Colony: The

conservatism became evident in both cultures during the
1660's and 1670's, manifested in a contraction of the electorate by legislative and executive action. Subsequently, the
electorate broadened in both England and the colonies, and for
many of the same reasons. Taking a different line of approach,
one finds that Hingham, Massachusetts, and similar provincial
towns became more rather than less homogeneous in the generation after 1650, more like old Hingham in England.[2]

English and French politics during the last three decades
of the seventeenth century were almost as unstable as colonial
politics. Moreover, the quest for political stability in England
between 1675 and 1725, recently examined by J. H. Plumb in
a book of that title, was matched by a similar search in the
colonies, and with comparable causes—notably the need for a
shift in constitutional arrangements. The Glorious Revolution
of 1688 quashed the Divine Right of Kings notion in Britain;
and after the colonial rebellions in 1689 a similar fate would
befall the pretensions of Proprietors there. Major changes in
the nature of English government between 1680 and 1720
were paralleled by comparable alterations in America.

The millennial and apocalyptic anxieties of Americans at
the close of the seventeenth century had their sources in similar
European apprehensions. And the social pietism characteristic
of the first decades of the eighteenth century constituted a
pan-Atlantic phenomenon. Between 1660 and 1760, the social
composition of indigenous military units in many of the colonies was changing—relying more on volunteers and merce-
naries, as in Europe, and less on the traditional militia.
Colonial currencies, especially eighteenth-century paper, were

---

Transformation of Provincial Massachusetts" (unpublished Ph.D. dissertation, Yale University, 1966); A. H. John: "The Course of Agricultural Change, 1660–1760," in *Essays in Agrarian History*, ed. W. E.
Minchinton (Newton Abbot, 1968), I, 226.

2. John J. Waters: "Hingham, Massachusetts, 1631–1661: An
East Anglian Oligarchy in the New World," *Journal of Social History*,
I (1968), 351–70; John Coolidge: "Hingham Builds a Meeting House,"
New England Quarterly, XXXIV (1961), 435–61.

relatively stable and serviceable. Consequently, the colonial economy was less primitive than historians have thought, just as colonial law and judicial activity were much more sophisticated than legal historians believed a generation ago.[3]

We have also begun to recognize that the Old World family lacked the stability and continuity historians have ascribed to it in devising "a convenient backdrop against which to portray the dynamic elements" of the changing family structure in the New World. Similarly, recent analyses of mobs and crowds in eighteenth-century Europe bear striking resemblance to our traditional understanding of mobs in the English colonies. "It now becomes more difficult to emphasize the peculiar rationality and discrimination of American mobs in their treatment of property. It is also hard to see how they were composed of more respectable, middle-class elements than their European counterparts. And it appears especially distorting to stress the unusual moderation and respect for lives displayed by American crowds."[4]

We have been led to understand that one of the most significant tendencies of colonial life was the dispersal of power to local sources, governmental and ecclesiastical. "Whether that involved the town, as in New England, or the local powers sitting in the vestry, as in Virginia, the characteristic political organization was decentralized." Oscar Handlin has further observed that colonial institutions were decisively shaped by the necessity of defining their connections to local power. True enough; but did these particular circumstances somehow give shape to a different kind of public life in America? Professor Plumb has recently demonstrated that local government was the basis of political power in Georgian England, too. If so, then the structure of politics and the vectors of power in Britain

3. See John W. Shy: "A New Look at Colonial Militia," *William and Mary Quarterly*, 3d series, XX (1963), 182–3; E. James Ferguson· "Currency Finance: An Interpretation of Colonial Monetary Practices," *ibid.*, X (1953), 153–80.

4. David J. Rothman: "A Note on the Study of the Colonial Family," *ibid.*, XXIII (1966), 632; Gordon S. Wood: "A Note on Mobs in the American Revolution," *ibid.*, 638.

and her colonies were not so very different, at least not in the ways we have believed.[5]

Finally, we have been told that the paucity and simplicity of society in the New World could not support the complexity and specialization of Old World professions. Consequently, the nature of vocational training and professionalism in America developed along new and different lines.[6] Recent research in European sources, however, has shown that general practitioners were not only common in early modern times, but that their medical training was scarcely superior to that received in the colonies. Historians have too often been misled by comparing colonial customs with those in London. The more sensible comparison is between the colonies and English provinces, where the practice of medicine was not very specialized at all in the seventeenth and eighteenth centuries.[7]

We confront the same difficulty in trying to understand the evolution of American law and its custodians. The administration of colonial justice does not bear much relationship to the King's courts at Westminster; but why should it? Much of early American law was derived from the outlying districts in England that produced colonial migrations. Therefore, colonial jurisprudence was comparable to its counterparts in the county, manor, and borough courts, as well as courts leet and quarter sessions.[8] By the same token, Professor Boorstin's portrait of the "lay lawyer" in colonial America is accurate enough

5. Handlin: "The Significance of the Seventeenth Century," in *Seventeenth-Century America. Essays in Colonial History*, ed. James M. Smith (Chapel Hill, 1959), 5; Plumb: *Sir Robert Walpole. The Making of a Statesman* (London, 1956), I, 42.

6. Boorstin: *Colonial Experience*, 191–202, 209–32.

7. F. N. L. Poynter, ed.: *The Evolution of Medical Practice in Britain* (London, 1961), 129–30, 135; Joseph F. Kett: *The Formation of the American Medical Profession. The Role of Institutions, 1780–1860* (New Haven, 1968), 5.

8. Julius Goebel, Jr.: "King's Law and Local Custom in Seventeenth-Century New England," *Columbia Law Review*, XXXI (1931), 416–48; Michael G. Kammen: "Colonial Court Records and the Study of Early American History," *American Historical Review*, LXX (1965), 738–9.

for the earlier eighteenth century, but inappropriate for later generations because it does not take into account the transformation of provincial bars during the four decades before Independence.[9] In brief, the professions were not so highly developed in Stuart and Hanoverian England as we have assumed; nor were they so primitive in provincial America as some had suspected.[1]

It would almost seem, then, that the comparative method has not served us well. It is only a tool, however, and can be no sharper than we make it. Certain deviations from English norms seem to have occurred early in the history of the colonies. Many of those deviations came eventually to be regarded as characteristically American. Yet "Americanisms" in politics or customs, like "Americanisms" in speech, often turn out to have been things quite English which died out in the Old World but still survived in the New. In many significant ways the colonies became more rather than less English in the century after 1660. In certain cases this occurred consciously, as part of an imitative process. In other spheres it occurred involuntarily, either because the colonies yielded to pressures from Parliament and the Privy Council, or because both England and America were subjected to common forces of change. Perhaps historians have been too eager to discern patterns and processes in colonial affairs that were uniquely American. If provincial legislatures were dominated by the politics of land distribution, Stuart and Georgian parliaments were deeply concerned with pressures of land enclosure. If interest groups and interest politics were unstable in the colonies, they were scarcely less so in England.

If the origins of American civilization are indeed implanted

9. See Murrin: "Anglicizing an American Colony," 256; Alan M. Smith: "Virginia Lawyers, 1680–1776: The Birth of an American Profession" (unpublished Ph.D. dissertation, Johns Hopkins University, 1968), esp. chs. 9–10.

1. See Edward Hughes: "The Professions in the Eighteenth Century," *Durham University Journal*, n.s., XIII (1952), 46–55; W. J. Reader: *Professional Men: The Rise of the Professional Classes in Nineteenth-Century England* (New York, 1966), ch. 1.

in the history of New World colonization, then that history set in comparative perspective may help us to judge whether the phoenix we seek derives from the very process of settlement itself, or from subsequent processes and phenomena in the American experience. Certainly, the fruits of English colonization had a very different color, texture, and flavor when compared with Spanish, Portuguese, French, and Dutch progeny. The hacienda, fazenda, and plantation developed differently. Bartolomé de Las Casas, Antônio Vieira, and John Eliot were different men in different contexts, though all shared a sense of compassion for the American Indian, and a desire to Christianize him in village communities. While Spanish colonization in the Caribbean tended to be relatively planned and systematic, English efforts there were usually executed haphazardly: settlement preceded the plan designed to guide it. And the so-called Forgotten Period of American history (1660–1760) bears virtually no resemblance to New Spain's comparable era, the Century of Depression (1580–1680).[2] Whereas New Spain suffered from disease, demographic declension, and economic stagnation, the colonies in North America prospered, expanded, and matured.

The English settlements would at once salvage and selvage their culture of origin—conserve it as well as extend its boundaries. But more, in seeking to preserve the past under difficult circumstances, the colonists would move, crablike, sideways into the future.

2. See David L. Niddrie: "An Attempt at Planned Settlement in St. Kitts in the Early 18th Century," *Caribbean Studies*, V (1966), 3–4; Woodrow Borah: *New Spain's Century of Depression* (Berkeley, 1951).

CHAPTER 2

THE QUEST FOR LEGITIMACY IN COLONIAL AMERICA

> Let this then be the distinctive mark of an American, that in cases of commotion he enlists under no man's banner, enquires for no man's name, but repairs to the standard of the laws.
>
> THOMAS JEFFERSON

IN 1691 KING WILLIAM III appointed Benjamin Fletcher to be governor of New York and also commander in chief of Connecticut's militia. When Fletcher reached the colonies in 1692, however, he found that Connecticut's assembly vigorously rejected his right to control their militia. Consequently, late in the crisp autumn of 1693, Fletcher hied himself to Hartford and caused his royal commission to be read publicly. The Yankee governor, Robert Treat, listened with disdain, then ordered the drums to be beaten in defiance. When Fletcher threatened Treat with imperial retribution, Connecticut's elected executive stepped forward, and with his hand on the hilt of his sword, declaimed: "If my drummers are again interrupted, I'll make sunlight shine through you. We deny and defy your authority." So the story is told.

That dramatic little confrontation epitomized several aspects of one of the central themes in early American history. I would like to suggest that an inquiry into the problem of legitimacy—the need to create and validate viable public institutions, statuses, and relationships—helps to clarify our conception of the colonies' relationship to England, helps to explain patterns of behavior, belief, instability, and subsequent events after Independence. It should also bring into meaningful juxtaposition various themes and issues—concerning religion, law, politics, and society—which have hitherto been regarded in compartmentalized fashion. Ultimately I hope to suggest that the criteria of legitimacy which eventually emerged after two centuries were "characteristically American," thereby helping to delineate, and sometimes sanction, possibilities of life in the new nation.

The most basic conception of legitimacy is "the condition of being in accordance with law, rule, or principle." Legitimate power is derived from some source of established authority that clearly allocates the right to command and the duty to obey. Compliance of the community is obtained when it affirms the belief that the rulers and their requirements constitute an acceptable order of custom and authority. Insofar as legitimacy is a psychological phenomenon, it depends upon the assumption that a particular set of institutions is appropriate for a certain society and that they function in a manner accepted or understood by the society.

There are various ways in which power may be legitimized and stability achieved: through personal confidence in the qualities of a charismatic leader; through the traditionalism which emanates over a long period of time from a system larger than any individual and faithful to "original principles" —what Max Weber called "the authority of the eternal yesterday"; and through belief in the validity of legal statute and functional competence based on rationally created rules.[1]

The sources of legitimacy in political society may be hereditary, aristocratic, democratic, elective, or a combination

1. See H. H. Gerth and C. Wright Mills, eds.: *From Max Weber: Essays in Sociology* (New York, 1958), 78–9, 294–5; Guglielmo Ferrero: *The Principles of Power* (New York, 1942); Robert A. Kann: *The Problem of Restoration. A Study in Comparative Political History* (Berkeley, 1968), 46–54.

thereof. Significantly, legitimacy in the English colonies inhered increasingly in democratic and elective sources, rather than in hereditary and titled origins. Nevertheless, the colonists recognized this reality with great reluctance because it signaled a serious departure from traditional European standards. In consequence, a considerable number of colonial governments and institutions achieved a condition of only quasi-legitimacy. They were necessary in order to prevent anarchy, and they were able to gain sufficiently wide acceptance so as not to be obliged to rely exclusively upon deception, corruption, and physical constraint; yet their acceptance was incomplete, grudging, and accompanied by mistrust. The reasons run deep in the American colonial experience, and were present from the outset.

Many of the seventeenth-century settlers found themselves living beyond the reach of sanctioned government, without charters or with patents of questionable validity. The Pilgrims held tenaciously but tenuously to their rock at Plymouth for three generations, unable to obtain a patent from the Crown; in 1692 they were absorbed by the Bay Colony. Connecticut and Rhode Island anxiously sought valid and valued charters, sending John Winthrop, Jr., and Roger Williams, their best men, repeatedly to London for that purpose. Even the patriarchal Puritan statesman, John Winthrop of Massachusetts, declared in 1635 that "we should do nothing hereafter but by commission out of England." [2] During the final quarter of the seventeenth century, a number of the early colonial charters—joint-stock as well as proprietary—came under attack by officials in London and were interpreted in contradictory ways. These challenges to the legitimacy of government in New England, New Jersey, Pennsylvania, Maryland, and Bermuda created and exacerbated severe political tensions.

2. William Bradford: *Of Plymouth Plantation, 1620–1647*, ed. Samuel Eliot Morison (New York, 1952), 75; James K. Hosmer, ed.: *Winthrop's Journal. History of New England, 1630–1649* (New York, 1908), I, 164.

Many of the colonists were troubled by their own illicit encroachment upon Indian lands. As one Pilgrim casuist asked, "What right have I to go live in the heathens' country?" He provided his brethren with the following answer:

> This then is a sufficient reason to prove our going thither to live lawful: their land is spacious and void, and there are few and do but run over the grass. . . . They are not industrious, neither have art, science, skill or faculty to use either the land or the commodities of it. . . . As the ancient patriarchs therefore removed from straiter places into more roomy, where the land lay idle and waste, and none used it . . . so it is lawful now to take a land which none useth, and make use of it.[3]

Perhaps some of the brethren were convinced; but I suspect that the casuist himself continued to have an uneasy conscience. From the beginning of American history, abuses marred the transfer of land titles from the Indians. Various colonial laws struck at the difficulty by declaring null and void all bargains made with the natives that did not have governmental approval. In part, such laws sought to remove causes of resentment among the Indians by preventing fraudulent purchases; but they also aimed at preserving the rights of the Crown or of proprietors to the land. The colonists' formal relations with the Indians lacked legitimacy—sometimes in the colonists' eyes, often in the Indians' eyes, frequently in ours—because treaties so often were predicated upon fraud and deception. Much of the Indian trade conducted in the eighteenth century was actually illicit, and white settlements constantly spilled over the boundary lines agreed upon.

Because the nations of western Europe had conflicting claims in the New World, colonial boundaries and territorial hegemony were often unclear. Witness the conflicts between

3. "Reasons and Considerations Touching the Lawfulness of Removing Out of England into the Parts of America," in Dwight B. Heath, ed.: *Mourt's Relation. A Relation or Journal of the English Plantation Settled at Plymouth in New England, by Certain English Adventurers, both Merchants and Others* (New York, 1963), 91–2.

Dutch and English over lands between the Hudson and Connecticut rivers. Pioneers of each nationality commonly charged their enemies with settling beyond the sanctions of clear title. In part, such moralistic-legalistic utterances served to assuage the colonizers' anxieties about visible lawlessness within their own precincts, or to disguise the disintegration of local governmental authority.

In early seventeenth-century England, the legal system stood in desperate need of rationalization and reform. The complexities and confusion of English law were transported to the colonies, however, ineluctably blurring even further the dimensions of legitimacy abroad. In addition, the Puritans of New England were charged with building a body of private, nonconstitutional law of their own—a code of laws out of line with English standards. Since no other seventeenth-century colony had so complete a compilation of law as Massachusetts, law was clearly a greater source of ambiguity than of well-defined orthodoxy. Common law simply could not function in the colonies in the same way it did in England. There were no trained lawyers, little attention to previous case law, and written judicial opinions virtually did not exist.[4]

Just as English lawyers had Sir Edward Coke's *Institutes of the Laws of England*, English Puritans had the *Institutes* of John Calvin. But European institutes were inadequate sources of intellectual legitimacy in the New World. The emphasis in American Puritanism upon an elaborate structure of covenants —between God and man, man and man, God and his chosen community of saints—indicates a form of ecclesiastical constitutionalism, or legalism, symptomatic of a quest for spiritual legitimacy. Having challenged the sanctity and propriety of the Church of England, New England's elect were doubly obliged to establish canons of orthodoxy. In this context, the

4. See Mark DeWolfe Howe: "The Sources and Nature of Law in Colonial Massachusetts," in *Law and Authority in Colonial America*, ed. George A. Billias (Barre, 1965), 11, 14; David H. Flaherty, ed.: *Essays in the History of Early American Law* (Chapel Hill, 1969), esp. chs. 2 and 3.

Half-Way Covenant of 1662 constituted a crisis of legitimacy in which elders, ministers, and churches were accused of being "irregular, illegal, & disorderly." Hence the periodic need of New England Congregationalists to convene synods, even though they smelled suspiciously Presbyterian. And all too often in all the colonies there were congregations without regular clergymen at all—"sheep without a shepherd," the Mennonites called themselves in the 1680's. "Since they had no preacher, they endeavored to admonish one another." [5]

Most of the public institutions which developed in the seventeenth-century colonies underwent this quest for integrity and recognition. The early assemblies, for example, existed on sufferance in many cases: Virginia's burgesses went unrecognized by the Crown from 1619 until 1639. The complex system of great and small burgher rights in New Netherland was designed to provide social legitimacy for the most important magistrates, officers, and ministers. Massachusetts Bay established Harvard College strictly on its own authority; therefore, whenever the colony's constitutional identity came under attack, Harvard's legal status fell into jeopardy as well. When the Bay Colony lost its charter in 1684, it was assumed that Harvard's charter of 1650 was also null and void. The failure of towns to develop in the Chesapeake colonies indicated to many—who judged by Old World standards—a lack of social legitimacy. Men associated towns with the presence of social control and good order. Cities would supposedly facilitate "good Discipline and careful tending . . . under faithful Teachers and Magistrates."

In 1689, when the constitutional kettle boiled to rebellion in many colonies, both the established governments *and* the insurrectionists seemed to lack proper credentials. Certainly the Dominion of New England, established by King James II in 1686, lacked integrity in the eyes of most New Englanders.

5. H. Shelton Smith, *et al.*, eds.: *American Christianity. An Historical Interpretation with Representative Documents* (New York, 1960), I, 272.

And when word of the Glorious Revolution in Britain reached Virginia, the news precipitated widespread chatter about the illegitimacy of royal government and sparked uprisings in the Northern Neck—"saying there was neither King, Laws nor Government." [6] In such unstable societies as these were, merely the menace of governmental illegitimacy posed a danger to public order. In Maryland, men in rebellion complained that "the Lawes are soe uncertaine and unknown that the people canot stere their Course with safetie in respect of them, which is a great greevance." [7]

The provisional governments established by various groups of malcontents, however, lacked legitimacy even more visibly than their predecessors. Jacob Leisler's twenty-month régime in New York had scarcely a shred of serious claim to exercise authority there; and Gershom Bulkeley's *Will and Doom*, the most important piece of political philosophy to emerge in response to the colonial rebellions, was explicitly designed to expose the new government of Connecticut as an illegitimate usurper. "They have no shadow of any warrant from their majesties," Bulkeley insisted, "for the exercise of this government to which they now pretend." [8]

The manifold crises of legitimacy in late seventeenth-century America were crises of change. At a time when new groups were seeking access to the political process, and at a time when new social assumptions were taking shape, countervailing legitimacy could not be located in the continuity of traditional integrative institutions. For some years prior to 1689, repeated deterioration in governmental effectiveness had made the stability of legitimate systems precarious at best. In

6. H. R. McIlwaine, ed.: *Executive Journals of the Council of Colonial Virginia, 1680–1699* (Richmond, 1925), I, 104–7.

7. Michael G. Hall, *et al.*, eds.: *The Glorious Revolution in America. Documents on the Colonial Crisis of 1689* (Chapel Hill, 1964), 54–5, 180.

8. Bulkeley: *Will and Doom, or the Miseries of Connecticut by and Under an Usurped and Arbitrary Power* (1692), in *Collections of the Connecticut Historical Society* (Hartford, 1895), III, 82, 94.

the years immediately following the rebellions, the most effective (albeit illegitimate) régimes proved to be even less
stable than their predecessors.

In 1694 Cotton Mather glanced retrospectively at the
history of New England, and used the image of a hedge to
describe the problem of achieving and preserving legitimacy in
the New World. He invoked the scriptural exhortation, "he
breaketh an Hedge and a Serpent shall bite him." Massachusetts Bay had been secure, said Mather, so long as "we had a
Royal Charter to be an Hedge about these Enjoyments." A
proper charter was a "Hedge whereby our Titles to our proper-
ties, and possessions, once questioned, are at once Confirmed." [9]
The period of England's greatest hostility to colonial charters
began in the 1680's and continued until about 1720. For half a
century thereafter, however, the colonists would zealously reprint editions of their original patents and seek charters of
incorporation to sanction their religious and economic enterprises.[1]

Ultimately, of course, the foremost fountain of legitimacy
for the colonies remained in England, drawing its resources
from the Privy Council, the Board of Trade, the Treasury, and
the King-in-Parliament. Bear in mind, for example, that colonial laws were not fully valid until approved in Whitehall. The
slowness of communications, however, tended to make these
final sources remote and unreal. Then, too, English opposition to Charles I, who first authorized many American enterprises, helped historically to undermine colonial constitutional
legitimacy. "I have found . . . a great Number of Pamphlets
printed from the Year 1630 to 1640," wrote Jonathan Swift,
"full of as bold and impious railing expressions against the
lawful Power of the Crown, and the Order of Bishops, as ever

9. Mather: *The Short History of New-England* (Boston, 1694),
14, 18.
1. See *The Charters of . . . Virginia, Maryland, Connecticut,
Rhode Island, Pennsylvania, Massachusetts Bay, and Georgia. . . .*
(London, 1766); Hugh Hastings, ed.: *Ecclesiastical Records. State of
New York* (Albany, 1905), VI, 4046–8.

were uttered during the Rebellion." [2] Then Cromwell's régime, itself stained with royal blood and the sweat of usurpation, made decisions affecting America which had to be undone in 1660 when monarchy reappeared. The Society for the Propagation of the Gospel in New England, established in 1649, had its charter declared invalid in 1661 and a new one granted on a different basis in 1662. Conversely, the Calvert family of Maryland, unseated from proprietary power by local Puritans in the 1650's, was restored to provincial control by King Charles II.

By contrast with the colonial scene, the problem of legitimacy ceased to be serious, or very troublesome, in England for more than a century after 1660. There were, to be sure, new constitutional arrangements to be made in the critical years 1689–1701; and there were brief episodic crises. But the vast majority of Georgian Englishmen were content with the status quo. They believed that theirs was the most perfect system of government ever devised, and that when the system functioned improperly it must have been because of poor personnel or faulty administration. People did die of disease, malnutrition, and gin in excess; the Tory critics did despise Sir Robert Walpole's "robinocracy" and the rise of the monied interest. But John Bull, by and large, was a very satisfied man.

EVER SINCE 1787, Americans have been able to seize upon concrete provisions of their written Constitution, and have lived within the structure of its legitimizing auspices. During the eighteenth century—to which we now should turn our attention —no colonial had more than a vague conception of the "constitution" under which he lived.[3] Not surprisingly, therefore, trivial matters frequently became inflated into great issues in-

---

2. Herbert Davis, ed.: *The Prose Writings of Jonathan Swift*, XII, *Irish Tracts, 1728–1733* (Oxford, 1955), 264.

3. See William Douglass: *A Summary, Historical and Political, of the First Planting, Progressive Improvements, and Present State of the British Settlements in North America* (Boston, 1749–51), I, 205–24 —"Concerning the general nature and constitution of the British North-American colonies."

volving first principles. In the absence of traditional and acceptable standards, cases of *lèse-majesté*—such as the libel trial of John Peter Zenger—were common occurrences. "How cautious then ought every one to be," wrote Cadwallader Colden in 1759, "in contributing anything towards the weakening of the legal powers of Government." [4]

Look for a moment at the fragility of all three major instruments of government. The royal governors lacked leverage. Their tenure was insecure and their decisions might easily be reversed "at home." They suffered, as Bernard Bailyn has remarked, from "swollen claims and shrunken powers." Whether a governor's royal instructions were in fact part of the law of the land was unclear, especially after 1715 when it was decided in London that an act passed by a provincial legislature and approved by the Crown took precedence over a royal instruction. [5] Then, too, no one really knew how to define the proper role and identity of the colonial council. It was not quite a cabinet, but not quite a counterpart of the House of Lords either. Because it had multiple functions, most of them were unclearly defined. And finally, the provincial assemblies' "quest for power" may be considered as simultaneously having been a quest for legitimacy as well. Endless squabbles between governors and burgesses over parliamentary privilege reveal the insecure bases on which both institutions rested. [6]

Every colonial assembly faced (or else self-consciously avoided) the difficult problem of relating the laws it passed to the legal system of Great Britain. And throughout the eight-

4. Colden to Alexander Colden, July 5, 1759, *Collections of the New-York Historical Society for the Year 1869* (New York, 1870), 203.

5. Bailyn: *The Origins of American Politics* (New York, 1968), 69, 88, 96; Leonard W. Labaree, ed.: *The Autobiography of Benjamin Franklin* (New Haven, 1964), 261–2.

6. Leonard W. Labaree: *Royal Government in America. A Study of the British Colonial System* (New York, 1958), 3, 167, 192–3; *Journals of the House of Representatives of Massachusetts, 1727–1729* and *1729–31* (Boston, 1927–28), VIII, 245–436, IX, 3–80 *passim;* Robert Zemsky: *Merchants, Farmers, and River Gods. An Essay on Eighteenth-Century American Politics* (Boston, 1971), 69–70, 239–40.

eenth century there was considerable ambiguity as to which English statutes were in effect overseas. In 1706, for example, the complex trial of the Reverend Francis Makemie threw New York into confusion over whether the penal laws of England did or did not extend to the plantations.[7] To make matters worse, few persons in these litigious provinces could be certain "what is law and what is not," or "how far the Legislative Authority is in the Assemblies." An anonymous Virginian made this matter a central issue in a striking disquisition published in 1701:

> It is a great Unhappiness, that no one can tell what is Law, and what is not, in the Plantations; some hold that the Law of *England* is chiefly to be respected, and where that is deficient, the Laws of the several Colonies are to take place; others are of Opinion, that the Laws of the Colonies are to take first place, and that the Law of *England* is of force only where they are silent; others there are, who contend for the Laws of the Colonies, in Conjunction with those that were in force in *England* at the first Settlement of the Colony, and lay down that as the measure of our Obedience, alleging, that we are not bound to observe any late Acts of Parliament made in *England*, except such only where the Reason of the Law is the same here, that it is in *England;* but this leaving too great a Latitude to the Judge; some others hold that no late Acts of Parliament of *England* do bind the Plantations, but those only, wherein the Plantations are particularly named. Thus are we left in the dark, in one of the most considerable Points of our Rights; and the Case being so doubtful, we are too often obliged to depend upon the Crooked Cord of a Judge's Discretion, in Matters of the greatest Moment and Value.[8]

7. St. George L. Sioussat: "The Theory of the Extension of English Statutes to the Plantations," in *Select Essays in Anglo-American Legal History* (Boston, 1907), I, 418, 420, 422, 425–6, 429; William Smith, Jr.: *The History of the Province of New-York* (London, 1757), 113, 247–9.

8. Louis B. Wright, ed.: *An Essay Upon the Government of the English Plantations on the Continent of America* (San Marino, 1945), 15–17, 23.

At intervals during the first half of the eighteenth century, Whitehall requested and insisted that the several colonies codify their laws and make clear digests available for use on both sides of the water. The colonies remained diffident, however, reluctant to expose their statutory deviations from the law of the realm. Finally, between 1750 and 1753 most of the colonies complied by compiling an up-to-date digest of laws in force. Only then, near the end of the colonial period, were provincial laws dignified and clarified by being given explicit public expression. In the process, however, indigenous alternatives to imperial authority were sanctified and publicized.[9]

The concept of legitimacy, and the legitimacy of law, have much to do with *who* can make, or discover, or apply the law. They also depend upon *how* the law is made, discovered, and applied, and upon the procedures which are used to bring the law into force. It is well known that the people of colonial America were a litigious lot, "on every little difference at law," as Cadwallader Colden said. Their litigiousness was a function and a symptom of the lack of clear criteria of legitimacy.[1] Characteristically, the famous Zenger case of 1735 hinged upon the validity of traditional interpretations of seditious libel; and the Morrisite faction in that affair took as its slogan "King George, Liberty, and Law." Authors of *The Independent Reflector*, an opposition weekly in New York in 1752–3, remarked upon the failure of magistrates to execute their public duties and enforce the laws. "Can it be presumed, that Persons sworn to execute the Laws, should openly counteract and violate them?"[2]

9. See *The Charlemagne Tower Collection of American Colonial Laws* (n.p., 1890), *passim;* Leonard W. Labaree, ed.: *Royal Instructions to British Colonial Governors, 1670–1776* (New York, 1935), I, 166–7.

1. There was considerable litigiousness in England and France, too, during the seventeenth and eighteenth centuries, in part a surrogate for the personal violence by which so many disputes were settled previously. In a sense, right replaced might as the criterion of legitimacy. What made colonial litigiousness special in this context was their unwillingness to accept adjudication as binding. Again and again the colonists ignored court decisions, or appealed them interminably.

2. *Collections of the New-York Historical Society for the Year 1869*, 208; James Alexander: *A Brief Narrative of the Case and*

In addition to the laws and their manner of enforcement, other regulations and reagents of human relationships also functioned in ways regarded as queer and unacceptable by European measures of judgment. The great problem with paper currency and banks of credit in colonial America was their apparent lack of legitimacy. The early American obsession with land titles and with surveying reveals their desperate concern with legitimizing property holdings and provincial boundaries. "We have, from the beginning," wrote an eighteenth-century historian, "been exposed to controversies about limits." Both the substantive and symbolic significance of boundaries in early America have been grossly neglected by modern historians. The quest for accurate boundaries—between New York and New Jersey, Massachusetts and New Hampshire, New Hampshire and New York, New York and Connecticut, Massachusetts and Rhode Island—was part and parcel of the quest for social and cultural norms and for stable political institutions. Accepted boundaries provide territorial hegemony at the least and geo-political legitimacy at best. Once the seventeenth century's sense of boundlessness had passed, men became deeply involved in the search for determinative land settlements. Thus Dr. William Douglass devoted the first chapter of his *Summary . . . and Present State of the Settlements* to a discussion of Anglo-French boundaries, and later passages to problems of provincial territoriality. Governor Thomas Hutchinson happened to write his *History of Massachusetts-Bay* because of work he did earlier on boundary commissions. William Byrd II wrote a classic essay, "The History of the Dividing Line," as a result of surveying the boundary between Virginia and North Carolina. Charles Mason and Jeremiah Dixon have been immortalized in American

Trial of John Peter Zenger, ed. Stanley N. Katz (Cambridge, Mass., 1963), 7, 26, 28, 33, 53, 82; William Livingston, *et al.: The Independent Reflector, or, Weekly Essays on Sundry Important Subjects More Particularly Adapted to the Province of New-York* [1753], ed. Milton M. Klein (Cambridge, Mass., 1963), 59, 85, 115–16, 148, 185–6, 195–7, 266–7.

history because they spent the years from 1763 until 1768 demarcating the long-disputed border between Pennsylvania, Maryland, and Delaware.[3] Although Americans have usually cared more about saving face than space, they have been passionately concerned about the destiny and domination of space. Never more so than in the eighteenth century.

If we turn our attention to the social institutions and assumptions of provincial America, we find that comparable conditions obtained. Although all of the colonies but three had established churches, they were not very securely established by European standards, and their legitimacy was therefore suspect. The recurrent episcopacy question in the eighteenth-century colonies—involving the Anglican quest for an American bishop—was profoundly symptomatic of the problem. In the absence of an American bishop, the Bishop of London had the colonies as part of his jurisdiction; but the nature and extent of his supervision remained unclear in practice, and ambiguous even in theory. A significant number of colonial religious groups looked to their European hierarchies as ultimate sources of authority. This was especially true of the Anglicans and Roman Catholics. The Dutch Reformed Church so relied upon the Classis of Amsterdam to supply colonial clergy that the Classis became accepted as the only source of legitimate ministerial authority. That assumption remained unchallenged until 1737, and operative until 1791 when the Dutch Reformed group in America finally asserted its independence.[4]

Clearly, there must have been for many denominations an

3. Smith: *History of the Province of New-York*, 186; Douglass: *Summary, Historical and Political . . . and Present State of the British Settlements in North America*, I, ch. 1, and 398–404, 415–19, 421–5; Byrd: "The History of the Dividing Line," in *The Prose Works of William Byrd of Westover*, ed. Louis B. Wright (Cambridge, Mass., 1966), 157–336; A. Hughlett Mason, ed.: *The Journal of Charles Mason and Jeremiah Dixon*, in *Memoirs of the American Philosophical Society* (Philadelphia, 1969), LXXVI.

4. John P. Luidens: "The Americanization of the Dutch Reformed Church" (unpublished Ph.D. dissertation, University of Oklahoma, 1969), 40, 47, 118–19, 122, 321.

awkward dichotomy between the formal locus of legitimate re-ligious authority and the immediacy of religious truth as each sect saw it. During the eighteenth century, dissenting groups in the southern colonies engaged in a long and arduous struggle to obtain an acceptable status in public law. Indeed, this issue was really the prime secular ingredient in the southern variant of the Great Awakening. In the middle colonies and in New England, Old Lights leveled the accusation at New Lights that they lacked theological legitimacy, and that they fostered "Dis-orders and Errors." New Lights, in their turn, accused the Old of lacking spiritual legitimacy: that was the great danger of an "unconverted ministry." Today we expect a psychoanalyst to have undergone analysis himself; in those days devout men expected their ministers to be converted.[5]

Understandably, matters of self-image and social legit-imacy were especially complex in colonial times. "In order to secure my Credit and Character as a Tradesman, I took care not only to be in *Reality* Industrious and frugal, but to avoid all *Appearances* of the Contrary." So wrote Benjamin Franklin in his *Autobiography*.[6] Certainly, there is something very Amer-ican about Franklin's emphasis upon industriousness and self-help; but most of all it is his quest for personal legitimacy—the attempt to make appearance and reality coincide—that rings true. Over the years England had dumped some of her most lawless inhabitants into the plantations. Not without cause were respectable Americans anxious to overcome the common view that most early colonists had been criminals. Even so, many servants had indeed arrived in the seventeenth-century settlements without written indentures, thereby creating a serious problem of ambiguous legal and social identities. Even-tually, each colony had to develop some standard, known as the "custom of the country," in order to specify the length of time which servants arriving without indenture should serve.

5. See Smith, *et al.*, eds.: *American Christianity . . . Representa-tive Documents*, I, 262–3.

6. Labaree, ed.: *Autobiography*, 125–6.

Sooner or later this "custom" became statutory law.[7] The momentum ran from expedience to acceptance to perpetuation.

The inevitable inflation of statuses in the colonies contributed to the quirkiness of social legitimacy there. In some situations, provincial governments tried to create artificial class distinctions by fiat, and in others they tried sumptuary laws. Governor Bernard of Massachusetts even proposed the establishment of an American nobility. None of these devices worked, of course; and as customary patterns of deference began to break down after 1740, the last real bulwark of traditional hierarchy crumbled. In consequence, the social order from mid-eighteenth to mid-nineteenth century was extremely fluid. Many Americans learned acceptable behavior from etiquette books, and symbols of status became important because they helped to make apparent the otherwise invisible ligaments of social order. Similarly, ceremonial and pageantry were important in the colonies in order to inform the populace that this office and that holiday were invested with special cachet. Hence the need for trumpets and cannons, or reading commissions aloud in public assemblies.

Europeans living primitively in the New World recognized that they faced a problem of maintaining traditional standards of "civilization." But with the passage of time it became difficult to determine just what the minimal or suitable standards were. For many, the lowest measure of civility became the American Indian. Colonists castigated one another with the admonition that they might sink to the barbaric level of the heathen. Positive criteria of social excellence and achievement, however, were much more difficult to ascertain. Eventually, and happily, personal qualities of merit became for many the critical test. "There is, perhaps, not a more dangerous Error, than to believe that we are bound to reverence Men for the Offices they sustain, without any Regard to their virtuous

7. Abbot E. Smith: *Colonists in Bondage. White Servitude and Convict Labor in America,* 1607–1776 (Chapel Hill, 1947), 19, 226–7, 229, 285–7.

Qualities, or useful Actions." So wrote William Livingston in 1753. "So in civil Life, nothing occurs more frequently, than to see an eminent Knave demanding the popular Esteem on Account of his Elevation. This ridiculous Respect paid to Men of superior Rank, without any Regard to their moral Character, is the Source of the most pernicious Consequences." [8]

Then too, the problem of social legitimacy in the colonies came down to the most literal levels, such as marriage and the family. In the seventeenth century, owing to the paucity of ministers, there were an extraordinary number of common law marriages—possibly more proportionately than in England. In consequence, some colonies passed legislation designed to legitimize retroactively common law marriages entered into during unsettled periods. In the Fundamental Constitutions of Carolina, first drafted in 1669, care was taken that "the Chamberlain's Court . . . shall have the care of all Ceremonies, Precedency, Heraldry . . . and Pedigrees; the Registries of all Births, Burials, and Marriages; legitimization and all cases concerning Matrimony or arising from it." All through the eighteenth century, clandestine and common law marriages remained commonplace despite the attendant ambiguities about the children of such relationships. Moreover, many believed that the religious enthusiasm of the Great Awakening had the unfortunate effect of stimulating unholy hormones. The Anglican Timothy Cutler called the Awakening a time when "our presses are forever teeming with books and our women with bastards." Cutler most likely was wrong about the erotic effects of enthusiasm, but merely the *belief* in rising illegitimacy caused social and psychological repercussions in colonial society. [9]

. . .

8. Livingston, *et al.: The Independent Reflector*, 360, 363.
9. James H. Cassedy: *Demography in Early America. Beginnings of the Statistical Mind*, 1600–1800 (Cambridge, Mass., 1969), 53, 57, 97n, 151–2, 155; Smith: *History of the Province of New-York*, 228; Labaree, ed.: *Autobiography of Benjamin Franklin*, 129–30.

IN SPANISH AMERICA and in Portuguese Brazil, personal and social legitimacy depended especially upon gentle birth; and statuses generally had sharper clarity than in the English colonies. During the first century of Spanish colonization, law and legality were significant concerns, and, unlike the English experience later, were determinative (though not necessarily mitigating) preoccupations in dealing with the Indians. The Spanish, who arrived in the New World first and therefore enjoyed the sanctions of priority, nevertheless looked ultimately to religious injunctions and natural law for their justification. The English, who arrived more than a century later and whose territorial claims were somewhat tenuous, turned to the Crown and to their charters for legitimacy. Given the chronology of European expansion, one might have expected a reversal among the two sets of rationalizations.[1]

Generally speaking, the problem of legitimacy did not appear in colonial Latin America in the same degree or forms it took in the English plantations. To be sure, when Cortez conquered the Aztecs he took along a notary who dutifully notarized everything the conquistadors did. Other Spanish conquerors were accompanied by lawyers. And, to be sure, the conquistadors' physical achievement was so great during the first two generations that they readily tended to challenge the rightfulness of royal decisions, and on occasion even the primacy of the Crown as an enabling force. After 1570, however, Philip II reasserted his full hegemony over the Spanish colonies. Since all legal statuses emanated from the royal person, Spain's colonial officialdom in the sixteenth and seventeenth centuries enjoyed greater prestige and stability than England's imperial bureaucracy. Because the Spanish monarchs kept tighter control over their plantations than the English, and because there was less institutional flexibility in the Iberian colonies, the legitimacy problem remained a manage-

1. Cf. Martin Needler: *Latin American Politics in Perspective* (Princeton, 1963), 35–9; Francisco José Moreno: *Legitimacy and Stability in Latin America. A Study of Chilean Political Culture* (New York, 1969), chs. 1–2.

able one right up until the movements for Independence at the close of the eighteenth century.[2]

INSECURE PEOPLE are quickest to find fault with others. Given the various crises of legitimacy in English America, therefore, and given the inevitable quest for constitutional, institutional, and social integrity, it is not surprising that colonists seized eagerly upon opportunities to challenge the rightfulness of Britain's dominion. They did so in a limited way in 1689, and would do so again more fully between 1765 and 1776. The prelude to the American Revolution first involved rejection of Parliament as an imperial legislative body, and ultimately even the moral legitimacy of the Crown. Until 1774, colonists tried to distinguish between legitimate powers of Parliament and those of the provincial assemblies. When Parliament denied the validity of such distinctions, the ideological crisis passed beyond the point of no return. Quite logically, the question of sovereignty became a vital issue of the American Revolution, for sovereignty is a critical quality of constitutional legitimacy.

John Dickinson of Pennsylvania, author in 1767 of the widely read *Farmer's Letters*, perceived the central sources of the American Revolution as creating a crisis of legitimacy. "There is a certain *confusion* in our laws," he wrote, "that is quite unknown in Great-Britain." Nevertheless, constitutionality in the colonies ultimately rested upon English pillars: "the government here is not only *mixt*, but *dependent*, which circumstance occasions *a peculiarity in its form*, of a very delicate nature." Dickinson anticipated that a conventional crisis of legitimacy would be compounded in the colonial context:

> A nation may change their King, or race of Kings, and, retaining their antient form of government, be gainers by changing. . . . But if once *we* are separated from

2. See C. R. Boxer: *The Golden Age of Brazil, 1695–1750. Growing Pains of a Colonial Society* (Berkeley, 1969), 83, 109, 111, 131; J. H. Parry: *The Spanish Seaborne Empire* (New York, 1966), esp. Part II.

our Mother country, what new form of government shall we adopt, or where shall we find another *Britain*, to supply our loss? Torn from the body, to which we are united by religion, liberty, laws, affections, relation, language and commerce, we must bleed at every vein.[3]

Between the Stamp Act Congress in 1765 and the Continental Congress in 1775, colonists convened many extra-legal bodies: there were committees of correspondence, "unwarrantable combinations" of colonial assemblies, circumstances such as the Boston town meeting calling a convention of all the Massachusetts towns, and the burgesses of Virginia meeting illegally as an "association." In 1776, the newly independent states established "anti-parliaments" of their own. No wonder moderate spokesmen of the patriot cause tried valiantly to couch their communications in the language of legitimacy. John Adams devoted himself to the rationalization of a "lawful revolution," and advocated scrupulous attention to legality. "I had good policy, as well as sound law, on my side, when I ventured to lay open before our people the laws against riots, routs, and unlawful assemblies. Mobs will never do to govern States and command armies."[4] The traditions of English constitutionalism, especially John Locke's famous statement of Whig principles in 1689, were repeatedly invoked to legitimize revolutionary recourses. Colonial lawyers, moreover, used the conservative common law as a weapon for constitutional emancipation and local autonomy. Theirs was thus a kind of conservative radicalism; or, as Richard B. Morris has put it, "revolutionary legalism." Understandably, then, Edmund Burke would remark of America that "in no country perhaps in the world is the law so general a study."[5]

3. *The Farmer's and Monitor's Letters to the Inhabitants of the British Colonies* (Williamsburg, 1769), 13, 19, 33, 36, 46, 77.

4. Adams to Benjamin Hichborn, January 27, 1787, in Charles F. Adams, ed.: *The Works of John Adams* (Boston, 1854), IX, 551. See also *ibid.*, II, 374.

5. Morris: "Legalism Versus Revolutionary Doctrine in New England," in Flaherty, ed.: *Essays in the History of Early American Law*, 418, 430–1.

It has been customary for some years to discuss the great authors of the American Renaissance—Emerson, Thoreau, Hawthorne, Melville, and Whitman—in terms of the dilemma they all faced: the lack of appropriate and indigenous literary sources, precedents, and styles. Patriotic politicians of the revolutionary era faced a similar quandary. Having rejected the implementation of English authority, they immediately embarked upon a new and different quest for republican legitimacy. "Whenever the Magistrate acts in Opposition to his political Power," William Livingston had written earlier, "he cannot do such Acts as Magistrate; but must be esteemed a Person exerting Strength without Power, that is, legal Power; which every Man of superior Strength hath, by the Law of Nature, a manifest Right to oppose. To resist in such a Case, is not resisting his Authority, but Force illegal and unauthoritative." They discovered, of course, that rejection was intellectually less demanding than regeneration. "Government is dissolved," Patrick Henry proclaimed in debate; "Where are your landmarks? your Boundaries of Colonies?" [6]

Illicit imperial authority might thus be branded and repudiated; but how to create and perpetuate new forms of governance? Therein lay the greatest crisis of legitimacy for revolutionaries. Nearly every state bill of rights written after 1776, following the example of Virginia, contained a formal denunciation of legal privilege based upon status. Thus the new Americans repudiated their forefathers' apparent dilemma in the realm of social legitimacy, leveling the criteria of both acceptability and opportunity. Thomas Jefferson, who criticized the illegitimacy of Virginia's new constitution—"a mere ordinance or statute with no permanent and binding power on the government"—yearned throughout the 1780's for a new

6. Livingston, *et al.*: *The Independent Reflector*, 326; Henry in Continental Congress, Sept. 5, 1774, in L. H. Butterfield, ed.: *The Diary and Autobiography of John Adams* (Cambridge, Mass., 1961), II, 124. See also George Chalmers: *Political Annals of the Present United Colonies, from Their Settlement to the Peace of 1763* (London, 1780), "Preface," para. 4 ("every principle of public law had been disputed") ff.

understanding of "constitutions." How could some absolute source of governmental authority be determined "on a bottom which none will dispute?"[7] The answer would not be worked out until 1787, and not fully even then.

In the meanwhile, between the Declaration of Independence and the federal Constitution, even such erstwhile radicals as Sam Adams had to come around and insist that

> There is Decency & Respect due to Constitutional Authority, and those Men, who under any Pretence or by any Means whatever, would lessen the Weight of Government lawfully exercised, must be Enemies to our happy Revolution & the Common Liberty. County Conventions & popular Committees servd an excellent Purpose when they were first in Practice. No one therefore needs to regret the Share he may then have had in them. But I candidly own it is my Opinion . . . that as we now have constitutional & regular Governments and all our Men in Authority depend upon the annual & free Elections of the People, we are safe without them. . . . If the publick Affairs are illy conducted, if dishonest or incapable Men have crept unawares into Government, it is happy for us, that under our American Constitutions the Remedy is at hand, & in the Power of the great Body of the People.[8]

Thus *the people* were now becoming the touchstone of legitimacy and power. "We the people. . . ."

Even so, the grand convention—self-consciously an extra-constitutional body—would meet in Philadelphia not so much in order to redefine the locus of authority, but because the Confederation government seemed to lack sovereign integrity as a nation. It could not ward off violations of its rights by foreigners; it could not control disorderly groups at home; and it could not pay its debts. Joel Barlow argued before a group of

7. Samuel Eliot Morison, ed.: *Sources and Documents Illustrating the American Revolution, 1764–1788, and the Forming of the Federal Constitution* (New York, 1965), 149; Jefferson: *Notes on the State of Virginia*, ed. Thomas P. Abernethy (New York, 1964), 117–19, 152, 197.

8. Adams to Noah Webster, April 30, 1784, in Harry A Cushing, ed.: *The Writings of Samuel Adams* (New York, 1908), IV, 305–6.

Connecticut lawyers in 1786 that new conditions required a new theory of legality. The Northwest Ordinance of 1787 was essential in order to rationalize and legitimize westward expansion. And James Madison's solution to the ubiquitous problem of factions was to legitimize them through a new theory of the proper relationship between interests, state, and society.

Madison, more than anyone else in 1787–8, faced directly and responsibly the most serious question arising from the new Constitution: what was *its* source of legitimacy, *its* enabling power? [9] For several decades past, growing numbers of Americans had been groping toward a notion of the people as constituent power and ultimate authority. As "Britannus Americanicus" had put it in urging resistance to the Stamp Act in 1765: "To overthrow it, nothing is wanting but your own Resolution, for great is the authority and Power of the People." In 1774, Ezra Stiles had similarly defended the legality of the Continental Congress:

> The King must know, the British Parliament must know, for the World will know it, that the American Continental Congress of September last was a regular legal patriotic Body . . . and that the *Mode of their Election* by a patriotic spontaneous selforigination from the People is defencible on the first Principles of Society and the English Constitution, and justifiable and glorious on the Principles of the Law of Nature and Nations and the finest Reasonings of the Jus civile.[1]

In August 1776 the new Constitution of Pennsylvania declared "that all power being originally inherent in, and consequently derived from, the people; therefore all officers of government . . . are their trustees and servants, and at all times

9. See Richard Hofstadter: *The Idea of a Party System. The Rise of Legitimate Opposition in the United States, 1780–1840* (Berkeley, 1969), 82, 85–6, 90, 98, 102–3.

1. "A serious Address to the Inhabitants of New-York," Dec. 17, 1765, Broadside Collection, New-York Historical Society; Franklin B. Dexter, ed.: *The Literary Diary of Ezra Stiles* (New York, 1901), I, 521.

accountable to them." And in 1783 it was the Reverend Stiles once again, student of the Enlightenment, who insisted excitedly that "a DEMOCRATICAL polity for millions, standing upon the broad basis of the people at large, amply charged with property, has not hitherto been exhibited." [2]

Madison took these various utterances, which grew in number, explicitness, and the complexity of their extrapolation between 1765 and 1787, and wove them into an enduring explication of the fountain and function of legitimacy in a democratic republic. In *The Federalist*, Number 39, he defined a republic as

> a government which derives all its powers directly or indirectly from the great body of the people, and is administered by persons holding their offices during pleasure, for a limited period, or during good behaviour. It is *essential* to such a government that it be derived from the great body of the society, not from an inconsiderable proportion, or a favoured class of it.

And when he introduced the first draft of the Bill of Rights in 1789, he observed:

> That all power is originally vested in, and consequently derived from, the people. That government is instituted and ought to be exercised for the benefit of the people . . . that the people have an indubitable, inalienable and indefeasible right to reform or change their Government, whenever it be found adverse or inadequate to the purposes of its institution.[3]

We have lived ever since, though not without vacillation and exception, within the framework of Madison's formulation.

The key figure in lending respectability and credibility to the new government, of course, was George Washington. Just as his very presence in Philadelphia in 1787 had helped to

2. Richard L. Perry, ed.: *Sources of Our Liberties* (New York, 1959), 329; Stiles: *The United States Elevated to Glory and Honor* (New Haven, 1783), 17.

3. Clinton Rossiter, ed.: *The Federalist Papers* (New York, 1961), 241, 243, 244; Gaillard Hunt, ed.: *The Writings of James Madison* (New York, 1904), V, 376–7.

sanctify that uncertain undertaking, his presence in New York, the new capital after 1789, legitimized the administration of executive power and, really, the entire experiment in republican government.

Members of Washington's cabinet obviously felt some sensitivity about that experiment. In 1792, following the execution of Louis XVI, Alexander Hamilton raised the question of French governmental legitimacy. Whereupon Jefferson gently reminded his colleague that "we certainly cannot deny to other nations that principle whereon our government is founded." One base-born progeny (in this case both the United States and Hamilton himself) ought not be too fastidious about the credentials of another. Even Jefferson as President, however, had to invoke criteria of constitutional integrity. "I deem no government safe," he wrote Gallatin in 1803, "which is under the vassalage of self-constituted authorities, or any other authority than that of the nation, or its regular functionaries." [4]

Yet even the existence of a written constitution did not guarantee unanimity on the foundations of the nation. As early as 1792, Fisher Ames complained that "the practice of crying out 'this is unconstitutional,' is a vice that has grown inveterate by indulgence." Nevertheless, men of different allegiances at least were in agreement as to which documents stood paramount in the pyramid of authority. "In my opinion," wrote Hamilton in 1802, "the present Constitution is the standard to which we are to cling. Under its banners, *bona fide*, must we combat our political foes, rejecting all changes but through [those] the channel itself provides for amendments." [5] Chief Justice John Marshall pounded the lesson home in his famous decision on *McCulloch* vs. *Maryland* (1819): "Let the end be legitimate, let it be within the scope of the Constitution, and

4. Merrill D. Peterson: *Thomas Jefferson and the New Nation* (New York, 1970), 482, 701.

5. *Ibid.*, 461; Hamilton to James A. Bayard, April 1802, in Henry Cabot Lodge, ed.: *The Works of Alexander Hamilton* (New York, 1886), VIII, 598; Adrienne Koch, ed.: *The American Enlightenment* (New York, 1965), 648–9.

all means which are appropriate, which are plainly adapted to that end, which are not prohibited, but consist with the letter and spirit of the Constitution, are constitutional."

As the nineteenth century opened, then, Federalists and Republicans had achieved a consensus that the surest source of sovereignty lay in the consent of the governed. Whereas nationalistic historical writing developed in Britain after 1790 in response to the external threat of Napoleonic France, in America it developed in response to an internal problem—the quest for legitimacy. "The American Revolution saved the colonies," said David Ramsay. "So necessary are occasional revolutions, to bring government back to first principles, and to teach rulers, *that the people are the fountain of all legitimate power*, and their happiness the object of all its delegations." [6]

All of which certainly makes for an awkward anomaly in American thought. Although the founders were themselves engaged in a continuous quest for modes of legitimacy appropriate to their times and needs, subsequent Americans have sought to validate their own aspirations by invoking the innovations and standards of our hallowed pantheon as unchanging verities. This nostalgic vision of the Golden Age actually conjures up an era when values were unclearly defined, when instability often seemed beyond control, when public rancor and private vituperation were rampant, and institutions frail and unformed.

6. Ramsay: *History of the United States from their First Settlement as English Colonies in 1607 to the Year 1808*. . . . (Philadelphia, 1816), I, 352. Italics mine.

CHAPTER 3

INVERTEBRATE AMERICA
The Problem of Unstable Pluralism

America, it would seem, is miraculously both singular
and plural, organized and scattered, united and diffused.

HENRY S. KARIEL,
The Decline of American Pluralism (1961)

THE QUEST for legitimacy in early America was complicated
by the presence of a kind of multi-dimensional pluralism.
Adapting the phrase of Ortega y Gasset, I find it useful to
envision the colonies, particularly in the period 1660–1760, as
invertebrate America: "a series of water-tight compartments,"
none of which felt very much "curiosity toward events in the
domain of the others." Taken together, the plantations lacked
a figurative spinal column. All too easily they slipped in and
out of relation to one another because they were not firmly
connected. They had not yet achieved the kind of collective
individualism whose motto would be struck by Theodore Parker
in 1848: "You are as good as I, and let us help one another." [1]

English colonial society, almost from the outset, underwent
both a remarkable degree of "horizontal" or simultaneous
pluralism (prodigious clusters of private groups, factionalism,

1. Parker: "The Political Destination of America and the Signs
of the Times," in *The Transcendentalists*, ed. Perry Miller (Garden
City, 1957), 357.

a fairly complex governmental apparatus) and of "vertical" or sequential pluralism. By the latter I mean simply the recurring nature of the transplantation experience, the repeated shocks to social relationships as wave after wave of swirling groups washed up along the eastern shores. Add the fact that many who came had already led disordered lives in Europe, and then note that the vastness of available space provided yet another major stimulus to heterogeneity in America. It has always been easier to deviate from canons of orthodoxy in this country, both because the canons have been so unclear and uncodified, and because people who thought "otherwise," like Roger Williams or Brigham Young, could go "elsewhere" and do so with impunity. Each sort of pluralism—the simultaneous and the sequential—intensified and reinforced the other, as new people from unstable situations added their uneasy presence to the fluidity of colonial society, and thereby made it even more so.

The depth and breadth of pluralism in America's experience have had many sources. Certainly, and unparadoxically, economic individualism has been a contributory factor, as well as the commitment (intermittently fulfilled) to uphold the dignity of individual persons and groups. Material opportunity has pushed sons toward an early independence, and disrupted the vocational and locational continuities of traditional European families. American fathers have held great expectations for their sons (and sometimes daughters), have wanted them to "do better than I did." Moreover, instability is especially likely to occur in a heterogeneous society where rapid change or improvement occurs in one sphere—in wealth, for example—without equally rapid change in other spheres, such as services, status, freedom, and power.

Over the past two decades, social scientists have been increasingly interested in the complexities of plural societies. Not surprisingly, they vary considerably (and often disagree) in their definitions and criteria for inclusion. For some, a plural society is one in which originally discrete cultures remain essentially separate and therefore fail to provide a cohesive basis for the "market situation" in which people of different ethnic groups must interact. For others, the various cultural patterns are seen as interpenetrating, thereby leading to the emergence of new forms. And for still others, the conflicting patterns of various groups are not cultural patterns in the usual sense, but "value patterns" comprising sets of activities which further both the interests and the ideals of groups brought together by economic, political, and social forces.[2]

We need not become engaged here in the conceptual archeology of the social sciences, particularly since the digging thus far has thrown up more rubble than it has revealed eternal foundations. Nevertheless, the work of social theorists does provide us with some formulations more precise or prescient than we are likely to stumble upon by serendipity. The very term "plural society," to begin with, is perhaps contradictory, for the idea of society, by dint of customary definition, implies unity—the antithesis of plurality. There is a sense, then, in which the central problem of plural societies lies in this contradiction: How can one be at once truly *plural* and yet literally a society?

We might resolve the dilemma by regarding plural societies as units of disparate parts, which owe their existence to external factors (such as tribalism or distinct historical origins) and lack a common social will. Multiple affiliations and loyalties have certainly been characteristic of plural societies, and often highly problematic to them. In 1767, when John Dickinson wrote the *Farmer's Letters*, he appealed to his fellow colonists to be guided by such "a spirit . . . that it will be impossible to determine whether an *American's* character is

2. See John Rex: "The Plural Society in Sociological Theory," *British Journal of Sociology*, X (1959), 114–24; H. I. McKenzie: "The Plural Society Debate," *Social and Economic Studies*, XV (1966), 53–60; Leo A. Despres: "Anthropological Theory, Cultural Pluralism, and the Study of Complex Societies," *Current Anthropology*, IX (1968), 3–26; Michael G. Smith and Leo Kuper, eds.: *Pluralism in Africa* (Los Angeles, 1968), esp. chs. 1–3; Michael G. Smith: *The Plural Society in the British West Indies* (Berkeley, 1965), esp. 75–91.

most distinguishable, for his loyalty to his Sovereign, his duty to his Mother Country, his love of freedom, or his affection for his native soil." [3]

I am most comfortable with an ordinary-language definition in which "plural society" connotes a polity containing distinct cleavages amongst diverse population groups. Often there will be a dispersion of power among groups bound together by cross-cutting loyalties, common values, and a competitive equilibrium or balance of power. Equally often there will be conflict between racial, tribal, religious, and regional groups, to such a degree that the whole must be maintained by regulation and force. Because of the role of authority in any system of domination, there is commonly a psychological pressure upon subordinate cultural segments to deny legitimacy to the imposed order, and to reject law and authority as such. Finally, I think it is particularly important to note that pluralism in less repressive societies has a built-in dynamic toward uncontrolled change. Certainly that has been true in the United States.

From the very beginning of American history, one might argue, our governmental and cultural impulses have been in the direction of uniformity and away from multiplicity. Yet our economic and social imperatives—the labor shortage, military requirements, and recruitment patterns for colonization—as well as geographical expanse, have all fostered pluralism. But why has pluralism been any more of a factor in the North American colonies than in many other settings? The answer, I think, is that ours has been *unstable* pluralism, and that the adjective here makes quite a difference. So many of the immigrants to the colonies came for anti-authoritarian reasons, came with hostilities against restraint already well formed. Moreover, plural societies gain in stability where major political parties cut across ethnic lines. Such has been the case in nineteenth- and twentieth-century America, where the history of party is remarkable for continuity and longevity. But such was not the case in colonial America, where there were Quaker

3. *The Farmer's and Monitor's Letters to the Inhabitants of the British Colonies* (Williamsburg, 1769), 12, 95.

parties, German parties, Presbyterian parties—where each group might have its own faction, each sect its own school, each dogmatist his own ideology.

Therefore, I must insist upon the fragile condition of unstable pluralism as being critical to an understanding of early, especially eighteenth-century, America. There have been, and are, polities characterized by stable pluralism, or by unstable homogeneity. The U.S.S.R. today is far more pluralistic in composition than the United States. But it is stable because of the intensity of centralized political repression there. Our own country, although less pluralistic, is also less stable because of the relative degree of permissiveness and toleration. Conversely, England between the coronation of James I in 1603 and that of Charles II in 1660 was not particularly stable; but the remarkable degree of social homogeneity enjoyed there made possible the passive reconciliation of the Restoration. Thereafter, stability would long endure because of the harmonious interplay between local and central institutions, between counties and the Crown, and because the gentry took seriously their political responsibilities and maintained order responsively. Social and political stability were prime desiderata in Hanoverian England, glorified at mid-century by David Hume; and the basic structure of Georgian politics was well tempered, steel-like in its strength and tenacity, even if it occasionally bent in the wind.

A case might be made, however, for the existence in colonial Latin America of both social pluralism and instability. It is a case I take seriously—and therefore hasten to get on to specifics, because only then will the particular dynamics of unstable pluralism in the English colonies become manifest. In the latter, pluralism developed from the unchecked density of ethnic, religious, and national groups of diverse origin. In the Spanish colonies, pluralism arose as a function of the conquest and subsequent sexual mingling of Iberian, Indian, and African peoples, a socio-racial pluralism institutionalized and stabilized by law and custom. Whereas pluralism in Latin America became a psychological phenomenon, having much to do with status and the perception of pigmentation, pluralism in North America was more a socio-political matter which complicated the fixity of institutions and public power.[4]

Let us look with some intensity, then, at the nature of unstable pluralism in British North America. And let us use "pluralism" in its most catholic sense: ethnic, regional, and chronological—all the possible encrustations of layer upon layer of humanity through time. For as Paul Tillich once wrote, "the mystery of the future and the mystery of the past are united in the mystery of the present. . . . But how can we have 'presence'? . . . Is not the present the ever-moving boundary line between past and future? *But a moving boundary is not a place to stand upon.*"[5] The metaphor is an ideal one for the study of American civilization through time, because our institutional, intellectual, and physical boundaries have been almost continually in motion. "Presence" has indeed been elusive where there was little stability and a surfeit of shifting changes in society.

IT SHOULD BE STRESSED that unstable pluralism, unlike the problem of legitimacy, was more prominently an eighteenth-century phenomenon than a seventeenth-century one. Recent studies by innovative social historians have in fact revealed that the colonies during their first two or three generations were much more stable than we had supposed.[6] Indeed, it may well transpire that some of our most sacred assumptions must be turned entirely upside down: that we not only shifted from

4. See Ronald C. Newton: "On 'Functional Groups,' 'Fragmentation,' and 'Pluralism' in Spanish American Political Society," *Hispanic American Historical Review*, L (1970), 1–29; Richard Morse: "Crosscurrents in New World History," in *Politics of Change in Latin America*, ed. Joseph Maier (New York, 1964), 54.

5. Tillich: *The Eternal Now* (New York, 1963), 130. Italics mine.

6. See Philip J. Greven, Jr.: *Four Generations. Population, Land and Family in Colonial Andover, Massachusetts* (Ithaca, 1970), 268–70; Kenneth A. Lockridge: *A New England Town. The First Hundred Years. Dedham, Massachusetts, 1636–1736* (New York, 1970), 165, 168–9.

being more "American" to less so as the seventeenth century progressed, but that the colonies also became *less* stable with the passage of decades.

Nonetheless, despite the eighteenth-century emphasis of this phenomenon, we ought to begin with some notion of earliest origins and anticipations. For the facts are that while Massachusetts, Connecticut, Virginia, and perhaps South Carolina were founded on the premise of stable homogeneity, and while Rhode Island, New York, New Jersey, Pennsylvania, Maryland, and Georgia were established with the expectation of stable heterogeneity, both sets of assumptions failed to be fulfilled.

The congregational churches of New England were to have enjoyed a kind of co-operative autonomy, an ecclesiastical polity of plural equilibrium. Serious doctrinal differences and dissension, however, emerged with effervescence by the 1640's, and synods were required irregularly for decades thereafter in order to prevent the full fragmentation of New England's orthodoxy. The Puritans of Massachusetts, moreover, as well as Quaker and German sectarians scattered elsewhere, acquired a state of mind and underwent a social process known as "tribalism." In becoming so exclusive and withdrawn, they were demonstrating one kind of defense mechanism against an unexpectedly plural society. They coped by refusing to cope, by abandoning all sense of mission save the salvation of their very own kind.

Ambiguities about the legitimacy of religious diversity in New Netherland were abundantly present from the very beginning. Dutch Reformed dominies insisted that the preservation of social stability required the strict enforcement of laws regulating religious practices. An orderly polity required religious orthodoxy and uniformity. Officials of the West India Company, however, took the side of Amsterdam's merchant aristocracy and supported *de facto* toleration. The Reverend John Megapolensis complained of "these godless rascals . . . Papists, Mennonites and Lutherans among the Dutch; also many Puritans or Independents, and many Atheists and various other servants of Baal among the English under this Government, who conceal themselves under the name of Christians; it would create a still greater confusion, if the obstinate and immovable Jews came to settle here." Even so, the company's directors reminded Governor Stuyvesant of the necessity for stable pluralism:

> Your last letter informed us that you had banished from the Province . . . a certain Quaker . . . Although we heartily desire, that these and other sectarians remained away from there, yet as they do not, we doubt very much, whether we can proceed against them rigorously without diminishing the population and stopping immigration, which must be favoured at a so tender stage of the country's existence. You may therefore shut your eyes, at least not force people's consciences, but allow every one to have his own belief, as long as he behaves quietly and legally, gives no offense to his neighbors and does not oppose the government.[7]

In the colony of East Jersey, developed a decade after this correspondence, the same imperatives obtained, with comparable results: Quakers and anti-Quakers, Scottish Quakers and Scottish Presbyterians, Puritans from Long Island in Elizabethtown, Puritans from New Hampshire in Piscataway, Dutch Calvinists in Bergen, Baptists and Quakers in Middletown and Navesink—a cacophony of discordant sectarians.

Sectarianism. The word should carry a heavy freight of import, and yet it has been strangely neglected by American cultural historians. We have long assumed that denominationalism is America's peculiar contribution to the history of religion, and that there is continuity in the configuration of American denominations from the colonial to the national period. I would like to suggest instead that sectarianism preceded denominationalism in American history, and that the differences are significant.

If I may be forgiven for defining what is Christ's in terms

7. Hugh Hastings, comp.: *Ecclesiastical Records. State of New York* (Albany, 1901), I, 335–6, 530.

of what is Caesar's, a sect is to a political faction as a denomination is to a party. Sects and factions tend to be unstable and impermanent, they lack the longevity, institutional apparatus, and coalition qualities of denominations and parties. Sects fluctuate, fragment, and feud among themselves. George Keith, the great Quaker controversialist of the 1690's, became an Anglican priest in 1702, while other erstwhile Keithian Quakers became Baptists. Francis Daniel Pastorius, the prominent Lutheran pietist, became a Quaker; and Count Zinzendorf, the German evangelical leader in Pennsylvania, was oft-criticized for constantly shifting his sectarian affiliation. Francis Makemie almost achieved martyrdom in fighting for Presbyterian liberties after 1700, yet he hated the Quakers who were waging the self-same struggle.[8]

Paradoxically, as one student has remarked, "the New World vision of the group and of group society entails an affirmation rather than a negation of individualism." America's pluralistic experience owes much to the enthusiastic and expansive drives of effulgent colonial communities. Inevitably, of course, pluralistic individualism would lead to sectarian cooperation, and ultimately to the stability of institutionalized denominationalism.[9] But not until after the Great Awakening had irrevocably shattered the remaining coherence of colonial Christendom. The religious revival was explicitly opposed as a threat to social and political stability. Connecticut's government claimed that revivals had a "natural tendency to disturb and destroy the peace and order" of the colony; and in 1743 the *Boston Evening Post* looked upon them as "the grand Engine of fomenting Divisions, and making Separations in our Churches." In New York the Awakening merely aggravated a condition of unstable pluralism long since out of control.

8. See H. Shelton Smith, *et al.*, eds.: *American Christianity. An Historical Interpretation with Representative Documents, 1607–1820* (New York, 1960), I, 252–3, 285, 296–7.
9. Darryl Baskin: "The Congregationalist Origins of American Pluralism," *Journal of Church and State*, XI (1969), 278, 280; Leonard W. Labaree, ed.: *The Autobiography of Benjamin Franklin* (New Haven, 1964), 194.

Because there is here perfect freedom of conscience for
all, except Papists, a spirit of confusion is ever blazing
up more and more. Everybody may do what seems
right in his own eyes. . . . Hence so many conven-
ticles exist. Hence so many are perplexed and misled;
while others neglect or scoff at the divine service, not
to speak of those who, on various wrong pretexts, entirely abstain from the Lord's Supper.[1]

By the 1740's, when this letter was written, inconstancies
of cultural pluralism were everywhere evident in provincial
America. Sectarian control over educational institutions receiv-
ing public support became particularly problematic. "An University hatched by the Heat of Sectaries," lamented William
Livingston of New York, "and cherished in the contracted
Bosom of furious zeal, shall be shewn to be the natural Consequence of a charter Government." And when Benjamin
Franklin decided to found a school in 1749, he was prompted
particularly by the presence in Pennsylvania of numerous
"foreigners unacquainted with our language, laws and customs." He especially hoped to see the Germans assimilated and
anglicized, and therefore would teach no foreign languages.
His school would be a homogenizing influence, not a diversi-
fying one.[2]

The sources, processes, and expressions of cultural pluralism all contributed to the creative variability of colonial life.
Even New England, the most homogeneous of regions, received
Huguenots by the 1680's, Irish after 1708, and significant
numbers of non-English immigrants by the 1720's. By the

1. David S. Lovejoy, ed.: *Religious Enthusiasm and the Great
Awakening* (Englewood Cliffs, 1969), 15; John E. Van de Wetering,
"The *Christian History* of the Great Awakening," *Journal of Presby-
terian History*, XLIV (1966), 128; Rev. Gualterus Du Bois to the
Classis of Amsterdam, May 14, 1741, in Hastings, *Ecclesiastical Rec-
ords. State of New York*, IV, 2756.
2. William Livingston, *et al.*: *The Independent Reflector, or
Weekly Essays on Sundry Important Subjects More Particularly
Adapted to the Province of New-York*, ed. Milton M. Klein (Cam-
bridge, Mass., 1963), 82–5, 178–9, 185, 207–14; Leonard W.
Labaree, ed.: *The Papers of Benjamin Franklin* (New Haven,
1959–   ), III, 386, V, 214–18.

1690's, immigrants could no longer be easily absorbed by Puritan society; between 1690 and 1740, sharp class differences and hostility emerged between established families and newcomers. Moreover, whereas British naturalization laws were designed to *minimize* immigration, protect the hegemony of the Church of England, and avert threats to political stability at home, colonial naturalization laws were intended to *encourage* immigration. Their permissiveness was an invitation to unstable pluralism: their openness to foreign Protestants, relatively liberal (albeit limited) welcome to Jews, growing acceptance of Roman Catholics, absence of religious rites, simpler procedures, and lower costs were all symptomatic and stimulating.[3]

Similarly, the proliferation of provincial newspapers after the 1720's was both a response to and a generator of unstable pluralism. They reprinted news from abroad as well as from other colonies, and thereby provided the beginnings of a more unified outlook. At the same time, however, newspapers were organs of factionalism and sectarianism, parochial, petty, and vituperative in their unsettling attacks. The famous case and trial of John Peter Zenger in 1734–5 arose from precisely these origins; and Zenger's canny lawyer, Andrew Hamilton, invoked a new kind of legal relativism appropriate to the circumstances of plural societies: "What is good law at one time and in one place," he contended, "is not so at another time and in another place."[4]

By the 1720's and 1730's there were also demographic changes which intensified mobility and contributed to change. People achieved physical maturity at a younger age, established economic independence and married earlier, were divorced more easily, and left their communities of origin with greater

3. Clifford K. Shipton: "Immigration to New England, 1680–1740," *Journal of Political Economy*, XLIV (1936), 225–39; Edward A. Hoyt: "Naturalization Under the American Colonies," *Political Science Quarterly*, LXVII (1952), 248–66.

4. James Alexander: *A Brief Narrative of the Case and Trial of John Peter Zenger, Printer of the New York Weekly Journal*, ed. Stanley N. Katz (Cambridge, Mass., 1963), 67–8.

frequency.[5] Because of economic growth and social diversity, the eighteenth-century colonies became less egalitarian and more stratified than the seventeenth had been. And when men moved, they moved to and through a plurality of ever-changing frontiers surrounding discrete and discontinuous areas of settlement.[6]

Because stability of any sort, homogeneous or heterogeneous, was so elusive to find and tenuous to keep, the settlers' public rhetoric played incessantly on themes of union and unity. "Union is the source of public happiness," Jonathan Mayhew insisted; "unity must subside and then it's plain what will follow," fumed the selectmen of Worcester, Massachusetts. "Our Ennemies never fail to take advantage of intestine divisions & confusion," wrote Cadwallader Colden in 1759, and the purpose of his exhortatory plea was clear.[7]

It had been equally manifest ever since the first generation that intercolonial co-operation was ephemeral at best and non-existent at worst. Material and religious differences kept the colonies at loggerheads except during moments of mutual crisis. Even then, conflicting interests and factions within each colony made joint military action difficult. In the eighteenth century, Virginia and Pennsylvania were at odds over trade rights in the Ohio Valley; Pennsylvania and New York over

5. Greven: *Four Generations*, 272–3; Lockridge: *A New England Town*, 172–3; Cadwallader Colden to Alexander Colden, June 15, 1759, *Collections of the New-York Historical Society for the Year 1868* (New York, 1868), 187.

6. James A. Henretta: "Economic Development and Social Structure in Colonial Boston," *William and Mary Quarterly*, 3d series, XXII (1965), 75–92; James T. Lemon and Gary B. Nash: "The Distribution of Wealth in 18th-Century America: A Century of Change in Chester County, Pennsylvania, 1693–1802," *Journal of Social History*, II (1968), 1–24; Fulmer Mood: "Studies in the History of American Settled Areas and Frontier Lines, 1625–1790," *Agricultural History*, XXVI (1952), 16–34.

7. Michael Zuckerman: *Peaceable Kingdoms. New England Towns in the Eighteenth Century* (New York, 1970), 67; Colden to Alexander Colden, July 5, 1759, in William Smith, Jr.: *The History of the Province of New-York*, ed. Michael Kammen (Cambridge, Mass., 1972), I, 295.

the Lake Erie trade; almost all of the colonies over boundary disputes, claims to western lands, and proper Indian policies. The Albany Congress, called in 1754 to organize a united front, ended in bickering and dissension. In 1757, Benjamin Tasker complained to Governor Horatio Sharpe of Maryland that

> The divided state of the Colonies is justly deplored by all sensible Men, who are Interested in their safety, and Prosperity; and animated with an Adequate Zeal for their welfare. The only Provision (amidst the distraction of such various views as are entertained in the different Colonies notwithstanding the Common danger) which has the least tendency towards an Union, or can conduce to an uniform Plan of Mutual assistance and defence, is that by which the Forces raised in the Respective Governments are subjected to an direction in their Military operations.[8]

The colonies were as restlessly unsteady amongst themselves as within themselves; and to complicate matters, they competed individually (and occasionally together, as "the North American interest") in the imperial arena for influence and exemption. After 1748, however, the system of interest politics centered in London became at once more plural and less stable, as new groups increasingly vied while Georgian ministries were decreasingly in control of the government and political situation. Witness Edmund Burke's description of Chatham's attempt in 1766 to form a ministry that would satisfy all factions:

> He made an administration so checkered and speckled; he put together a piece of joinery, so crossly indented and whimsically dovetailed; a cabinet so variously inlaid; such a piece of diversified Mosaic: such a tesselated pavement without cement; here a bit of black stone, and there a bit of white; patriots and courtiers, kings friends and republicans; whigs and tories; treacherous friends and open enemies: that it was in-

8. Quoted in Harry M. Ward: *"Unite or Die." Intercolony Relations, 1690–1763* (Port Washington, 1971), 42–3.

deed a very curious show; but utterly unsafe to touch, and unsure to stand on.[9]

Wherefore I am inclined to alter the imagery and suggest that the coming of the American Revolution—like the firing of a flint-lock gun—resulted in considerable part from the striking of a British flint against a colonial hammer, thereby producing sufficient sparks to ignite the priming. Unstable English politics in the 1760's—the most severe since the 1680's—acted upon colonial communities themselves too long in motion, thereby firing ideologies latent for more than a generation.

For nearly a century, English officials had been bothered by the diversity, untidiness, and instability they saw in colonial life, laws, and polities. Again and again abortive efforts were made to impose uniformity. Hence the Dominion of New England, the sporadic revocation of colonial charters, repeated requests for codification of colonial laws, resentment of provincial paper currencies, parliamentary passage of the Naturalization Act of 1740, creation of the entire navigation system, and the administrative reforms which came in 1764–5 and caused so much trouble. Hence one imperial official's denunciation in 1752 of the "false Policy, that calls Factions and Parties, and Checks, and independent Interests, and such Stuff Constitutional." Hence Thomas Hutchinson's lament in 1767 that "we shall never be all of one mind in our political principles." Hence Daniel Leonard, the polemical opponent of John Adams, wrote in 1775 that "the provincial constitutions, considered as subordinate, are generally well adapted to those purposes of government, for which they were intended, that is, to regulate the internal police of the several colonies; *but [they] have no principle of stability within themselves.*"[1]

9. See Michael Kammen: *Empire and Interest. The American Colonies and the Politics of Mercantilism* (Philadelphia, 1970), chs. 4 and 5; John Almon, ed.: *Anecdotes of the Life of the Right Hon. William Pitt, Earl of Chatham* (London, 1810), III, 373.

1. Thomas Pownall: *Principles of Polity, being the Grounds and Reasons of Civil Empire* (London, 1752), 37; Hutchinson: *The History of the Colony and Province of Massachusetts-Bay*, ed. L. S. Mayo

While conservatives decried the abominations of diversity and instability, a few farsighted colonials began to envision and rationalize alternatives to the conventional wisdom. Away back in 1659, John Eliot, New England's foremost missionary, had argued that if a person migrated to a remote place, "meet it is that he do change his Rulers." A man should only undertake colonization with the "approbation of the Rulers whence he goeth, and with the acceptance of those to whom he removeth, lest by unstable changes they . . . slip out from under the Government of the Lord." Eliot's formulation was neither fully developed nor very characteristic of colonial thought before the 1760's: merely a glimmering. Thereafter, however, American Whigs warned one another that pluralism weakened their subordinate position severely in coping with imperial pressures, for Whitehall would take advantage of colonial differences to play one off against another. "Specious fallacies will be drest up with all the arts of delusion," wrote John Dickinson in 1767,

> to persuade one colony to distinguish herself from another, by unbecoming condescentions, which will serve the ambitious purposes of great men at home. . . . Opposition can never be effectual, *unless it is the united effort of these provinces*—that therefore BENEVOLENCE *of temper towards each other*, and UNANIMITY *of counsels*, are essential to the welfare of the whole.[2]

During the Revolution itself, newly independent states seemed to have reached their *ne plus ultra* of unsteadiness. "Unstable democracy," wrote Alexander Hamilton in 1777, "is an epithet frequently in the mouths of politicians. . . . When the deliberative or judicial powers are vested wholly or partly in the collective body of the people, you must expect error, confusion and instability." The Marquis de Chastellux

---

(Cambridge, Mass., 1936), II, xi; Leonard: *Massachusettensis* (Boston, 1775), 44 (italics mine).

2. Eliot: *The Christian Commonwealth: or, The Civil Policy of the Rising Kingdom of Jesus Christ* (1659), in *Collections of the Massachusetts Historical Society*, series 3, IX (1846), 149; Dickinson: *The Farmer's and Monitor's Letters*, 53–4 (emphasis Dickinson's).

summed up the postwar situation eloquently and briefly in
1782: "In a nation which is in a perpetual state of growth,
everything favors this general tendency; everything divides
and multiplies." [3]

By the mid-1780's, those men we now call Founding
Fathers—Fathers of the Nation because they were Sons of the
Revolution—were primarily obsessed with achieving and ra-
tionalizing a system of stable pluralism. That aim prompted
John Adams to write his vast *Defence of the Constitutions of
Government of the United States* in 1786. That aim motivated
Jefferson to advocate a society where diverse men might be
free to inquire, worship, and express their beliefs openly. That
aim inspired Benjamin Franklin to write of parties in 1786
that "such will exist wherever there is liberty; perhaps they
help to preserve it. By the collision of different sentiments,
sparks of truth are struck out, and political light is obtained." [4]

Even the most ardent republicans, however, wondered anxiously whether stability and security could be achieved in a
large, extended polity; and this issue became a central consideration for those assembled in Philadelphia during the summer of 1787. As Madison put it in the opening of *The Federalist*, Number 10: "complaints are everywhere heard from our
most considerate & virtuous citizens . . . that our governments are too unstable." Both the Federalists and the Anti-
Federalists explicitly desired a balanced political pluralism—
variously called consolidation, confederation, decentralized na-

3. Hamilton to Gouverneur Morris, May 19, 1777, in H. C. Syrett,
ed.: *The Papers of Alexander Hamilton* (New York, 1961), I, 255;
Chastellux: *Travels in North America in the Years 1780, 1781 and
1782*, ed. Howard C. Rice, Jr. (Williamsburg, 1963), II, 506.

4. Adrienne Koch: *Power, Morals, and the Founding Fathers*
(Ithaca, 1961), 41, 88, 100; Jefferson to Madison, Dec. 20, 1787, in
Julian P. Boyd, ed.: *The Papers of Thomas Jefferson* (Princeton,
1955), XII, 442; Verner W. Crane, ed.: "Franklin's 'The Internal
State of America' (1786)," *William and Mary Quarterly*, 3d series,
XV (1958), 226. For a similar formulation with respect to sectarian-
ism, by Ezra Stiles in 1767, see Edmund S. Morgan: *The Gentle
Puritan. A Life of Ezra Stiles, 1727–1795* (New Haven, 1962), 252.

tionalism, as well as other casual epithets. They simply could not agree on how best to achieve that goal structurally.[5]

Madison, more than any other participant, addressed himself to this matter directly. "What we wished," he recorded in his notes on the 1787 debates, "was to give to the Govt. that stability which was every where called for, and which the Enemies of the Republican form alleged to be inconsistent with its nature." His central concern in *The Federalist Papers* was to demonstrate how a republic, traditionally regarded as the most volatile form of political organization, could be rendered reliable and enduring. A confederation could, he contended, produce sufficient stability to permit popular sovereignty and liberty to be maximized. In 1788, when Philip Mazzei asked Madison why he supported the proposed Constitution, Madison replied directly that he

> thought it safe to the liberties of the people, and the best that could be obtained from the jarring interests of States, and the miscellaneous opinions of Politicians; and because experience has proved that the real danger to America & to liberty lies in the defect of *energy & stability* in the present establishment of the United States.[6]

The concept of balanced government which emerged so vitally in 1787–8 embodied institutional means whereby a viable political system could be maintained in a diffuse society. And so it was that American colonial history, which had begun with a quest for purity and homogeneity, ended with a sophisticated rationale for pluralism and heterogeneity. What had happened was not really so paradoxical as it may seem, for the so-called melting pot had been a boiling cauldron all along, from Jamestown to James Madison. There is a very real sense

5. See "Debates in the Federal Convention of 1787," in Charles C. Tansill, ed.: *Documents Illustrative of the Formation of the Union of the American States* (Washington, D.C., 1927), 162, 302, 631.

6. *Ibid.*, 196; Madison to Mazzei, October 8, 1788, in Gaillard Hunt, ed.: *The Writings of James Madison* (New York, 1904), V, 267 (italics Madison's).

in which the American nation emerged, not in response to new-found national unity, but rather in response to provincial disunity, in response to a historical problem of long duration: how best to control unstable pluralism, how best to balance the areas of compulsion and freedom in American life.

WHAT HAPPENED TO this complicated matter thereafter is a large and unwieldy story, beyond the bounds of what can properly be told here. I ought, however, to give at least a glimpse of what transpired beyond 1790, for the problem of unstable pluralism does indeed make contact with the exigencies of more recent times.

The remarkable permissiveness of regional, social, and political pluralism still nagged at the serenity of many in federal America. "Our country is too big for union," whined Fisher Ames in 1803, "too sordid for patriotism, too democratic for liberty. What is to become of it, he who made it best knows." Timothy Dwight, the peripatetic president of Yale College, feared disunion among the states and collapse of the republic.[7]

In fact, most of those engaged in educational enterprises in the young nation believed, with George Washington, that "the more homogeneous our citizens can be made . . . the greater will be our prospect of permanent union." So Noah Webster sought "uniformity & purity of language," and Thomas Jefferson most admired those "who have been educated [at home], and whose manners, morals, and habits are perfectly homogeneous with those of the country." Benjamin Rush advocated a federal university where "the youth of all the states may be melted (as it were) together into one mass of citizens." [8] They all hoped to achieve a common citizenship based upon cultural

7. Ames to Thomas Dwight, October 26, 1803, in Seth Ames, ed.: *Works of Fisher Ames* (Boston, 1854), I, 328; *President Dwight's Decisions of Questions Discussed by the Senior Class in Yale College, in 1813 and 1814* (New York, 1833), 51–2, 74, 103.

8. David Tyack: "Forming the National Character: Paradox in the Educational Thought of the Revolutionary Generation," *Harvard Educational Review*, XXXVI (1966), 31–2, 37.

unity and well-ordered liberty. The free American would sensibly subordinate his identity to the larger, singular character envisioned for the nation. Collective individualism, it might be called.

Physical expansion and the injection of new immigrants made Jacksonian America far more heterogeneous than anything Jefferson, Rush, or Webster might wildly have envisioned. After the 1820's, when manhood suffrage became widespread, ethnic and religious differences tended to become the more important sources of political conflict. By the 1840's a nativist reaction reflexively screamed shrill notes of alarm at the prospect of unstable pluralism verging upon chaos. The words of the *American Republican* are representative:

> Our country presents many inducements to foreigners to come here; and the past policy of the government has given a too easy and indiscriminate admission to it. . . . In the early period of our national existence, there may have been reasons for the free admission of foreigners which do not exist now; and if the reasons have changed or ceased to exist, the practice founded on them should also be changed.[9]

Agreement on constitutional fundamentals seems to have encouraged every lesser social conflict to find political expression.

Diversity within the southern states, and attendant anxieties, were equally prevalent though less commonly noticed. "So many and so various have been the sources from which Carolina has derived her population," wrote David Ramsay in 1809, "that a considerable period must elapse, before the people amalgamate into a mass possessing an uniform national character." By the 1830's and 1840's, however, convolutions of southern thought had become more arcane and distinctive. Southern spokesmen insisted upon pluralism nationally combined with monolithic regionalism. They contended that slavery was a sectional institution over which Congress had no control,

9. See Lee Benson: *The Concept of Jacksonian Democracy. New York as a Test Case* (Princeton, 1961), viii, 42, 112–13, 115, 118–19, 165, 275–6; *American Republican*, August 10, 1844, 2.

but would brook no deviations or dissent *within* their localities.[1]

Daniel Webster captured the contradictory tendencies at work in ante-bellum America better than most, and articulated them into a political philosophy of collective individualism on the national scale. "This united system is held together by strong tendencies to union," he wrote in 1843, "at the same time that it is kept from too much leaning toward consolidation by a strong tendency in the several States to support each its own power and consideration." In 1851, Webster quoted these lines of poetry to a farmer in Georgia. "The States are united, confederated;—"

> Not, chaos-like, together crushed and bruised,
> But, like the world, harmoniously confused;
> Where order in variety we see,
> And where, though all things differ, all agree.[2]

Since the Civil War we have vacillated between self-praise for being a "nation of immigrants" and self-hate for the stations of restless locomotion through which we daily pass. The greenback era and the gilded age agonized over issues which were resolved, when they were not simply brushed aside, by the interaction of many social and economic forces. The agrarian movements of the final quarter of the nineteenth century involved unstable coalitions of groups whose particularistic interests were always in evidence, and often worked against the achievement of effective national organization. The urban mind in America has actually been like the eye of the fly under a microscope, composed of thousands of glittering facets. Not surprisingly, we have had sporadic outbursts such as this state-

1. Ramsay: *History of South Carolina, from Its First Settlement in 1670 to the Year 1808* (Newberry, S.C., 1858), 12; and see William W. Freehling: *Prelude to Civil War. The Nullification Controversy in South Carolina, 1816–1836* (New York, 1966), ch. 4.

2. Webster to the New England Society of New York, Dec. 22, 1843; Webster to Mark A. Cooper, Oct. 6, 1851, in *The Writings and Speeches of Daniel Webster . . . National Edition* (Boston, 1903), III, 209, XII, 274. Although Webster's letter does not identify the source of these lines, they are from *Windsor Forest* by Alexander Pope.

ment from the Commissioner of the Common Schools of New York City in 1896:

> I consider it the paramount duty of our public schools, apart from the educational knowledge to be instilled into our pupils, to form American citizens of them, to take up and gather together all the heterogeneous elements of this cosmopolitan population, and through the crucible of the public school to fuse and weld them into one homogeneous mass, obliterating from the very earliest moment all the distinguishing foreign characteristics and traits, which the beginners may bring with them, as obstructive, warring, and irritating elements.[3]

Clearly then, the political phenomenon of many states and one union balancing their sovereignties—the problem of legitimacy again—has been paralleled by the phenomenon of uneasy socio-political pluralism. The nation has simultaneously managed to develop both a multi-culture and the unifying characteristics of a mono-culture.

Because of our conformist diversity, our style may perhaps be located less in specific characteristics than in a common condition of compromise, or hybridization. There is certainly a quality of heterogeneity-within-homogeneity in modern America. Our political and ideological affiliations are conditioned by a host of secondary social differences reflecting the wide range of regional, occupational, and cultural variations found in the United States. The pressures on a system of competing coalitions comprised of diverse groups compel them all to behave in certain compromising ways.[4] Hence my fondness for an excessively cynical poem by Tom Moore, an Irish liberal turned Tory who lived in the United States during Jefferson's second administration.

3. Jacob W. Mack to Mayor William Strong, April 16, 1896, Strong Papers, New York City Municipal Archives. I am indebted for this reference to Professor Samuel McSeveney of Vanderbilt University.

4. See Daniel Bell: "Unstable America. Transitory and Permanent Factors in a National Crisis," *Encounter*, XXXIV (June 1970), 11–26; Charles Sellers: "The Equilibrium Cycle in Two-Party Politics," *The Public Opinion Quarterly*, XXIX (1965), 16–38.

> Who can, with patience, for a moment see
> The medley mass of pride and misery,
> Of whips and charters, manacles and rights,
> Of slaving blacks and democratic whites,
> And all the piebald polity that reigns
> In free confusion o'er Columbia's plains?

And again:

> Take Christians, Mohawks, democrats, and all
> From the rude wigwam to the congress-hall,
> From man the savage, whether slav'd or free,
> To man the civiliz'd, less tame than he,—
> 'Tis one dull chaos, one unfertile strife
> Betwixt half-polish'd and half-barbarous life;
> Where every ill the ancient world could brew
> Is mix'd with every grossness of the new.[5]

Moore managed to catch both the golden dream and the disturbing reality.

5. *Epistles, Odes, and Other Poems* (1806), in *The Poetical Works of Thomas Moore* (Boston, n.d.), 6 vols. in 3, I, 76–7, 95–6.

EPILOGISM
Some Interconnections

In visions fair the scenes of fate unroll,
And Massachusetts opens on my soul;
There Chaos, Anarch old, asserts his sway,
And mobs in myriads blacken all the way:

. . . .

Lo, THE COURT FALLS, th'affrighted judges run,
Clerks, Lawyers, Sheriffs, every mother's son.
The stocks, the gallows lose th'expected prize,
See the jails open, and the thieves arise.
Thy constitution, Chaos, is restor'd;
Law sinks before thy uncreating word.

DAVID HUMPHREYS and LEMUEL HOPKINS,
The Anarchiad (1786)

BEFORE PLUNGING into a related set of considerations concerning the origins of American civilization, we might well pause for a moment in order to reflect upon some interconnections between the quest for legitimacy and the problem of unstable pluralism. It has been strategically useful, I think, to isolate both and examine them *in vacuo*. Nevertheless, they must historically have had a synergistic relationship—the mutual action of agents which, when taken together, increase each other's effectiveness.

A congruence of legitimacy and stability is basic to the life of any sound political society. Stability will be more easily achieved where members of a community, large or small, approve of the institutional arrangements which determine their lives. A government will be more viable if its pattern of authority dovetails with the other, parallel patterns in the society of which it is a part. Where there is uncertainty about norms and forms of legitimacy, various options are opened which encourage or aggravate unstable pluralism. As Fenimore Cooper had Judge Temple say in *The Pioneers:* "living as we do . . . on the skirts of society, it becomes doubly necessary to protect the minister of the law." The very presence of instability and pluralism is a challenge to many modes of legitimacy, and lack of the latter will stimulate the former.

It may well be that Roger Williams, a peculiarly near-sighted visionary, perceived these interworkings more clearly than any other seventeenth-century colonist. He persistently sought a charter for Rhode Island, denounced illicit dealings with the Indians, sought spiritual legitimacy and a viable accommodation between Church and State. In every case, significantly, Williams's solutions to the problem of legitimacy also provided a rationale for stable pluralism, a way for men of diverse origins and persuasions to live harmoniously together.

But Williams's solutions went unheeded for a very long time, and so the tension in colonial society between personal liberty and social order long remained stretched and strained. Here is a characteristic complaint from Justus Falckner of Germantown, Pennsylvania, in 1701:

> The local Christian minority . . . is divided into almost innumerable sects, which pre-eminently may be called sects and hordes, as Quakers, Anabaptists, Naturalists, Rationalists, Independents, Sabbatarians and many others, especially secret insinuating sects, whom one does not know what to make of, but who, nevertheless, are all united in these beautiful principles, if it please the Gods (*si Dis placet*): Do away with all good order, and live for yourself as it pleases you! [1]

1. Falckner to Rev. Heinrich Muhlen, Aug. 1, 1701, in *Pa. Mag. Hist. & Biog.*, XXI (1897), 218; see also the German Reformed Elders of Pennsylvania to the Classis of Amsterdam, July 1728, in

The concept of liberty is felt less urgently in a homogeneous society where the values of the individual are predominantly those of the social order also. Freedom becomes a cherished ideal, however, in a complex society where the individual may hold conflicting values derived from various sources.

In colonial America, the spiritual communities—"churches" in the original meaning of that word—ceased rather early to coincide with the physical communities of citizens and inhabitants. That disjunction contributed to a particularly heady sort of pluralism which undermined one of the traditional canons of legitimacy in the Old World.

Moreover, especially in the eighteenth century, a remarkable degree of geographical mobility intensified the condition of unstable pluralism, and thereby contributed to confusion about the legitimacy of provincial social structures and statuses. Physical fluidity and upward mobility tended to undermine older criteria of constitutional government, as well. Where discrete social classes were difficult to identify, assumptions about "mixed government"—their time-honored formula for the proper relationship between Estates and political power—were thrown into confusion, and eventually forced a major adjustment in American political theory.

I find it strikingly symptomatic that the colonists so often sought specific demographic data about their societies. The presence of many diverse and energetic people made it imperative to keep reasonably good vital records, as well as census and immigration information. Significantly, the leading exponents of early American demography were residents of two of the most heterogeneous colonies: Benjamin Franklin of Pennsylvania and Ezra Stiles of Rhode Island.[2]

Equally interesting is the way in which social diversity forced provincials to legitimize the formal statuses of indi-

---

William J. Hinke, ed.: *Life and Letters of the Rev. John Philip Boehm . . . 1683–1749* (Philadelphia, 1916), 155–8, 160–4, 168–9.

2. See James H. Cassedy: *Demography in Early America. Beginnings of the Statistical Mind, 1600–1800* (Cambridge, Mass., 1969), 107, 110–13, 167–8.

vidual immigrants on an ad hoc basis. The several settlements simply *assumed* the right to naturalize aliens, since none of their royal charters granted that right explicitly. The interpenetration of points of legitimacy and pluralism on this matter would cause problems in defining allegiance and national identity, and eventually lead to unpleasant forms of xenophobia.

Certainly, two of the most critical problems in American life have concerned conformity and race, regimentation and pigmentation. Their myths and consequences converge ironically when we consider the melting pot image so often used by politicians, naïve pluralists, and social scientists. The melting pot is hardly a suitable metaphor for a system characterized by unstable pluralism. But—bitter irony—isn't there a sense in which the melting pot notion is more applicable within the black American nation than within the white? There was great diversity in the African origins of American Negroes: regional, linguistic, and tribal differences, as well as in their prior condition of freedom (some had been previously enslaved in Africa; others were first enslaved by Europeans). Despite this diversity, however, Africans were forcibly homogenized after several generations into a fairly singular Afro-American mold with common folkways. Thus, the only American melting pot has perhaps been a black one, though in this case the putative pot has been reluctant to call the kettle black.

A MAJOR ATTRIBUTE of the Great Awakening, according to some of its most astute observers, was that it permanently reversed, or completed the reversal, of a traditional relationship between rulers—whether ecclesiastical or political—and subjects.[3] After the 1740's, a guiding rule of American communities would be their own welfare as decided and articulated by Mr. Everyman. Leaders thereafter would have to accommodate themselves to the imperatives of society's impulses because

3. See Perry Miller: "Jonathan Edwards and the Great Awakening," in *Errand into the Wilderness* (Cambridge, Mass., 1956), 161–5; Wesley M. Gewehr: *The Great Awakening in Virginia, 1740–1790* (Durham, 1930), ch. 8.

legitimacy would be perceived as emanating from the bottom up, rather than radiating from the top down. Yet the inversion could hardly be accomplished smoothly because America was steadily becoming more heterogeneous. As the "bottom" became more diffuse and less cohesive, as Americans became less and less able to agree on methods and goals appropriate to the good society, it became ever more difficult to achieve legitimacy, in any functional sense, from the bottom up.

As diversity developed at every level, the quest for valid and viable institutions became more taxing and urgent. Thus the various plans of intercolonial union invariably dealt with the need for singular standards of legitimacy in a pluralistic portion of the empire seeking mutuality: a single value for coinage in all the colonies, a colonial mint, uniform laws to deal with runaways and debtors, uniform naturalization proceedings, uniform control over marriage, extradition, and trade disputes.[4]

Even so, as late as 1775 a fair number of colonial Cassandras shared grave anxieties about the likelihood of a successful resistance movement on the part of such dissimilar societies. Here is the testimony of Robert Beverley of Virginia:

> We are an infant Country, unconnected in Interest and naturally disunited by Inclination. Our Forms of Government differ egregiously, but our religious Tenets still more so. Our modes of Life vary, and our Articles of Commerce interfere prodigiously. Nor are we naturally more disjointed in Situation than in Temper. It is true indeed there seems to be a Sort of Union at present, but I am afraid it is only in Appearance. Ambition, Resentment, and Interest may have united us for a Moment, but be assured, when Interests shall interfere and a Dispute shall arise concerning Superiority, a Code of Laws, and all the Concomitants of a new Government, that that Union will soon be converted

4. See Frederick D. Stone, comp.: "Plans for the Union of the British Colonies of North America, 1643–1776," in *History of the Celebration of the One Hundredth Anniversary of the Promulgation of the Constitution of the United States*, ed. Hampton L. Carson (Philadelphia, 1889), II, 439–503.

into Envy, Malevolence, and Faction, and most probably will introduce a greater degree of Opposition than even now prevails against the Mother Country.[5]

Beverley proved in the long run to be excessively pessimistic, but he was certainly prophetic about the next fourteen years of American history, 1775 until 1789. During those years especially, when legitimacy and stability were both so elusive, there were multiple confusions, claims, and counterclaims about identities and labels. In Pennsylvania politics, for example, moderates called themselves the Republican Society while the radicals, paradoxically, adopted the name of the Constitutional Society. Similarly in 1787–8, the Federalists were truly nationalists (strong centralizers) and the Anti-Federalists were in fact the real federalists (advocates of decentralization). The pattern of ambiguity would endure so long as its underlying imperatives remained.

Moreover, where legitimacy is lacking and pluralism predominates, delicate compromises must be reached in order to resolve tensions arising from contradictory tendencies. Hence James Madison's ingenious effort to define the nature of national supremacy in a federal republic:

> I hold it for a fundamental point, that an individual independence of the States is utterly irreconcilable with the idea of an aggregate sovereignty. I think, at the same time, that a consolidation of the States into one simple republic is not less unattainable than it would be inexpedient. Let it be tried, then, whether any middle ground can be taken, which will at once support a due supremacy of the national authority, and leave in force the local authorities so far as they can be subordinately useful.[6]

5. Beverley to William Fitzhugh, July 20, 1775, quoted in Robert M. Calhoon, ed.: " 'A Sorrowful Spectator of These Tumultuous Times,' " *Va. Mag. Hist. & Biog.*, LXXIII (1965), 52.

6. Madison to Edmund Randolph, April 8, 1787, in Gaillard Hunt, ed.: *The Writings of James Madison* (New York, 1901), II, 337–8. See also Gouverneur Morris's proposition in the Federal Convention, August 29, 1787: "Full faith ought to be given in each State to the public acts, records, and judicial proceedings of every other

There is, I think, something essentially American about this delicate quest for political equipoise, for a "middle ground," for both aggregate sovereignty and decentralized republicanism, as I shall try to show in the chapters to come.

Stable pluralism requires a strong *underpinning* of legitimacy. A plural society is best insured by the rule of law—law made within the framework of an explicit constitution by elected representatives, executed by a partially autonomous administrative staff, and adjudicated by an independent judiciary. Insofar as all of these were created in 1787 and achieved in 1789, those dates do distinguish a genuine watershed in American history.

But stable pluralism in a democracy also requires a strong and lasting inventory of psychological legitimacy: understanding, acceptance, and pervasive confidence in the composite system necessary to make it run smoothly rather than by fits and starts. Americans continue to celebrate pluralism in the past, but are reluctant to honor it in the present. Have we fully accepted the legitimacy of pluralism? How highly do we value cultural, moral, and regional autonomy, absolute toleration, community control over education, the continued integrity of divergent groups? Partially: some of us, some of these, in some places, at some times. Our ambiguity about the implications of our own system—"the huge, unrecorded hum of implication" —ought to prompt us to look more closely than we have at the historical background of our ambivalence.

State." Charles C. Tansill, ed.: *Documents Illustrative of the Formation of the Union of the American States* (Washington, D.C., 1927), 633.

PART TWO

A Strange Hybrid, Indeed

❧ · ❧

A strange hybrid, indeed, did circumstances beget, here in the New World, upon the old Puritan stock, and the earth never before saw such mystic-practicalism, such niggard-geniality, such calculating-fanaticism, such cast-iron-enthusiasm, such sour-faced-humor, such close-fisted-generosity.

JAMES RUSSELL LOWELL

PROLEGOMENON

> I have sundry doubts to clear away, questions to resolve, and paradoxes to explain before I permit you to range at random; but these difficulties once overcome, we shall be enabled to jog on right merrily through the rest of our history.
>
> WASHINGTON IRVING,
> *Knickerbocker's History of New York* (1809)

I AM INCLINED to depict the history of American civilization as a triptych: a picture in three compartments side by side, commonly hinged so that the two lateral scenes may fold in toward the central one. Quite obviously, to me, the quest for legitimacy—something we lacked and sought—is the subject of one lateral panel; and the problem of unstable pluralism—something we had in excess—is the subject of the other. What then is the subject of the central scene?

To answer that question adequately will consume the next three chapters of this essay. To answer it summarily, I might invoke here an ugly word of classical origin—syzygy—meaning the conjunction of two organisms without loss of identity, a pair of correlative things, a paradoxical coupling of opposites. An easier word—concept, but one almost as ugly, is biformity, a concept which provides the frame of reference for my next chapter.

I am disposed to believe that the condition of syzygy and the presence of biformities are central to a proper perspective upon American civilization. They help us to feel both the resonance and the dissonance in our culture. I am also disposed to believe that problems of legitimacy and unstable pluralism helped to produce biformities in abundance. Henry Burlingame, III, that fabulous creature of John Barth, identified part of the nexus with reference to colonial America:

> There is a freedom there that's both a blessing and a curse, for't means both liberty and lawlessness. . . . 'Tis philosophic liberty I speak of, that comes from want of history. It throws one on his own resources, that freedom—makes every man an orphan like myself and can as well demoralize as elevate.[1]

Let me take a moment to suggest some ways in which the lack of legitimacy and excess of unstable pluralism contributed to strange sorts of hybrids, noted above by James Russell Lowell, which have proliferated in the United States. Doing so may help to clarify the relationship between Parts One and Two of this essay, and enable us to proceed more easily to a conceptual discussion of biformity, to the conflicts and crises of early modern England, and to contradictory tendencies characteristic of colonial America.

Where traditional structures of social hierarchy were undermined or altogether lacking, clearly defined statuses became elusive; and some of the attendant ambiguities acquired permanence as biformities; our "bourgeois aristocracy," for example. In Calvinist New England, the uncertainty of individual salvation threatened the security of a social order based upon the

---

1. *The Sot-Weed Factor* (New York, 1960), 181. Nathaniel Hawthorne was equally sensitive to the same situation. He remarked that Hester Prynne "had wandered, without rule or guidance, in a moral wilderness; as vast, as intricate and shadowy, as the untamed forest." He also had Chillingworth, Hester's husband, say of Pearl that "there is no law, nor reverence for authority, no regard for human ordinances or opinions, right or wrong, mixed up with that child's composition." To which Dimmesdale, the adulterer, replies: "None,—save the freedom of a broken law." *The Scarlet Letter* (1850: Centenary Edition [Indianapolis, 1963]), 128–9, 189.

collective worth of individuals bound together by a national covenant.[2] Turning to more secular illustrations, the colonial penchant for constitutionalism helped to make provincial protests fairly restrained phenomena, on the whole: "moderate rebellions." Also, the relative fragility of governmental legitimacy caused colonial allegiances to be dualistic and ambiguous— simultaneously a source of anti-authoritarianism as well as an American search for super-legitimacy.[3] The creation of a federal government *de novo* in 1789, and its subsequent legitimization, contributed to national incongruity by imposing a new network of institutions and assumptions upon well-established older ones.

The whole process seems circular, I suppose; for if the inability to achieve legitimacy produces contradictory tendencies, the need to resolve those anomalies also stimulates the search for legitimacy. Which leads me to believe that some tensions are in a sense functional, that is, both creative and perhaps resolvable, while others are not. Some biformities are produced by the successful resolution of contradictory tendencies, while other dualisms are produced precisely by the failure to resolve certain tensions. When a paradox persists for a very long time, the perplexity of its immediate issue becomes a permanently fixed tension, or polarity.

Hawthorne caught hold of all this more tangibly when he saw that "troubled joy" at Merrymount resulted from conflicting life styles in a "moral wilderness." I am persuaded that a plethora of dualisms, functional and dysfunctional alike, encourages very rapid change—social, political, and attitudinal— and that inconsistencies in American thought persistently pro-

2. See, for example, Robert G. Pope: *The Half-Way Covenant. Church Membership in Puritan New England* (Princeton, 1969), ch. 4.
3. The problem of trying civilians in military courts during the American Revolution aroused fears that "whilst we are strugling for the Sacred Name of Liberty we are establishing the fatal Tendency to Despotism." See *Calendar of New York Historical Manuscripts, Relating to the War of the Revolution, in the Office of the Secretary of State, Albany, N.Y.* (Albany, 1868), II, 182.

vide the basis for unanticipated shifts in feeling and perception.[4] More on this in a moment, for it is the specific subject of Chapter 4. Let's return once more to the proper focus of this prolegomenon—the interlacing of legitimacy, unstable pluralism, and syzygy.

Insofar as there has been a cult of consensus in American history, a desire for togetherness if not uniformity, that cult has developed both from the quest for legitimacy and from the desire to reconcile our restless pluralities. Perhaps the cult of consensus has worshipped at a hollow shrine, however, for pluralism really cannot be reduced to a singular position, ideology, or system. It is the singular-collective postulate of numerous positions: conservatism *and* liberalism, individualism *and* corporatism, hierarchy *and* equalitarianism, emotionalism *and* rationalism, autonomy *and* co-operation are all integral to the mutuality of pluralism. Thus the exigencies of democratic politics in America have constantly forced partisan groups to assume some of the coloring of their opponents. "We are all republicans: we are all federalists," declared Jefferson at his first inaugural. And in 1840 the Whigs outdid themselves to be more democratic than the Democrats.

The matrix of paradoxy in American life—unstable pluralism—has constantly been expanded and stretched by new groups and individuals who somehow had to be accommodated. Simple recognition of this ineluctable fact may have occurred in the English colonies before it appeared anywhere else in modern history. Benjamin Franklin's "Apology for Printers," published in *The Pennsylvania Gazette* in 1731, declared that the opinions of men were diverse; therefore "both Sides ought equally to have the Advantage of being heard by the Publick. . . . *So many Men, so many Minds*." [5] Similarly, when John Randolph accepted the speakership of Virginia's House of

---

4. For a pertinent psychological study, see Michael Landmann: *Pluralität und Antinomie. Kulturelle Grundlagen Seelischer Konflikte* (Munich, 1963).

5. Leonard W. Labaree, ed.: *The Papers of Benjamin Franklin* (New Haven, 1959–   ), I, 194–5, II, 260. Italics Franklin's.

Burgesses in 1734, he expressed emphatically the view that counterpointed opinions were necessary and "of all things the most useful." Why? Because "then we shall hear one another patiently, put the Weight of every Man's Reason in the Ballance against our own, and at last form a Judgment upon the whole matter." [6]

Politicians and professional people in all the provinces often made a virtue out of necessity. Where diversity and multiplicity were everywhere apparent, where counterpointed tendencies were inevitable, both society and polity could benefit from healthy tensions embodied in a natural system of checks and balances. "So different are the private Interests of Men," Ebenezer Devotion reminded the rulers of Connecticut, "so various and headstrong their Passions and Lusts, that good Laws and a strict Execution of them, will probably bring upon you the Odium of many." [7] Where society was so pluralistic, and men so ambitious, that government really was *not* best which governed least; but not everyone accepted that conclusion.

The perplexity of pluralism appears with special clarity when we examine conflicting attitudes held by colonial leaders concerning the proper relationship between educating the young and achieving the good society. Take, for example, Jonathan Edwards, Benjamin Franklin, and Samuel Johnson. For Johnson, first president of King's College, the immediate aim of education was obedience; the means of achievement was religion; the sanctions were law and authority; the social goal was stability; and the final desideratum was communal well-being. For Edwards, the immediate aim of education was morality; the means of achievement was piety; the sanctions were sin and damnation; the social goal was a gracious community; and the final desideratum was glorification of God. For Franklin, the immediate aim was personal nurture; the

6. H. R. McIlwaine, ed.: *Journals of the House of Burgesses of Virginia, 1727–1740* (Richmond, 1910), 176.

7. *The Civil Ruler . . . A Sermon Preached Before the General Assembly of the Colony of Connecticut. . . .* (New London, 1753), 49.

means of achievement was public education; the proper sanction was conscience; the social goal was a civilized community; and the ultimate desideratum was individual wisdom and personal happiness.[8] How differently these three contemporaries envisioned the good society! In America, henceforth, there could be no singular Society—only societies conceived by communities of unlike-minded men.

But how, amidst bewildering, fluctuating pluralism, could such communities even be envisioned? Despite the anti-institutionalism of revivalists and evangelicals, the Great Awakening caused a proliferation of religious institutions. Following the Awakening, New Divinity men hither and yon addressed themselves to one another even more than to their congregations. By exploring and explaining new subtleties in their theological systems, they neglected some of the central problems of Christianity and society. In the process they achieved a measure of cerebral success but lost contact with the populace. Indeed, one of the most bitter-sweet paradoxes of the Great Awakening lay in the disruption of communities and the loss of clerical prestige precisely because of an extended religious revival.

If the earliest élites in American history, the formative and determinative groups, were capable of shaping their own life styles, those styles have nevertheless been challenged by the subsequent deracination of American society; that is to say, by the influx of other ethnic and interest groups. "Nativism from the beginning of the nineteenth century to our own times," remarks a foreign observer,

> expresses the tension created by two competing types
> of national consciousness, the first universalistic in out-
> look, the second based on an awareness of belonging to
> a national organic community whose values are to a

8. The critical document for Johnson is his essay "Raphael" (ca. 1763), printed in Herbert Schneider, ed.: *Samuel Johnson, President of King's College: His Career and Writings* (New York, 1929), II, 542–60. For Franklin, in addition to his *Autobiography*, see his "Proposals Relating to the Education of Youth in Pennsylvania" (1749), in *Papers of Benjamin Franklin*, III, 397–421.

certain degree not transferable and whose aim is to determine the character of the nation and the activities of the state according to its own ideals. The interplay between these two tendencies has determined to a large degree the structure and course of American nationalism.[9]

In nineteenth- and twentieth-century America, the most obvious biformity born of pluralism would be the bilingual condition known as hyphenated Americanism, defined in the following manner by *The Random House Dictionary of the English Language:* "noting a naturalized citizen of the U.S. believed to be ambivalent in his loyalty: so called because of the tendency to style himself according to his former and present nationalities, using a hyphen; e.g., 'German-American.'" Recall Mr. Dooley's immortal remarks on the Anglo-Saxon "hurtage":

An Anglo-Saxon, Hinnissy, is a German that's forgot who was his parents. . . . I'm an Anglo-Saxon. . . . Th' name iv Dooley has been th' proudest Anglo-Saxon name in th' County Roscommon f'r many years. . . . Pether Bowbeen down be th' Frinch church is formin' th' Circle Francaize Anglo Saxon club, an' me ol' frind Dominigo . . . will march at th' head iv th' Dago Anglo-Saxons whin th' time comes. There ar-re twinty thousan' Rooshian Jews at a quarther a vote in th' Sivinth Ward; an', ar-rmed with rag hooks, they'd be a tur-r-ble thing f'r anny inimy iv th' Anglo-Saxon 'lieance to face. Th' Bohemians an' Pole Anglo-Saxons may be a little slow in wakin' up to what th' pa-apers calls our common hurtage, but ye may be sure they'll be all r-right whin they're called on . . . I tell ye, whin th' Clan an' th' Sons iv Sweden an' th' Banana Club an' th' Circle Francaize an' th' Pollacky Benivolent Society an' th' Rooshian Sons of Dinnymite an' th' Benny Brith an' th' Coffee Clutch that Schwartzmeister r-runs an' th' Tur-rnd'yemind an' th' Holland society an' th' Afro-Americans an' th' other Anglo-Saxons begin f'r to raise their Anglo-Saxon battle-cry, it'll be

9. Yehoshua Arieli: *Individualism and Nationalism in American Ideology* (Cambridge, Mass., 1964), 24, 27–8.

all day with th' eight or nine people in th' wurruld that has th' misfortune iv not bein' brought up Anglo-Saxons.[1]

Immigration, pluralism, dualism. The American whey of life does not separate easily from its curd.

1. Finley P. Dunne: *Mr. Dooley in Peace and War* (Boston, 1898), 54–6.

CHAPTER 4

BIFORMITY
A Frame of Reference

It is a commonplace to state that whatever one may come to consider a truly American trait can be shown to have its equally characteristic opposite. This, one suspects, is true of all "national characters," or (as I would prefer to call them) national identities—so true, in fact, that one may begin rather than end with the proposition that a nation's identity is derived from the ways in which history has, as it were, counterpointed certain opposite potentialities; the ways in which it lifts this counterpoint to a unique style of civilization, or lets it disintegrate into mere contradiction. This dynamic country subjects its inhabitants to more extreme contrasts and abrupt changes during a lifetime or a generation than is normally the case with other great nations.

ERIK H. ERIKSON, *Childhood and Society* (1950)

ANY QUEST for national character, culture, or style plunges one into a tangle of complex historical considerations. "Seminal ideas received in childhood," wrote Edward Eggleston in 1900, "standards of feeling and thinking and living handed down from one overlapping generation to another, make the man English or French or German in the rudimentary outfit of his mind."[1] Nonetheless, writers interested in the American quarry

1. *The Transit of Civilization from England to America in the Seventeenth Century* (2nd ed., Boston, 1959), 1.

of this quest have usually sought to simplify and generalize by expounding the importance of this or that particular factor.

Thus we are free to choose from among an enormous catalog of single-factor explanations: the intellectual inheritance of western Europe; the English tradition of liberty, which has produced distinctive political institutions; the Anglo-Saxon tradition of law, language, religion, and custom; the process and psychological impact of immigration; the interplay of inheritance and environment; economic abundance; immigration and abundance in tandem; migration and mobility; the westward movement of the frontier; "the American dream": the desire for liberty, opportunity, and land; the universal passion for physical prosperity; freedom of enterprise; the democratic faith or dogma; "the American conscience": the dominant body of opinion; our mode of conformity; generosity and the philanthropic impulse; our modes of child rearing; and the antithesis between highbrow and lowbrow, to mention a few.

One way to reconcile such a bewildering welter of plausible explanations might be to ascertain a style or state of mind receptive to them all, yet having a certain thrust and weight of its own. Erik Erikson, the distinguished psychoanalyst, has pointed the way and suggested such a state of mind in the observation quoted above. Most Americans, he believes, are faced with alternatives posed by such polarities as: open roads of innovation and jealous islands of tradition; outgoing internationalism and defiant isolationism; boisterous competition and self-effacing co-operation. "Thus the functioning American, as the heir of a history of extreme contrasts and abrupt changes, bases his final ego identity on some tentative combination of dynamic polarities such as migratory and sedentary, individualistic and standardized, competitive and co-operative, pious and freethinking, responsible and cynical, etc." [2]

Erikson's schema seems to me far more meaningful than singular approaches to culture through particular inheritances, processes, or attributes. Moreover, Erikson's insight may be

2. *Childhood and Society* (2nd ed., New York, 1963), 285–6.

reinforced with observations by perceptive observers from many fields of interest. Ethologists, for example, have recently noted that the existence of opposing impulses does not necessitate anxiety or dissolution, but may instead create tensions which stiffen a particular character. Philosophers have shown that "the actual focus of any history is a problem that has been generated by a tension developed between newer and older human ways of acting and believing." Students of art and taste have piloted the same channel with great success: "The history of styles as well as the cultural geography of nations can only be successful—that is approach truth—if it is conducted in terms of polarities, that is in pairs of apparently contradictory qualities. English art is Constable and Turner, it is the formal house and the informal, picturesque garden surrounding it." [3]

American historians on the whole have been uninterested in this more European way of perceiving culture and character. Instead, they have debated endlessly the relative merits of what they call conflict and consensus historiography, worrying whether our history has been most striking for unity or disunity—jarring Jeffersonian and Hamiltonian traditions, or harmonious fellow travelers all preferring the back of the church, the front of the bar, and the middle of the road. Disputes about how best to interpret power struggles between radicals and moderates, conservatives and liberals, have blinded us to the larger and internalized tensions within the society as a whole, as well as within many of those individuals who comprise it. Since World War II, it is true, some brilliant practitioners of the "American studies approach" to history and literature have tended to explain our frictions and uniqueness through the analytical leverage of myth and paradox, thereby minimizing to some extent the objective reality of conflict. [4]

3. John Herman Randall, Jr., quoted in Fred Somkin: *Unquiet Eagle. Memory and Desire in the Idea of American Freedom 1815–1860* (Ithaca, 1967), xiv; Nikolaus Pevsner: *The Englishness of English Art* (London, 1956), 18, 31, 117.

4. See David Brion Davis: "Some Recent Directions in American Cultural History," *American Historical Review*, LXXIII (1968), 700–3.

Somehow we must go beyond, as well as get beneath, the conflict versus consensus polarity. We must also appreciate the inconsistencies and paradoxes without losing sight of the very real struggles that have taken place.

One obstruction to clearer vision in this matter has been an enduring element of ambiguity in American historical writing —not at all surprising in a culture particularly perplexed by ambivalence and contradictory tendencies. There are some superficial ironies which are easily explained; but more perplexing and intriguing are the ambiguities one finds in the writings of such major figures as Frederick Jackson Turner, Charles A. Beard, Perry Miller, and others. In Beard's most famous book, for example, it is not at all clear whether he was saying that the Founding Fathers framed the Constitution because they expected to profit by it, or rather that the ways in which the Fathers made their profits predisposed them to look at political and constitutional issues from a certain perspective. Beneath this equivocation in Beard's historical statement lay a real ambiguity in thought; and both were rooted in a decided dualism in Beard's position as scholar and publicist of the Progressive era.[5]

Curiously enough, American historians have been less sensitive to contradictory tendencies in the national style than foreign observers, philosophers, theologians, high-level journalists, and scholars of the interdisciplinary "American studies" movement. The latter group has indeed stressed antinomies in the American character, as well as anomalies inherent in many indigenous circumstances. But their concern has belletristic origins, has largely located its manifestations in the literary culture, and has been almost exclusively preoccupied with nineteenth- and twentieth-century situations, to the neglect of colonial origins.

By contrast, Reinhold Niebuhr ranged through the length

5. See Lee Benson: *Turner and Beard. American Historical Writing Reconsidered* (New York, 1960), 96–101; Richard Hofstadter: "Beard and the Constitution: the History of an Idea," *American Quarterly*, II (1950), 196, 204–8.

and breadth of our experience in order to depict persuasively the irony of American history. "Our age is involved in irony," he wrote,

> because so many dreams of our nation have been so cruelly refuted by history. . . . Our idealists are divided between those who would renounce the responsibilities of power for the sake of preserving the purity of our soul and those who are ready to cover every ambiguity of good and evil in our actions by the frantic insistence that any measure taken in a good cause must be unequivocally virtuous.[6]

It is vitally important to recognize, however, that ours is not the only culture characterized by biformities. This condition occurs universally, especially in colonial circumstances. But in diverse cultures the tensions take various forms and are resolved in different ways, if at all. In addition, foreign observers have been noting for generations what Erik Erikson also believes, namely, that "this dynamic country [in particular] subjects its inhabitants to more extreme contrasts and abrupt changes during a lifetime or a generation than is normally the case with other great nations." James Fullarton Muirhead, an Englishman who spent the years 1890–93 here preparing *Baedeker's Handbook to the United States*, put it this way:

> It may well be that a long list of inconsistencies might be made out for any country, just as for any individual; but so far as my knowledge goes the United States stands out as preëminently the "Land of Contrasts"— the land of stark, staring, and stimulating inconsistency; at once the home of enlightenment and the happy hunting ground of the charlatan and the quack; a land in which nothing happens but the unexpected; the home of Hyperion, but no less the haunt of the satyr; always the land of promise, but not invariably the land of performance; a land which may be bounded by the aurora borealis, but which has also undeniable acquaintance with the flames of the bottomless pit; a land which is

6. *The Irony of American History* (New York, 1952), 2, 4.

laved at once by the rivers of Paradise and the leaden waters of Acheron.[7]

What we must do is ask whether these inconsistencies have, in fact, been more pronounced in American history than elsewhere, and inquire as to the nature of our paradoxes and their historical sources. In order to do this we must first have some clear notion of "un-American" societies, their uncertainties and biformities. There is no assurance; but when we know what we are not, we may also know better what we are.

I HAVE REMARKED that societal tensions and counterpoised inclinations tend to become accentuated or aggravated when transplanted into colonial settings. The reasons and manifestations of this are important, though not at all obvious. Therefore, we might briefly examine the circumstances of New Spain and New France with an eye especially to our developing frame of reference.

When Spain turned westward at the close of the fifteenth century, her recent unification barely concealed significant sectional and psychic differences. Isabella of Castile, the intensely Catholic queen, felt concern about the absolute assertion of spiritual authority. Until 1492 the hierarchical Castilian state had physically confronted Moorish Granada, and of necessity retained its medieval orientation. By contrast her husband, Ferdinand of Aragón, a secular Renaissance ruler, was more oriented to the east and north. Whereas Isabella presented the unity of spiritually intransigent Christendom to infidel and pagan, Ferdinand was more committed to the shifting, amoral statecraft of competitive princes. Managing with personal verve and cunning, he was Machiavellian in every sense.

The point, then, is that Spanish conquistadors, catechizers, and colonists carried with them to the New World this dual heritage of contemporary tendencies in tension: Medieval and Thomistic versus Renaissance and Machiavellian. Conse-

7. *The Land of Contrasts. A Briton's View of His American Kin* (Boston, 1898), 7.

quently, the conquest developed as a kind of dual revelation.[8] One result was that the American Indian was viewed bifocally: through the eyes of the self-assured knight errant, and also through those of the inquisitive humanist. The tragic fate of the Indian under Iberian dominion owed much to this inevitably myopic ambivalence.

There was still another, related dualism characteristic of Spain on the eve of colonization. On the one hand a militant nobility and dependent peasantry shared a common desire for riches by warfare. The aristocracy sought prestige and plundered wealth, while the peasants, soldier-cultivators, hoped for land. On the other hand, meanwhile, the town-based bourgeoisie looked to capital accumulation through commerce and industry. Such entrepreneurs existed in all the peninsular towns. But only in eastern Spain, especially Catalonia, had they gained sufficient power to restrain the expansionist tendencies of the militants. By 1492 these two Spains were moving toward collision, a conflict which might well have altered the face of Spain but for the discovery of America. The New World offered vast expanses of land, unheard-of wealth, and enormous brigades of disciplined labor. Paradoxically, however, new chests of wealth from the Indies would eventually ruin Spanish trade and industry. Ironically also, the new frontier helped to destroy the very class which might have brought a commercial renaissance to Spain. Instead, the merchant-entrepreneur receded into obscurity, while the knight-adventurer, the visionary of wealth through conquest, gained new impetus.[9] Thus colonization resolved a major tension in early modern Spain in ways exactly opposite to the pattern in Stuart England, where the bourgeoisie and capitalism flourished in response to the stimulus of overseas expansion.

Once the settlement of New Spain got under way, a fresh configuration of conflicts and anomalies emerged. The first of

8. See Richard M. Morse: "Toward a Theory of Spanish American Government," *Journal of the History of Ideas*, XV (1954), 72–7.

9. Eric Wolf: *Sons of the Shaking Earth* (Chicago, 1959), 157–62.

these grew simply from the fact that conquerors and colonizers were urban types whose task nevertheless was to make contact with the soil, from which all wealth would flow, given the available labor of millions of Africans and American Indians.[1] Then the conquistador on the threshold of capitalism found himself all too soon in a vise which bore the peculiar marks of a contradiction, caught between past and future. His Utopia of gold and freedom was threatened by the tension between personal aggrandizement and demands of an increasingly centralized imperial system under Charles V and then Philip II. The tendency of conquistadors to form local enclaves and élites ran up against the Crown's burgeoning bureaucracy. An irresistible force had apparently met an immovable body.[2]

Meanwhile, the Crown's dual aims of revenue and converted Indians were only theoretically compatible. Bartolomé de Las Casas's awareness of the tension was evident in his appeals (on behalf of the Indian) to both fiscal needs and the royal conscience. Inevitably, however, conflicts grew between the humanitarian compassion of Spanish administrators and what seemed to be the practical realities and necessities of colonial life. Inexorably the city of man, peopled by avaricious Spaniards, would destroy the City of God that friars and Indians together were beginning to build.[3]

Whereas wars of rebellion and independence ultimately resolved some of Latin America's colonial contradictions, the English conquest of New France in 1759–60, and her subsequent patterns of administration and control, perpetuated dualisms which have persisted and fascinated historians from Francis Parkman's time until our own. Parkman saw in the

---

1. Richard M. Morse: "Latin American Cities: Aspects of Function and Structure," *Comparative Studies in Society and History*, IV (1962), 473.

2. Wolf: *Sons of the Shaking Earth*, 166–7; Fernando Benítez: *The Century After Cortés* (Chicago, 1965), 179; Irving A. Leonard: *Baroque Times in Old Mexico* (Ann Arbor, 1959), ch. 3.

3. See J. H. Parry: *The Spanish Seaborne Empire* (New York, 1966), 173–91; John Leddy Phelan: *The Millennial Kingdom of the Franciscans in the New World* (Berkeley and Los Angeles, 1956), 87.

history of New France a struggle between "barren absolutism" and "a liberty, crude, incoherent, and chaotic, yet full of prolific vitality." As a counter-influence to absolute authority there lay the great interior wilderness. "Rudely and wildly antagonistic," the domain of savage freedom beckoned the "disfranchised, half-starved seigneur, and the discouraged *habitant* who could find no market for his produce." [4]

Like New Spain, New France also had a dual intellectual inheritance. The stronger of the two strains was the Jansenist-inspired pietism of the seventeenth century; the weaker, but important nonetheless, was the more tolerant spirit of the Enlightenment. Pietism won out, yet libertinism would recur repeatedly in French-Canadian writing. The Jansenist strain appears in the efforts of French Jesuits to civilize the Indian; but the religious absolutism of the Jesuits was curiously combined with a surprising sense of cultural relativism. In consequence, cassocked conquistadors tended to permit the heathens great latitude in the sphere of natural conduct while insisting upon absolute conformity in the sphere of supernatural religion. Although the Jesuits eventually sanctioned conquest and colonization in the interest of conversion, they periodically objected to the military and mercantilist concomitants of such programs. [5]

As the fringes of settlement slowly grew in New France, so did the tension between European expectations and emerging realities—the conflict between old prescriptions and new imperatives. Even royal authorities recognized that a vast discrepancy had developed, for example, between the real position of the seigneur and the one ascribed to him. The pressure of new economic necessities would prove to be a more powerful

4. Wilbur R. Jacobs, ed.: *Letters of Francis Parkman* (Norman, 1960), I, li; Samuel Eliot Morison, ed.: *The Parkman Reader* (Boston, 1955), 266–7. See also Mason Wade, ed.: *Canadian Dualism. Studies of French-English Relations* (Toronto, 1960).

5. John C. Rule: "The Old Regime in America: A Review of Recent Interpretations of France in America," *William and Mary Quarterly*, 3d series, XIX (1962), 592; J. H. Kennedy: *Jesuit and Savage in New France* (New Haven, 1950), 100–4.

determinant of social behavior than schemes of imperial administrators.[6] Resolution of these problems only began to emerge when what had once been regarded as deviance came to be recognized as in fact the norm. Thus Brisay de Denonville, Governor General of New France, would eventually write to his superior "that Monseigneur should not determine to cease to give letters of nobility; but that it would be well to give them only to those who will . . . enter into whatever commerce makes a noble in this country."[7]

Even so, tensions between feudal rights and royal absolutism continued to cause the same unrest in New France as it did in old. Intendants and governors kept up their fierce but subtle enmities in the eighteenth century. And as one would expect, there emerged from the conquest of 1759 two distinct styles of life and taste. One was French, Catholic, conquered, leaderless, and ruled by the law of the Custom of Paris. The other was English, Protestant, vigorous, triumphant, and ruled by the common law tradition. Within this biformity the new French-Canadian, already nascent, would be finally molded.[8]

I do not mean to suggest, then, that citizens of the United States are uniquely a people of paradox. Polarities may be found in many cultures the world over. I do insist that members of colonial societies are especially susceptible to both the inconsistencies they inherit and those they form anew. Although I have taken New Spain and New France as examples, one finds similar evidence, say, in Anglo-Dutch South Africa or in Portuguese Brazil. In the formation of Brazilian society

6. Sigmund Diamond: "An Experiment in 'Feudalism': French Canada in the Seventeenth Century," *William and Mary Quarterly*, 3d series, XVIII (1961), 25–6; Guy Frégault: *La Civilisation de la Nouvelle France* (1713–1744) (Montreal, 1944), 219–20.

7. Quoted in Diamond: "An Experiment in 'Feudalism,' " 31–2; see also L. R. MacDonald: "France and New France: The Internal Contradictions," *Canadian Historical Review*, LII (1971), 121–43.

8. Rule: "The Old Regime in America," 590–1, 593; A. R. M. Lower: "Two Ways of Life: The Primary Antithesis of Canadian History," in Canadian Historical Association *Report* (1943), 5–18; A. R. M. Lower: "Two Ways of Life: the Spirit of Our Institutions," *Canadian Historical Review*, XXVIII (1947), 383–400.

the process of balancing off antagonisms has been central: between the African and the native; between agrarian and mining regions; between Catholic and heretic; Jesuit and *fazendeiro; bandeirante* and plantation owner; *Paulista* and *emboaba,* Pernambucan and *mascate.*[9]

I would be among the first, then, to recognize that many of the polarities I shall point to have their counterparts elsewhere. What finally matters, I think, is *the particular configuration of tensions within a national setting*, as well as the behavioral, intellectual, and emotional consequences of that configuration. Perhaps one difference among styles depends upon the degree to which a given nation recognizes and accepts its dualisms. Americans more than most, I believe, have historically tended to ignore their biformities, for they feel that inconsistency is a bad thing. But should we not be aware, though not necessarily beware and bemoan our biformities? For the least attractive of them may have become deformities, and the most monotonous uniformities.

I am also inclined to think, however, that denizens of these United States and their forebears have been unusually and profoundly perplexed by ambivalence and contradictory pulls. I agree with Leo Marx that "the dialectical tendency of mind—the habit of seeing life as a collision of radically opposed forces and values—has been accentuated by certain special conditions of experience in America." More than a merely Manichean view is involved, more than the common American habit of creating false or exaggerated disjunctions. Edward Shils has suggested that there exists a broadly antinomian strain, such that our basic respect for institutions and the rights of others is often punctuated by periods of exceptional disrespect for law and irreverence toward individuals.[1]

9. See Richard M. Morse: "Some Themes of Brazilian History," *South Atlantic Quarterly,* LXI (1962), 159–82; Gilberto Freyre: *The Masters and the Slaves. A Study in the Development of Brazilian Civilization* (1st English ed., New York, 1946), 7–8, 79–80; Leonard M. Thompson: "The South African Dilemma," in *The Founding of New Societies,* ed. Louis Hartz (New York, 1964), 178–218.
1. See Marx: "Two Kingdoms of Force," *The Massachusetts Re-*

Ultimately, doesn't any national style depend upon the interaction of two fundamental factors: the human condition and contextual conditions; or, the customary and the environmental? In most societies the former has had a certain fixity and has mattered enormously. In the United States, the human condition—which is everywhere paradoxical, to be sure—has been given unusual freedom to vacillate permissively between possible poles. Thus environment has here been efficacious because its very vastness and diversity have served to exacerbate and expand those contradictory tendencies inherent in the human condition.

THE UNITED STATES is commonly represented by two images or icons. Both are used on posters and in cartoons, though it is not at all clear which is most appropriate to any particular circumstance. One is an extremely tall, thin old man, his beard trimmed to an old-fashioned goatee, his formal suit cut from a Betsy Ross creation. The other is a portly, maternal woman draped in flowing robes of the classical style, crowned with a diadem, and holding a torch aloft in one hand. Uncle Sam symbolizes the government: demanding, negotiating, asking for sacrifices. The Goddess of Liberty, or Columbia, represents the land of freedom and opportunity: America as a bountiful cornucopia. The national iconography seems to be sensitive to what America offers her people and the world, as well as to what the government requires of its citizens.[2]

Symbols such as these have long fascinated foreign observers of the American scene. The most distinguished of them all, Alexis de Tocqueville, recognized that individualism and idealism were somehow just as characteristic of the American style as conformity and materialism. He discerned two tendencies within the principle of equality: "the one leading the mind of every man to untried thoughts, the other inclined to prohibit

view, I (1959), 84; Shils: *The Torment of Secrecy. The Background and Consequences of American Security Policies* (Glencoe, 1956), 161.

2. See Geoffrey Gorer: *The American People. A Study in National Character* (New York, 1948), 50–3.

him from thinking at all." If the principle of equality predisposed men to change, it also suggested to them certain interests which could not be satisfied without a settled order of things. "Equality urges them on, but at the same time it holds them back; it spurs them, but fastens them to earth;—it kindles their desires, but limits their powers." Tocqueville admitted to being surprised by two facets of the United States in 1831: "the mutability of the greater part of human actions, and the singular stability of certain principles." Men were constantly and restlessly in motion; but their minds were fixed. Once an opinion took root, no power on earth might dislodge it.[3]

James Bryce, the perceptive Englishman who visited here half a century after Tocqueville, remarked that if Americans were shrewd and tough-minded, they were also very impressionable; that if they were restless and unsettled, they were also rather associative. "Although the atoms are in constant motion, they have a strong attraction for one another." He found them a vacillating people, and again resorted to scientific metaphor to make his meaning clear: "they have what chemists call low specific heat; they grow warm suddenly and cool as suddenly." Despite their inclination to change mood and place so readily, Bryce also noted the power of habit, tenacity, and tradition among Americans, and therefore concluded that "it may seem a paradox to add that the Americans are a conservative people."[4]

Students of American culture, much influenced by Bryce and Tocqueville, have occasionally remarked that racial discrimination, civic corruption, and violence are just as much American traditions as equality, morality, and the rule of law. They have noted that Americans tend to be more smug and complacent than other peoples, yet more self-critical too, and conscience-stricken; that a moral dualism in the United States couples passionate concern for private, material prosperity with a propensity for periodic public moral renewal and re-

3. Quoted in Richard L. Rapson, ed.: *Individualism and Conformity in the American Character* (Boston, 1967), 9–10, 14.
4. *The American Commonwealth* (2nd ed., London, 1891), II, 281–3.

ligious enthusiasm. By constantly breaking with the past and
conforming to transitory norms and fashions, the American
seems to be both anti-traditionalist and highly conformist. He
is also embarrassed by another moral dualism: the conflict
between high ethical standards and the ethos of the market
place. Perhaps because of a bad conscience he is extraordinarily
generous, yet always afraid of "being played for a sucker."
Inevitably, the American has been obliged to reconcile morality
and expediency. Thus if generous actions motivated by compassionate considerations are accepted without gratitude, mis-
interpreted, or unrequited, a cynical repudiation of humanitarianism may follow.[5]

The American has also held conflicting attitudes toward
intellectual and manual labor. When the life of the mind has
obviously promoted material well-being, it has generally been
appreciated and rewarded. But when it has appeared to
threaten established norms and comfortable ways of thinking,
or the power and influence of entrenched groups, it has been
resented and disparaged. Southern ambivalence about labor,
leisure, and laziness—beginning way back with Captain John
Smith's jeremiad against "idleness and sloth" at Jamestown—
is part of a larger configuration of southern images, each of
which has its obverse. The other side of chivalry is arrogance,
of paternalism is racism. In short, it would seem that the American has been unable to elude the ancient and equivocal tension
between authority and the individual.[6]

Some of which—to the everlasting credit of American
authors—has become staple fare in our literature and formal
thought. George Santayana found the American "an idealist
working on matter." Van Wyck Brooks, in his first excited report on the condition of American culture, saw a frank accept-

5. See Hans Kohn: *American Nationalism. An Interpretive Essay*
(New York, 1957), 74; Gabriel Almond: *The American People and
Foreign Policy* (New York, 1960), 32, 43, 45–6, 52.
6. Merle Curti: *American Paradox: The Conflict of Thought and
Action* (New Brunswick, 1956), viii and *passim;* C. Vann Woodward:
"The Southern Ethic in a Puritan World," *William and Mary Quar-
terly*, 3d series, XXV (1968), 343–5, 370.

ance of linked values which no one expected to have anything in common: high ideals and catchpenny realities. "Between university ethics and business ethics, between American culture and American humor, between Good Government and Tammany, between academic pedantry and pavement slang, there is no community, no genial middle ground." Brooks found that colonial literature of the seventeenth century was "composed in equal parts . . . of piety and advertisement." Hence from the very beginning there may have been two main currents running parallel through American minds: the transcendental current, elevated by Jonathan Edwards, refined by Ralph Waldo Emerson; and the practical current which Benjamin Franklin made into a philosophy of common sense, and which nineteenth-century humorists raised to a style of entertainment.[7]

In Robert Lowell's recent trilogy, *The Old Glory*, based upon traditional American literary and historical materials, the poet explores certain tensions and antonyms arising from the hidden painfulness of American origins. In *Endecott and the Red Cross*, adapted from Hawthorne's story about Massachusetts Bay during the 1630's, Thomas Morton and Governor Endecott are set as archetypal American rivals—libertine and Puritan, Dionysiac and Apollonian, the establishmentarian and the nonconformist. Lowell has perceived and presented a movingly bifarious view of the North American experience and sensibility.[8]

IF THE PENETRATING INSIGHTS of so many observers are essentially on target, as I believe they are, then we are obliged to raise four crucial questions. Has America been marked by different biformities than other nations? Has their configuration been unusual? If so, why? And what have been the consequences?

7. Santayana: *Character and Opinion in the United States* (New York, 1920), 175; Brooks: *America's Coming of Age* (New York, 1915), 17–20.

8. *The Old Glory* (New York, 1965); see Richard Gilman's interview with Lowell, *The New York Times*, May 5, 1968, D1 and D5.

Americans and foreigners seem to agree, in varying degrees, with the Italian author Raoul Romoli-Venturi that "all the tensions of the world have been imported by the United States." Jacques Maritain, a philosophical visitor, puts it this way:

> the feelings and instinct of community are much stronger in this country than in Europe . . . the result of which is a tension, perpetually varying in intensity, between the sense of the community and the sense of individual freedom. Such tension, to my mind, is normal and fecund in itself. Of course, it happens to create conflicts, especially when the community feels that it is threatened in its very life, and reacts . . . with "posses" which hunt men who are not necessarily criminals. Then a counteraction follows as a rule, in the name of moral tenets such as individual freedom and civil rights, without which the very existence and unity of the nation cannot hold.[9]

From the very beginnings of settlement at Jamestown, Plymouth, Salem, and St. Mary's City, there has been contention over the meaning of America. Was it to be a conglomeration of individuals, each going his own way, or a well-ordered society of generally co-operative groups? The very vastness of the landscape made the former almost inevitable, but the latter nearly a necessity. Because the cultural forces of western Europe were transplanted to circumstances of relative isolation, "they reverberated like loud voices in an empty room; and they fell into new relationships." Constance Rourke has said it with admirable grace:

> Thus the psychological intensities of Calvinism were greatly deepened in the New England colonies as compared with the practice of Calvinism in English communities, which tended to fringe off into groups of a quite different character and thus to become modified. And these peculiar inner intensities fell into conjunction with wholly primitive influences here. All through the colonial period up to the French and Indian War

9. *Time* (June 14, 1968), 26; Maritain: *Reflections on America* (New York, 1958), 21–2, 163.

the colonists fought savage foes and even adopted some of their forms of savagery, against a background of this intricate inner quest. . . . These forces were all but antiphonal, one set completely against the other.[1]

Why should we be this way? Why should biformities be so pervasive in the American style? There are many reasons. The first in point of time (and the subject of my next chapter) is that England during her great age of colonization and cultural transmission was peculiarly racked by tensions and contradictory tendencies. The conflict of generations in "Jacobethan" times, Mary versus Elizabeth, Catholic versus Protestant, Cavalier versus Roundhead, the ambiguous issue of overpopulation are just a few illustrations.

A second reason rests in the very process of uprooting and immigrating. Many colonists migrated in order to escape anxieties at home; but by coming they activated others and created some anew, such as the tension between inherited ideas and environmental realities, which demanded some sort of accommodation.

A third reason also has to do with our being a nation of immigrants. Multiple origins, ethnic diversity, and social heterogeneity have produced discomforting strains. In the guise of Poor Richard, a certain cosmopolitan provincial publicly extolled the colonies as places of refuge for Europe's aged, ill, aliens, and dissenters; but as Benjamin Franklin he privately expressed his fear of German immigration to Pennsylvania. The Germans "under-live, and are thereby enabled to under-work and under-sell the English; who are thereby extremely incommoded and consequently disgusted."[2] Walt Whitman would put this problem posed by uneasy pluralism most simply a century later in *Leaves of Grass:*

> Do I contradict myself?
> Very well then I contradict myself,
> (I am large, I contain multitudes.)

1. *The Roots of American Culture, and Other Essays* (New York, 1942), 54–6.

2. Quoted in Max Savelle: *Seeds of Liberty. The Genesis of the American Mind* (Seattle, 1965), 567–8.

A fourth factor may be found in the ambivalence of English attitudes and imperial policies during the colonial era. Provincials were not supposed to deviate, for example, from institutional norms at home; but neither were they to imitate the House of Commons too slavishly, or demand its privileges and prerogatives. Thus for a century and a half the colonists, who were at once English and New English, developed a delicate equipoise of dual loyalties. In consequence, the meaning of liberty developed in America not so much in opposition to force but as a pattern of ways in which force was to be applied. "The safeguards of liberty lay not in the denial of the use of force, but in the establishment of appropriate procedures for its use." [3]

A fifth reason is simply that *America Was Promises*, as Archibald MacLeish put it thirty years ago. Ever since John Cotton's 1630 sermon, "God's Promise to His Plantations," men have expected much of America: greater freedom, opportunity, and bounty than was ever offered man in all of known history. Those are difficult expectations to fulfill consistently, making frustration inevitable.

The sixth reason is a related one, almost an appendage to the fifth. Our principles and ideals have been so loftily elevated that we have often been unable to live by them consistently or realize even an approximation of them. "American history is a paradox if not a contradiction," writes John W. Caughey. "Ours was the first nation to dedicate itself at the outset to a regime of freedom. . . . Yet as a nation and as a people we have all too often strayed from this path." [4]

Seventh and eighth causes of our biformities are also closely linked. Rapid physical and social mobility have brought people quickly from one region to another and from one status to another, subjecting them to unexpected circumstances and

3. Oscar and Mary Handlin: *The Dimensions of Liberty* (Cambridge, Mass., 1961), 21, 37, 87.
4. "Our Chosen Destiny," *Journal of American History*, LII (1965), 251.

requiring accommodation among diverse possibilities. The plight of Clyde Griffiths in Dreiser's *American Tragedy*, or of the southern rural Negro transplanted to Chicago's South Side, are typical. Meanwhile the intense pace of life and rapidity of change subject Americans to tensions and uncertainties not found elsewhere, or at least not in the same degree. "But what is the American?" asked Fenimore Cooper in 1845: "A jumble of the same senseless contradictions in his social habits, as he is fast getting to be in his political creeds and political practices; being that is *in transitu*, pressed by circumstances on the one side, and by the habit of imitation on the other." [5] The United States may very well be the first large-scale society to have built innovation and change into its culture as a constant variable, so that a kind of "creative destruction" continually alters the face of American life.

A ninth reason has been defined by Perry Miller as "an unreconcilable opposition between Nature and Civilization—which is to say, between forest and town, spontaneity and calculation." Where else is the citizen torn so powerfully between the vastness and beauty of the natural world on one side, and the overwhelming influence of urbanization and technology on the other? [6]

Finally, we have had to reconcile individualism and conformity, and so have developed a curious amalgam, a collective individualism, described perfectly by Ralph Barton Perry:

> American self-reliance is a plural, collective, self-reliance—not "*I* can," but "*we* can." But it is still individualistic—a togetherness of several and not the isolation of one, or the absorption of all into a higher unity. The appropriate term is not "organism" but "organization"; *ad hoc* organization, extemporized to meet emer-

5. Cooper: *Satanstoe* (Lincoln, 1962), 55.
6. Miller: "The Shaping of the American Character," and "The Romantic Dilemma in American Nationalism and the Concept of Nature," in *Nature's Nation* (Cambridge, Mass., 1965), 1–13, 197–207; Leo Marx: *The Machine in the Garden. Technology and the Pastoral Ideal in America* (New York, 1964).

gencies, and multiple organization in which the same individuals join many and surrender themselves to none.[7]

Collective individualism is only one among a large cluster of biformities which express the contradictory tendencies of our contrapuntal civilization. There are also the conservative liberalism of our political life, the pragmatic idealism of our cerebral life, the emotional rationalism of our spiritual life, and godly materialism of our acquisitive life.

The English colonies were established by Calvinists who believed that in and of himself man could do little to save his own soul, and that gaining the world conferred no profit; yet Americans have behaved ever since as though he who strives shall indeed gain the world, and save his soul in the bargain. Many of the Founding Fathers believed in national perfectibility despite their deeply pessimistic appraisal of the particular state of mankind. Many of the utopian and communitarian experiments of the mid-nineteenth century were essentially devised as anti-institutional institutions, swerving erratically between extremes of anarchism and collectivism. Progressives early in this century tried desperately to reconcile within themselves an ethic of communal responsibility with one of unrestrained individualism. And two sorts of liberalism have become solidly entrenched in modern America: laissez-faire liberalism and welfare state liberalism. Witness the New Nationalism of Theodore Roosevelt and the New Freedom of Woodrow Wilson; contrast the first and second phases of the New Deal under Franklin Delano Roosevelt.

In short, the push-pull of both wanting to belong and seeking to be free has been the ambivalent condition of life in America, the nurture of a contrapuntal civilization.

7. *Characteristically American* (New York, 1949), 13.

CHAPTER 5

CONFLICT, CRISIS, AND CHANGE
The Context
of English Colonization

> I find there are many pieces in this one fabrick of
> man; this frame is raised upon a mass of Antipathies. I am
> one methinks, but as the World; wherein notwithstanding
> there are a swarm of distinct essences, and in them another
> World of Contrarieties, we carry private and domestic
> enemies within, public and more hostile adversaries with-
> out. . . . Let me be nothing, if within the compass of
> my self I do not find the battail of Lepanto, Passion against
> Reason, Reason against Faith, Faith against the Devil,
> and my conscience against all. There's another man within
> me, that's angry with me, rebukes, commands and dastards
> me.
>
> SIR THOMAS BROWNE, *Religio Medici* (1642)

BETWEEN the abortive Armada in 1588 and conclusion of
the Thirty Years' War in 1648, Europe was a fascinating but
fearful place. Transitional paroxysms of the later Renaissance
and uncontrolled tremors of several sorts were felt everywhere
in western Christendom. In England especially, for more than
sixty years, there were profound crises of mind and spirit, reflected in religion, literature, and political thought. Social

change became too rapid, uncontrollable, and readily apparent both within and between gradations of English society. Amidst industrial and economic change, demographic debates over population problems, and intergenerational hostility, Puritanism emerged as a dynamic, disruptive force while the aristocracy and gentry were being transformed. Because the nation divided against itself, its polity was torn apart and then rebuilt. Not just in England, but in Scotland, Ireland, and the North American "plantations" as well. For against the background of this half century of tumult and transition at home, England began to expand across the sea. Not surprisingly, those brave but leaky ships sailing westward with the sun carried not only milch cows and ratsbane, but ambivalent attitudes toward primitive peoples and plantations as well.

IT HAS BEEN the traditional (albeit trite) prerogative of historians to label periods of peculiar perplexity as "transitional." There does, however, seem to be an overwhelming consensus that Europe in the later sixteenth and earlier seventeenth century was indeed a delicately poised place in a pivotal time. Consequently, J. H. Hexter has urged us to examine the era in terms of "polar pairs, pulling men in opposite directions and therefore creating tensions": Church-State; Catholic-Protestant; lay-clerical; secular-religious; dynasty-region; court-country; *Realpolitik*-legitimacy; absolutism-constitutionalism; town-hinterland; and the mixture of love and fear by which Renaissance princes were obliged to rule. As Hexter has observed, the tensions in early modern society created by the pulls of each polar pair sometimes emerged as conflicts between organized groups, but ofttimes as the "uncertainties, unresolved dilemmas and inconsistencies of individual men." [1]

Why should this have been especially so in the later sixteenth and early seventeenth century? One reason lies in the

1. J. H. Hexter: *Reappraisals in History* (New York, 1963), 13, 32–42, 208–11.

very nature of those elusive, overlapping phenomena we call Renaissance, Reformation, and Scientific Revolution. Each, as Professor Trevor-Roper suggests, had a Janus-face. "The Renaissance was a revival not only of pagan letters but of pagan mystery-religion. The Reformation was a return not only to the unforgettable century of the Apostles but also to the unedifying centuries of the Hebrew kings. The Scientific Revolution was shot through with Pythagorean mysticism and cosmological fantasy." In short, the new intellectual forces at work in Europe were themselves ambiguous.[2]

Scholars have recently demonstrated that between 1560 and 1660, especially during the second half of that period, Europe underwent a general crisis consisting of several component elements. In part, it grew from the exigencies of monarchical development—discrepancies between the theory of absolutism and the inability of kings to enforce their will readily. Because rulers lacked firm control, they were forced to rely on the nobility in ways that compromised their absolutist inclinations. Simultaneously, an antithesis emerged between two alternative systems: the fiscal one of princes, which might encourage state capitalism but squeeze out free enterprise, and the mercantile system of the major cities, which required a more flexible type of monarchy.[3]

The general European crisis of the earlier seventeenth century manifested itself in England in many ways. Because James I and his son Charles lacked the political savvy of Elizabeth, and because they refused to reform their court, they ran into ultimate disaster. Most of their antagonists were not opposed to monarchy as such, or even to economic traditionalism. They were gentry, powerful in the counties and in Parliament, who resented the high burden of taxation they had been obliged

2. H. R. Trevor-Roper: *Religion, The Reformation and Social Change* (London, 1967), 90, 134.

3. Trevor Aston, ed.: *Crisis in Europe, 1560–1660* (New York, 1967); Margaret A. Judson: *The Crisis of the Constitution* (New Brunswick, 1949).

to carry, and who despised the extensive number of parasitic leeches which had grown up around the throne and on the economy of England.

As one might expect, Machiavelli was much studied during these decades in England, where readers recognized his (and their own) contradictions. The political technician and passionate republican strain ambivalently against each other in *The Prince* and in *The Discourses*.[4] Just so, Sir Walter Raleigh, fascinating figure of late Elizabethan times, vacillated between the universe of St. Augustine and the world ascribed to Machiavelli's mind, between idealism and calculating materialism; for this practical man of affairs was also an unstable dreamer.

What, then, was most deeply troubling the England of Elizabeth and James I? The question is important, for as Tocqueville remarked:

> at the period when the peoples of Europe landed in the New World, their national characteristics were already completely formed; each of them had a physiognomy of its own; and as they had already attained that stage of civilization at which men are led to study themselves, they have transmitted to us a faithful picture of their opinions, their manners, and their laws.[5]

BETWEEN THE CLOSING YEARS of the sixteenth century and the middle of the seventeenth, between John Donne and John Milton, between *King Lear* and the Christian paradox of man's fortunate fall in *Paradise Lost*, educated Englishmen were obsessed with paradox as a literary form. The essence of the metaphysical lyric is paradox: sharp antitheses, incongruous objects connected, agonizing questions, contrasts between desire and possibility. Donne called on God to

> Take me to you, imprison me, for I,
> Except you enthrall me, never shall be free,
> Nor ever chaste, except you ravish me.

4. See Felix Raab: *The English Face of Machiavelli. A Changing Interpretation, 1500–1700* (London, 1964), 255–8, 260–3.

5. Phillips Bradley, ed.: *Democracy in America* (New York, 1945), I, 28.

And Thomas Percy, Donne's older contemporary, observed that

> Everye white will have its blacke,
> And every sweete its sowre.

William Prynne produced precious essays on such themes as *Healthes Sicknesse* and *The Unlovelinesse of Love-lockes*, both published in 1628. Fourteen years later, Edward Browne called for political moderation in *A Paradox Usefull for the Times*, "that oftentimes good doth come of evill, wisdome from folly, and light out of darknesse." That same year Sir Thomas Browne's *Religio Medici* appeared, sadly lamenting that "for the world I count it not an Inn, but a Hospital, and a place not to live but to die in." [6]

Why this fascination, sustained intensely over half a century, with a curious art form? Surely, beneath the symptomatic and compulsive use of this particular trope lay anxiety and ambivalence. Paradoxes equivocate. They involve dialectic, often to challenge some orthodoxy or another. They are often self-critical. They may involve many different figures of speech, but essentially they reflect an ambiguity of thought. They may occur in any place or period of cerebral speculation; but they especially tend to accumulate in periods of intense intellectual activity, when many different ideas and systems compete with one another, and make men sensitive to the doubleness of human perception. [7]

Thus the years from 1598 until 1602, when John Donne wrote his *Paradoxes and Problemes*, were years of disillusionment and intrigue for Donne, and for England as well. Accordingly, his third paradox suggested "That by Discord Things Increase." In 1627 Walter Cary bemoaned *The Present State of England, Expressed in this Paradox: Our Fathers Were Very Rich With Little, And We Poor With Much*. Cary

6. Literature concerning paradox in late Renaissance England is so considerable and unwieldy that I have reserved citations for the Bibliographical Suggestions, p. 304 below.

7. See Rosalie L. Colie: *Paradoxia Epidemica. The Renaissance Tradition of Paradox* (Princeton, 1966), 6–7, 10, 12, 22, 33, 169–89, 461–81, 508, 518–20.

examined three phenomena of his times—law suits, drunken-ness, and ostentatious dress—in arguing that "we use our Much ill, and they used their Little well."

While paradoxy prevailed as an aesthetic flourish between the late 1590's and 1650's, there were deep-rooted underlying causes. A literary convention does not become fashionable un-less it reflects the mood of an age. To perceive and perpetrate paradoxes one must have both confidence and cynicism. These were, indeed, quintessential to Jacobean and Caroline England. In *Old Fortunatus* (1600) and *Satiromastix* (1602), Thomas Dekker brought the paradoxical encomium to the English stage, but with little attempt yet to give it dramatic signifi-cance. "Weele feede our selves with paradoxes," says Ande-locia, leading his companion to make a mock oration on hunger. "A dish of Paradoxes is a feast of strange opinion." In *Mon-sieur d'Olive* (1605), George Chapman used the convention with more dramatic effect. The character for whom the play is named takes pride in his skill as a talker, and his use of paradoxy provides an opportunity for proving his ability in discourse. Plays of Ben Jonson, especially *Volpone* (1606), completely assimilate the convention of paradoxical encomium into the author's themes.[8]

On the eve of English colonization in the New World, many traditional assumptions were being challenged. In *King Lear*, feudal and patriarchal loyalties are confronted by the blind individualism of Goneril, Regan, and Edmund. Leitmo-tifs of *The Merchant of Venice* and *Coriolanus* are similar. In writings of the later Elizabethans there is continuous oscilla-tion between extremes of pessimism and hopefulness. Edmund Spenser found it impossible in *The Faerie Queene* to reconcile medieval chivalry with Puritan restraints. Nor could Sir Philip Sidney fully keep intact the several faces of ideal man in his

---

8. Alexander H. Sackton: "The Paradoxical Encomium in Eliza-bethan Drama," *University of Texas Studies in English*, XXVIII (1949), 87, 90, 94, 97, 104; Henry Knight Miller: "The Paradoxical Encomium with Special Reference to Its Vogue in England, 1600–1800," *Modern Philology*, LIII (1956), 156–7, 172.

age. Hence his deterioration into contradiction: the poet who must not publish, the Platonist entangled with earthly beauty, the patron eternally in debt—in short, the "shepherd knight." As crises mounted early in the seventeenth century, so did a sharp antagonism between the humanistic, secular spirit of the Renaissance, and the revived spirit of early Christianity: Puritan if not ascetic, other-worldly, inflexible. What distinguished the Jacobean age from the Elizabethan was its more exact, more searching, more detailed inquiry into moral and political questions, and its interest in analyzing mysteries and ambiguities of the human mind.[9]

Where the decades from 1585 until 1615 witnessed astounding literary productivity in England, the period 1615–40 did not. Exuberance and national pride gave way to gloom and introspection. The fashionable psychic malady of these years was melancholia. It received more literary attention than any other humour, and required all sorts of queer and obscure scientific theories. One cause of such gloom was the cluster of conflicting philosophies uncovered by the new Renaissance learning. When man has grown accustomed to one course of thought, to one system universally accepted, it is not easy for him to adapt to several.[1]

Fear of mutability and decay had occasionally been expressed during the later sixteenth century. After 1600, however, exacerbated by the new astronomy, such notions began to exert an influence upon the popular imagination. John Donne caught the essence of this in *An Anatomie of the World:*

> And new Philosophy calls all in doubt,
> The Element of fire is quite put out;

9. Sir Herbert Grierson: *Cross Currents in English Literature of the 17th Century; or, The World, The Flesh, and the Spirit, Their Actions and Reactions* (London, 1929); Roger Howell: *Sir Philip Sidney: The Shepherd Knight* (Boston, 1968); F. P. Wilson: *Elizabethan and Jacobean* (Oxford, 1945).

1. Don Cameron Allen: "The Degeneration of Man and Renaissance Pessimism," *Studies in Philology,* XXXV (1938), 206, 211; Lawrence Babb: *The Elizabethan Malady: A Study of Melancholia in English Literature from 1580 to 1642* (East Lansing, 1951).

The Sun is lost, and th'earth, and no mans wit
Can well direct him where to looke for it.
And freely men confesse that this world's spent,
When in the Planets, and the Firmament
They seeke so many new; they see that this
Is crumbled out againe to his Atomies.

'Tis all in peeces, all cohaerence gone;
All just supply, and all Relation.[2]

Thus the intellectual life of Jacobean England was characterized by confusion and ferment. The vision of reality that had supported the rational consciousness of man for hundreds of years was fading. In retrospect, the Renaissance and Reformation, discovery of America, and the new astronomy had been more successful in undermining old assumptions and prejudices than in substituting new verities. The consequence was a profound spiritual crisis, a *crise de conscience*, in which man's "double heart" was repeatedly emphasized and analyzed.

T. S. Eliot has delineated a dissociation of sensibility, a split between thought and feeling, during the Stuart century in England. The metaphysical poets and Cambridge Platonists were especially exemplary and conscious of this tension between secular and spiritual, between mysticism and baroque rationalism. Such Christian skeptics as Sir Thomas Browne, Jeremy Taylor, and Joseph Glanvill were extraordinarily sensitive to dualisms of their day, and were attracted to paradox as the expressive form in which the complexity of truth could most closely be approached. Hence John Donne's "subtile knot which makes us men" reflected his awareness of the fundamental dualism of flesh and spirit.[3]

This dissociation of sensibility had its genesis, in part, in the reformed Church of England, for the Elizabethan ecclesi-

2. See George Williamson: "Mutability, Decay, and Seventeenth-Century Melancholy," *ELH. A Journal of English Literary History*, II (1935), 121–50; Victor Harris: *All Coherence Gone* (Chicago, 1949), esp. 1–7, 129.

3. Margaret L. Wiley: *The Subtle Knot. Creative Scepticism in Seventeenth-century England* (London, 1952), 79–88, 127–30, 151–8, 184–8, 205–8, 211–13, 246–9, 261–3; S. L. Bethell: *The Cultural Revolution of the Seventeenth Century* (London, 1951), esp. chs. 2–4.

astical settlement had been a cautious compromise in which Calvinist and Catholic elements were combined. The Thirty-Nine Articles, for example, were so framed as to enable members to believe either in predestination or free will, as they preferred. A similar ambiguity surrounded the significance of the sacrament in the communion service. The established Church managed to be a baroque breezeway between Catholicism and Protestantism, "firmly attached to both, but too open either to obstruct the passing zephyr or be permanently injured by offering too rigid a resistance to the hurricane." [4]

During the first third of the seventeenth century, as Puritanism neared its ascendancy, the Church of England acquired a troublesome theological biformity. Anglicanism separated God from natural man by elevating Him above human nature, yet joined God to man through the activity of free justification. Divine perfection was at once accessible to man but also kept away from him; God could elevate man to Heaven by offering him grace through the Church sacraments. Puritanism, in contrast, "assumed that grace and nature were two theaters of one Divine plan, each distinct and yet each involved with the other, incommensurate realms held in dialectical tension, inextricably entwined, wrestling in the universe and in the souls of men." [5] (This concept is summed up in the title of one of Richard Sibbes's works: *The Soul's Conflict With Itself and Victory Over Itself by Faith.*) The many and varied causes of conflict between Anglican and Puritan are well known: use of the surplice, ecclesiastical government, communalism, discipline, and forms of worship. What is less clearly established is the deeply felt tension within Puritanism itself.

Alongside a sincere desire to remain within the Church, Puritanism also contained factors undermining that very urge. It was this unresolved tension, rather than the activity of small

4. Sidney E. Mead: "The Rise of the Evangelical Conception of the Ministry in America (1607–1850)," in *The Ministry in Historical Perspective*, ed. H. R. Niebuhr and D. D. Williams (New York, 1956), 209.

5. John F. H. New: *Anglican and Puritan. The Basis of Their Opposition*, 1558–1640 (Stanford, 1964), 103–4, 108, 111.

scparatist sects, that offered a real danger to the Church of England. R. H. Tawney put it a little differently in his classic essay:

> There was in Puritanism an element which was conservative and traditionalist, and an element which was revolutionary; a collectivism which grasped at an iron discipline, and an individualism which spurned the savourless mess of human ordinances; a sober prudence which would garner the fruits of this world, and a divine recklessness which would make all things new.[6]

Alongside these spiritual uncertainties, dualisms in Jacobean political thought seem less self-destructive. They were pervasive, however, and equally determinative of biformities in American origins. To begin, the English Reformation had left a crucial ambiguity in the matter of ecclesiastical organization: whether papal power over the Church had been assumed by the Crown alone or by the King-in-Parliament. Then, during the later sixteenth century, and even more under the early Stuarts, royal authority was being challenged from three sides: by Roman Catholics, Puritans, and Parliament. There was also the menace of invasion from abroad. The inevitable response took the form of a royalist reaction, which claimed that the King possessed the throne and its powers by divine and hereditary right. Calvinists, in turn, sought a concept that would separate spiritual and temporal power, and so moved toward a theory of the duality of authority.[7]

Christian casuists, meanwhile, attempted to harmonize the Machiavellian political mentality (pervaded by considerations of policy, opportunity, and power) with sustained dedication to God's purposes. The framework of Christian ethics had somehow to be adapted to meet new situations and dangers, for, as George Mosse has remarked, so long "as tensions between religious presuppositions and realities of life exist, such casuis-

6. *Religion and the Rise of Capitalism* (London, 1926), 212.
7. W. H. Greenleaf: *Order, Empiricism and Politics. Two Traditions of English Political Thought. 1500–1700* (London, 1964), 39–41; C. H. McIlwain, ed.: *The Political Works of James I* (Cambridge, Mass., 1918), xxi–xxvi and *passim*.

tic thought will always have great relevance in attempting to adjust the Christian tradition to various forms of worldly wisdom and secular necessities." Hence the advice of one pamphleteer to James I, that if his people became unreasonable, he must bring them to do his bidding through "some craft or by some holy pretence." [8] Somewhat altered by circumstance and the man, this notion would become central in the Massachusetts governorship of John Winthrop, and would emerge as one element in an American style: pragmatic idealism.

The Jacobean mind was divided over more than just political and religious questions, though those spheres were certainly the most controversial. Historical, philosophical, and social thought were also undergoing changes, with unsettling consequences for the expansion of English minds overseas. There seem to have been two important schools of historical thought in Stuart England: the common lawyers, with their belief that the Constitution was immemorial; and their opponents, who suggested that it had once been altered by feudal principles. Then too, Tudor conceptions of education, especially higher education, were giving way to newer notions, but not without a struggle, just as philosophical notions of certainty and constructive skepticism were being transformed by William Chillingworth, John Tillotson, John Wilkins, and Joseph Glanvill. The complexities and occasional absurdities of this age, however, were not simply the manifestations of troubled minds and souls. They also reflected the realities of social conflict and change. [9]

ENGLAND IN 1650 did not *appear* to be so very different than fifty or a hundred years before. The western slopes of the Cotswolds, along the Severn estuary, the moorlands of the north, and hamlets in Gloucestershire and Worcestershire

8. Mosse: *The Holy Pretence. A Study in Christianity and Reason of State from William Perkins to John Winthrop* (Oxford, 1957), 5, 12–13, 154.

9. J. G. A. Pocock: *The Ancient Constitution and the Feudal Law* (Cambridge, 1957), 36–7; Henry G. Van Leeuwen: *The Problem of Certainty in English Thought, 1630–1690* (The Hague, 1963).

looked as they long had. Children still ran at barleybreak and women danced to a tabor and pipe beside half-timber buildings. But much that shaped their lives was indeed profoundly different. Change had rarely in fact been more rapid in English history. We see it with especial clarity in the conflict between youth and middle age during the later Elizabethan era. Fathers tended toward prudent conservatism and self-effacing duty in public affairs, while sons, such as Philip Sidney, Edmund Spenser, Robert Cecil, and Robert Devereux, admired ambition, fashioned a cult of honor for themselves, and sought to live by it. Many of those who survived into the seventeenth century reached their fullness of years just as English America was being colonized. Their personal ambitions, bitter frustrations, and worldliness would set a special seal upon their time, particularly since conflicts with their fathers had encompassed and altered the contradictions of Elizabethan England. What were those contradictions? Daring innovation and nostalgic traditionalism; chivalrous gentlemen who were also crass materialists, to mention only two.[1]

Hiram Haydn has helped to clarify the dichotomies in later Elizabethan society by postulating the existence of a Counter-Renaissance, a movement which emerged in the sixteenth century in protest against both medieval scholasticism and the humanistic revival as well. Some "enigmatic Elizabethans" mounted extensive opposition to the accustomed systematization of the universe, to right reason and virtue as the basis of human conduct. In essence, theirs was an intellectual rebellion against social change so rapid as to be inscrutable. Their legacy for Jacobean times was consequently a constellation of counterpoised inclinations: lustiness and piety, doubt and affirmation, confidence and despair. So John Donne, poet of the early lyrics and of the erotic *Elegies*, became the revered Dean of St.

1. Wallace T. MacCaffrey: *The Shaping of the Elizabethan Regime* (Princeton, 1968), 4–5; Anthony Esler: *The Aspiring Mind of the Elizabethan Younger Generation* (Durham, 1966), ix, 3–4, 203–8, 222, 225–30, 239–41; Patrick Cruttwell: *The Shakespearean Moment and Its Place in the Poetry of the 17th Century* (London, 1954), 251–2.

Paul's who thundered damnation at the very Inns of Court where he had squandered his youth. So Donne's radical skepticism and his passionate desire for certainty. So Sir Francis Bacon's need to reconcile the expedient careerist and the impresario of new science, the pragmatic and the mystical. So Walter Raleigh's poem "The Lie," showing the discrepancy between principles professed and actual practices. So in the same men, indeed in the same passages, one finds affirmation and rebellion, idealism and cynicism, delicacy and grossness.[2]

The social changes responsible for these tensions were many and varied. We have become accustomed to assume that England's aristocracy and gentry, whether rising or falling, were assuredly undergoing the profoundest crises. There was unprecedented economic mobility among the middle landowning groups, with families moving up and down in remarkable numbers. In consequence, the gentry was changing its composition with unusual rapidity. Therefore, an intense acquisitive pressure built up for outward marks of social distinction—all the more so because a gentleman, by definition, pursued no profession or occupation systematically. Excessive expenditures, characteristic of the Jacobean age, sprang from an attitude of mind which put generosity and display above thrift and economy. One might say that two conflicting social ethics were at odds: a capitalist-Protestant ethos and an aristocratic one. On the one hand, self-improvement, independence, thrift, hard work, sobriety, competition, and the association of poverty with moral weakness; on the other hand, generous hospitality, clear class distinctions, social stability, tolerance toward sins of the flesh, service to the state, arrogant self-confidence, a patronizing attitude toward economic inferiors, and an acceptance of poverty in the lower classes as part of the natural order of things. As Lawrence Stone has written, "if in this age of confusion and turmoil many men—even Cromwell himself—seem

2. *The Counter-Renaissance* (New York, 1950), 1–26; Charles Blitzer: *An Immortal Commonwealth. The Political Thought of James Harrington* (New Haven, 1960), xiii–iv, 187–8; Lawrence Stone: *The Crisis of the Aristocracy, 1558–1641* (Oxford, 1965), 27.

to straddle the two ideals, this does nothing to minimize the essential contradiction between them." [3]

Under these bifurcated circumstances, the power of the nobility gradually lessened, and the political as well as financial stability of England became precariously poised during the first third of the seventeenth century. By the reign of Charles I, notions of harmony within the Commonwealth had understandably broken down, and the words "Court" and "Country" had come to connote political, psychological, and moral antitheses. By the 1630's, when the great Puritan migration to North America occurred, England was experiencing all the tensions created by the development within a single society of two distinct cultures. Professor Stone has once again summed them up admirably:

> The one was adopted by the majority of the nobility and a tiny handful of court gentry; the other by the majority of the gentry and a minority of country peers. Dekker was ranged against Massinger; Milton against Davenant; Robert Walker against Van Dyck; Artisan Mannerism against Inigo Jones; suspicion and hatred of Italy as vicious and popish against a passionate admiration for its aesthetic splendours; a belief in the virtues of country living against the sophistication of the London man-about-town; a strong moral antipathy to sexual license, gambling, stage-plays, hard drinking, duelling, and running into debt, against a natural weakness for all these worldly pleasures and vices; a dark suspicion of ritual and ornament in church worship against a ready acceptance of the beauty of holiness advocated by Laud; and lastly a deeply felt fear and hatred of Papists and Popery against an easy-going toleration for well-connected recusants and a sneaking admiration for Inigo Jones's chapel in Saint James's, got up in full Counter-Reformation fig for the use of Henrietta Maria and her Catholic friends.[4]

3. *Crisis of the Aristocracy*, 8–9, 11, 581–6, 669, 722–4, 728; Hexter: *Reappraisals in History*, 117–49.
4. *Crisis of the Aristocracy*, 269–70, 488, 502.

Curiously enough, the demographic pressures of this period worked in almost whimsical ways. There had been steady population growth, which led to pressure on the means of subsistence, which in turn could have been met by an expansion of industrial production and of areas under cultivation. But the early Stuart governments resolutely opposed these solutions. Consequently England, though not really overpopulated, was *relatively* so because the population was greater than the economy as then organized could absorb. To contemporaries horrified by poverty and terrified by vagabondage, overpopulation seemed excessive and something had to be done.[5]

Thus there were no secure monoliths in Jacobean and Caroline England. Instead, there was unremitting ideological tension, and always the forces of mobility and growth were pulling against the strength of inertia, the forces of enterprise against those of custom. That fragile antiphonal could not long endure.

IN MANY PHASES of English history, no person or place provides such dramatic focus for an age as the monarchy itself. James I, who inherited the English throne four years before Jamestown was planted, stood in many respects as the central figure of England in his time. Called "the wisest fool in Christendom" by a French statesman, he combined in his effete person an extraordinary mass of contradictions. If he was quick-witted, intelligent, and learned, he was also vain, superstitious, and lazy. He was cautious, at times cowardly, yet capable of exhibiting his mother's courage and defying public opinion. He was likely to lecture his subjects at one moment and yield to them in another. Because of his unhappy, loveless childhood, he has been described as "an old young man." In his *Basilikon*

5. Mildred Campbell: " 'Of People Either Too Few or Too Many.' The Conflict of Opinion on Population and Its Relation to Emigration," in *Conflict in Stuart England. Essays in Honour of Wallace Notestein*, ed. W. A. Aiken and B. D. Henning (London, 1960), 171–201.

Doron (1598), James deplored sodomy, swearing, drunkenness, and blasphemy; nevertheless, he engaged extensively in all four during his lifetime. His court was a haven for sexual deviants, and his reign scarred by scandal.[6]

Turning to James as a politician, we must be careful not to exaggerate the newness of conflict between the early Stuarts and their parliaments. Elizabeth had been *politique;* her Commons doctrinaire and fanatical. They wanted to advance beyond the Anglican Church Settlement. She was determined to move no further. They wanted to settle the succession to the throne as a guarantee against reversion to Catholicism. She saw dangers in that policy and preferred to do nothing. Invariably they wanted action while she preferred inaction. But these and other issues deepened and intensified in Jacobean times, caught between two "ancient and undoubted rights": on the one hand, royal prerogative raised high by the doctrine of divine right; on the other, the privileges of the people exercised through their representatives. Sir John Eliot, the great parliamentarian, was nonetheless torn between his love for the Commons and his firm belief that the King could do no wrong. A great many among his contemporaries shared his ambivalence.[7]

Throughout the brooding decades before 1640, the House of Commons was often indecisive in defining authority and using power. Moreover, parliamentary leaders in these years liked to think of themselves as conservatives. They did not believe they were militant reformers, but rather men who would repair an ancient constitution. It was indeed John Pym who maintained that "the form of government in any state cannot be altered without apparent danger of ruin to that state." In 1628, the Commons was radical in the name of conservatism, demanding in the Petition of Right their lawful due based on precedent. "Their hands may have been the hands of

6. Maurice P. Ashley: *The Stuarts in Love* (London, 1963), 9, 43, 96–9, 109; W. L. McElwee: *The Wisest Fool in Christendom* (London, 1958).

7. J. E. Neale: *Elizabeth I and Her Parliaments, 1559–1581* (London, 1953), 28; Harold Hulme: *The Life of Sir John Eliot, 1592–1632* (London, 1957).

Esau," notes Maurice Ashley, "but the voice was the voice of Jacob." [8]

Inevitably, these dualisms began to polarize around the terminological realities of Court and Country. Their sharpening antagonism would help to determine the political strife and paralysis of nearly forty years. The Court denoted a network of ministers, courtiers, officials, their clients and connections throughout the land. The Country was composed of landed proprietors, both peers and gentry, as well as merchants beyond the range of Court benefits or antagonized by its policies. The elements adhering to these configurations were by no means fixed. Within each there were shifting groups, and men did pass from Court to Country, as Sir John Eliot did, and from Country to Court, as Sir Thomas Wentworth did. Needless to say, only a minority of the nation as a whole was oriented in any conscious and definite way to either party. Only in the later 1630's, as Charles and his opposition moved on a collision course, would an unprecedented political stirring occur, and alignments become general. [9]

So there would be a civil war, but one which brought neither side immediate release from the aches of ambivalence. Throughout the war, individuals and communities were torn by the conflict between local and national loyalties. In Kent, for example, important landowning families opposed with equal tenacity the centralizing power of King Charles, the Long Parliament, and Cromwell: a plague upon them all. [1] In 1650, Gerrard Winstanley's pamphlet, *England's Spirit Unfoulded*, dealt with the thorny issues of obligation and al-

8. Hexter: *Reappraisals in History*, 137; Ashley: *England in the Seventeenth Century* (Harmondsworth, 1952), 45, 65–6, 76.

9. Perez Zagorin: "The Court and the Country: A Note on Political Terminology in the Earlier Seventeenth Century," *English Historical Review*, LXXVII (1962), 306–11; Zagorin: "The Social Interpretation of the English Revolution," *Journal of Economic History*, XIX (1959), 376–401.

1. Alan Everitt: *The Community of Kent and the Great Rebellion, 1640–1660* (New York, 1966); Roger Howell, Jr.: *Newcastle Upon Tyne and the Puritan Revolution: A Study of the Civil War in North England* (New York, 1967).

legiance. What support should the man of principle give to a régime which contains some of the prerequisites for bringing about a more just social order, yet is characterized by backsliding and human frailty? Puritan policymakers were torn throughout their régime by conflicting social considerations of individualism and collectivism.[2]

Ideological conflict proliferated during the 1640's as men divided their allegiances; and ubiquitous utopian movements added to the intellectual confusion. English Presbyterians, with some clerical and a few lay exceptions, were in reality moderate Anglicans who believed in a temperate, lay-controlled Elizabethan episcopacy. In addition, Cromwell's Protectorate actually comprised a fusion of two elements in English political society. There were the men responsible for revolution, men who formed the solid core of the Independents, and dominated the army. But there were also members of the original aristocratic opposition of 1640 who, though compelled to political radicalism, would have been happy with the settlements of 1641 or 1647. These men had generally stood aside from the revolutionary acts of 1649–53, but then rallied to Cromwell as a "saviour of society" when he became Protector.

Praisegod Barebone's Parliament would disappoint Cromwell's hopes, but he could not have been too surprised, for seeds of trouble were there from the outset. One group of members saw themselves as heirs of the historic Parliament and caretakers of its traditions until it could be properly restored. Another thought only of fulfilling Daniel's Old Testament prophecy that "the Saints shall take the kingdom and possess it." Cromwell, the great parliament man, could not get on with parliaments anyway; but neither could he get along without them! By 1657, with a new, written constitution called the Humble Petition and Advice, England had a monarchy without a monarch. No wonder an M.P. said that "the

2. G. E. Aylmer, ed.: "A Newly Discovered Pamphlet by Gerrard Winstanley," *Past and Present*, No. 40 (1968), 3–15; Margaret James: *Social Problems and Policy During the Puritan Revolution, 1640–1660* (London, 1930), 10–15.

Providences of God are like a two-edged sword, which may be used both ways." [3]

Who, in the end, could quite say what had happened? The effects of the decades 1640–60 seem contradictory. A great revolution took place, but a very incomplete one, with many apparent reversions to the status quo when all was said and done. James Harrington may have got some clear perspective, for he was an enemy of monarchy but a friend of King Charles, a republican who denounced the republic as an oligarchy. He knew that England (and Europe) had been out of joint for more than a generation. He recognized that the Crown had lost its estates but continued to claim power derived from them. He knew the nobility had been bought out but would not abdicate its privileges. He saw that much of the yeomanry had lost their hold on the land, but continued to cling to rights they could no longer enforce. The results might be tyranny, or oligarchy, or anarchy; but vast social dislocation surely. An aristocratic commonwealthman, Harrington had enough historical detachment to see that Europe's bloody crisis began to provide some resolution to the ambiguities of feudal constitutionalism. The medieval order, "the Gothick hallance," had finally collapsed.[4]

With the Restoration of Charles II in 1660, a slow process of healing and reconciliation began. The results were not immediately apparent; for a deep chasm lay between the Catholic temper of Charles's court and Parliament's dislike of popery. Charles himself was attracted both to astrology and astronomy, to chemistry and alchemy, to science and superstition. Whigs and Tories emerged, but they were not so far apart as Cavaliers and Roundheads had been. After all, "Whig" originally

3. Willson H. Coates: "An Analysis of Major Conflicts in Seventeenth-Century England," in *Conflict in Stuart England*, 19, 28–30; Trevor-Roper: *Religion, the Reformation, and Social Change*, 406–7, 462; A. H. Woolrych: "The Calling of Barebone's Parliament," *English Historical Review*, LXXX (1965), 492–513.

4. R. H. Tawney: "Harrington's Interpretation of His Age," *Proceedings of the British Academy 1941*, XXVII, 203, 209–11; Blitzer: *An Immortal Commonwealth*, xiii–iv, 3–5, 22–3, 187–8.

meant a Scottish outlaw, and "Tory" an Irish robber! Not so very different. There developed a cult of the golden mean in later Restoration times, epitomized by George Savile, Marquess of Halifax, "the Great Trimmer." Moderation was his watchword, and the state a ship at sea in which the balance of safety would be preserved by keeping passengers to the middle. Halifax even saw God as a Trimmer, "divided between his two great attributes, his mercy and his justice." [5]

England's polity had been disrupted and rebuilt. When the job was ultimately done, with the Revolution Settlement and Act of Union with Scotland, the polity became Great Britain. By the time union was achieved in 1707, most of the more excessive ambiguities and anomalies of British culture had been resolved—or else transplanted to America.

BECAUSE HISTORIANS often suffer from taxonomic illusions, we are accustomed to labeling the later Renaissance as an era of fiercely felt nationalisms. Yet the context of exploration and transplantation reveals endless exceptions and anomalies; for stark conflicts between nationalism and opportunism provided a major source of ambiguities at the very outset of modern colonization. Christopher Columbus merely provides the most famous example. Giovanni Verrazzano, a Florentine, was employed by the French monarch Francis I. John Cabot was a Genoese in the service of England's Henry VII. Ferdinand Magellan was a Portuguese in the Spanish service; another Portuguese, Diego Ribero, was royal cosmographer at the Spanish court. Samuel Champlain, father of New France, had served in the Spanish navy. The English Hudson's Bay Company was founded by two French traders, Pierre Esprit Radisson and Sieur de Groseilliers, who had become disgruntled with fur-trading restrictions in New France. In 1665 they simply presented an exploitative scheme to Charles II, and he sent a vessel to Hudson's Bay. The great company was soon chartered.

5. Ashley: *England in the Seventeenth Century*, 135, 140, 148, 155, 165–6.

Henry Hudson himself, an English navigator, had made voyages in 1607 and 1608 for the English Muscovy Company. But once these attempts to locate a northeast passage to the Orient failed, his services were sought by merchants of the Dutch East India Company who also hoped to discover such a route. While negotiations were temporarily broken, Hudson was approached by another Dutch merchant in Amsterdam to undertake a voyage for the newly formed French East India Company. When Hudson's *Half Moon* finally sailed in 1609, on behalf of the Amsterdam chamber of the Dutch East India Company, it carried a mixed crew of English and Dutch sailors —not at all unusual for such voyages. In 1610, Hudson was once again in England's service, this time commanding a voyage sponsored by the Muscovy Company, the East India Company, and some independent merchants. Sir Thomas Gates and Sir Thomas Dale, of Jamestown notoriety, both were captains of Dutch companies who later received special permission from the States-General to participate in the Virginia Company venture.[6]

Similarly, the great financiers and entrepreneurs in the age of European expansion were generally more opportunistic than nationalistic. The Dutch, especially Flemings and Liégeois, spread everywhere in the seventeenth century: into France under Henry IV and Richelieu, actively pushing for the formation of chartered companies. They would also be found in Denmark, in Sweden, and in some of the Hanseatic towns. The Dutch supplied ships' captains and, when it was not formally forbidden by their government, even some of the ships. It was not unusual to find Netherlanders among the high officials in other countries' colonies. Capitalists invested their money wherever it promised the best return. In France under Richelieu some companies even received financial help from hated England; and under Colbert they got assistance from Germany. Understandably then—given the political and religious displacement of Europeans, and given the ubiquitous quest for wealth—

6. E. B. O'Callaghan, ed.: *Documents Relative to the Colonial History of the State of New-York* (Albany, 1856), I, 1–3, 9–10.

loyalties, necessities, and opportunities were frequently brought into abrasive juxtaposition and conflict.[7]

Although the Renaissance and Reformation both provided stimuli for colonization, the two phenomena had different origins and orientations. Consequently, influences arising from them often emerged as contradictory tendencies strapped together by the demands of time and place. One thinks immediately of the tension arising from the emphasis upon living fully in this world while trying to achieve the next. Then, too, religious diversity, the heritage of the Reformation, was not easily acceptable in later Renaissance England. In the first phases of Stuart colonization, therefore, the dilemma arose whether to seek reasonable uniformity at home and permit religious diversity overseas, or to tolerate unsettling diversity at home and insist upon cohesion in the colonies in order to ensure their survival. Neither alternative was wholly satisfactory, nor was a *via media* either. Therein lay a source of strain for the English Protestant Church. Colonization seemed one way to resolve such tensions bred from pluralism; but it would sometimes aggravate them instead, and ofttimes create new ones from the old matrix.[8]

IN 1603 THE VIRGIN QUEEN who had suffered from syphilis was dead; James VI of Scotland became James I of England as well. In 1604 five Jacobean courtiers sat, like so many ruffed

7. See Thomas J. Condon: *New York Beginnings. The Commercial Origins of New Netherland* (New York, 1968), 13–14; E. L. J. Coornaert: "European Economic Institutions and the New World; the Chartered Companies," in *The Cambridge Economic History of Europe*, ed. E. E. Rich and C. H. Wilson (Cambridge, 1967), IV, 244–5.

8. Conrad Russell: "Arguments for Religious Unity in England, 1530–1650," *Journal of Ecclesiastical History*, XVIII (1967), 201–26; Edward Arber, ed.: *Travels and Works of Captain John Smith* (2nd ed., Edinburgh, 1910), II, 959; Franklin B. Dexter: "The Pilgrim Church and Plymouth Colony," in Justin Winsor, ed.: *Narrative and Critical History of America* (Cambridge, 1884), III, 264. For the same problem in Dutch New Netherland, see John Webb Pratt: *Religion, Politics, and Diversity. The Church-State Theme in New York History* (Ithaca, 1967), 25.

grouse displaying, at the Somerset House Peace Conference; Spain and England relaxed their hatreds, at least for a while. And so English entrepreneurs began to muster their money and men for overseas plantations. But why would people go? Why would they leave the comfort of things known for the insecurity of the inscrutable? We assume too readily that immigrants were always attracted to the colonies, when in reality they often were repelled by Europe. With the decline of feudal localism, people gained mobility. Agricultural transformations forced many peasants off the land. When industrialization came, many rural folk simply had to move to towns or else seek farm land in the New World. In short, they weren't always pulled to America, they were often pushed out of Europe.

More than that, however, a great many came explicitly in order to escape the contradictory tendencies of a troubled time and place. Roger Williams, for example, had been distressed by the vacillations of Church–State relations in post-Reformation England. "Who knowes not," he asked,

> how easie it is to turne, and turne, and turne againe whole Nations from one Religion to another? Who knowes not that within the compasse of one poore span of 12 yeares revolution, all England hath become from halfe Papist, half Protestant, to be absolute Protestants; from absolute Protestants to absolute Papists; from absolute Papists (changing as fashions) to absolute Protestants? [9]

A great many would indeed emigrate to avoid such tortured twisting; so that colonization, in one sense, helped to provide a resolution for some of them. In yet another sense, however, the early English colonies were liberal offshoots of a deeply divided society. By contrast, New France was more nearly the controlled projection of a highly centralized and basically unified régime.

9. *The Bloudy Tenent, of Persecution, for cause of Conscience, Discussed in a Conference Betweene Truth and Peace* (London, 1644), in *The Complete Writings of Roger Williams* (New York, 1963), III, 325–6.

It has been observed that the first great age of English colonization "was driven by the twin spirits of adventure and control, and while 'adventurous Elizabethans' embarked upon voyages of discovery overseas, many others embarked upon inward voyages of discovery." [1] Some men, like William Bradford and John Winthrop, were to do both. Colonization would help to relieve the strain, partly real and partly imagined, between underemployment and overpopulation in England. So, too, it would help to alleviate the tension between commerce and piety that had frayed the nerves of many Elizabethans. There was a place for both in the planting of colonies, and Richard Hakluyt, the Bristol publicist, told them so. Colonizing would make it possible to convert Indians to Christianity; but it would also provide a means of re-establishing merchants who had gone bankrupt and were in debtors' prisons. [2]

In short, the New World would hopefully dissolve dilemmas of the Old. In reality, however, colonies would fertilize and reproduce those dilemmas, exacerbate some and produce others fundamentally new. A promotional tract urging Scots to settle in East Jersey explained that no man might purchase more than a twenty-fourth share of the entire colony, so that no individual would gain excessive power over the rest. Nevertheless, neither could any settler alienate too much of his land without losing title to it, so "that Dominion may follow Property, and the inconveniency of a Beggarly Nobility and Gentry may be avoided." [3] The colonists did succeed in avoiding a beggarly nobility, but developed instead a bourgeois aristocracy.

England's experience in colonizing Ireland during Tudor times had been fraught with ambivalent implications that

1. Winthrop D. Jordan: *White Over Black. American Attitudes Toward the Negro, 1550–1812* (Chapel Hill, 1968), 40.

2. See Louis B. Wright: *Religion and Empire: The Alliance Between Piety and Commerce in English Expansion, 1558–1625* (Chapel Hill, 1943).

3. George Scot: *The Model of the Government of the Province of East-New-Jersey in America* (Edinburgh, 1685), in *Collections of the New Jersey Historical Society*, ed. William A. Whitehead (New York, 1846), I, 268.

An Ecclesiastical Biformity in Stuart England

1. *A British Janus: Anglicè a Timeserver*, a High Church caricature from the later seventeenth century.

A similar engraving in 1689 represented "A Trimmer" as a bisected compound of contradictory ecclesiastical opposites. It was accompanied by the following verses:

> A true blew Priest, a Lincey Woolsey Brother.
> One Legg a Pulpitt holds, a Tubb the other.
> An orthodox, grave, moderate, Presbyterian.
> Half Surplice, Cloake, half Priest, half Puritan;
> Made up of all these halfes, hee cannot pass
> For any thing, intirely, but an Ass.

Colonial Ambivalence About the Indians

2. *Penn's Treaty with the Indians*, by Edward Hicks, c. 1830. Oil on wood panel.

Hicks painted at least nine versions of this theme, one as a signboard for Bogart's Inn in Doylestown, Pennsylvania. For so long as the sign hung from a pole in front, the tavern was known as "The Sign of Penn's Treaty." The primitive composition was based upon a popular engraving of Benjamin West's 1772 painting (now in the Pennsylvania Academy of Fine Arts). West's painting—commissioned by the Penn family—compromised between the high style of history painting in England and a more straightforward representation.

Under the great elm at Shackamaxon, William Penn dispenses peace and yard goods to the Indians. The painting's mood combines smug piety with the stolid respectability of successful bourgeois. Note the contrast between the overlarge heads and wooden gestures of the Indians and Hicks's effort to give true likenesses to Penn and his cluster of Friends.

The statement on the scroll reads as follows: "Charter of Pennsylvania

in North America. Treaty with the Indians in 1681 without an oath. Wm. Penn, Thos. Lloyd, James Logan, Thos. Story, Thos. Janney, William Markham."

3. *Copper Weathervane*, by Shem Drowne, 1716.

An Indian archer made by Drowne to crown the turret of Boston's Province House, palace of the royal governors (1716–76). The archer became such a beloved landmark that Paul Revere used it in an engraving (1768) as a symbol of Boston itself.

Nathaniel Hawthorne later wrote a charming, cryptic tale, called "Drowne's Wooden Image," about the ambiguities of art and the artist in eighteenth-century America.

"Backwoods Baroque" in Colonial Culture

4. *A Grand Plat of the City and Port of Annapolis*, drawn in 1718 by James Stoddert and copied in 1748.

This innovative plan for Annapolis is almost a caricature of European baroque city planning. With its two great circles, the imposing "Bloomsbury Square," and radiating diagonal streets, the scheme introduced new urban notions to the colonies. Governor Francis Nicholson, who was primarily responsible for the development of Annapolis, must have had in mind the achievements of French baroque designers: first applied to garden layout (as at Versailles), then to town expansion and remodeling on the continent, and subsequently adapted by Christopher Wren and John Evelyn in rebuilding London after the Great Fire of 1666.

In theory Nicholson planned to combine the English residential square and the French *rond-point*. But he apparently did not comprehend one of the basic aims of baroque design: to create as many terminal vistas as possible by ending each diagonal street at a great public building or monument, with the center line of the street precisely on axis with the center of the structure.

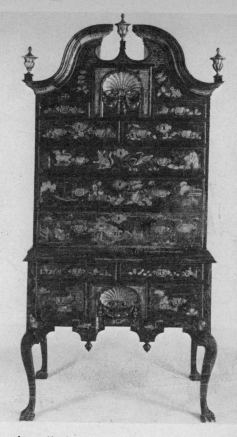

For the phrase "backwoods baroque," I am indebted to the superb work of my colleague, John Reps: *The Making of Urban America. A History of City Planning in the United States* (Princeton, 1965), 106–8.

5. *High Chest of Drawers, Japanned Maple and Pine*, made in Boston by John Pimm (active 1736–73) for Joshua Loring; probably painted by Thomas Johnson.

Here is a prime example of the baroque joined with oriental decoration on a rococo Queen Anne frame. There is a similar highboy, also with japanned decoration and made in Boston around 1735, in the Early American Wing, Metropolitan Museum of Art, New York City (item 40.37.1).

The full baroque style, pre-eminently suited for the service of absolute monarchies or the Roman Catholic Church, seems heavy and a bit ludicrous in the more egalitarian colonies. For Georgian-baroque architecture in early Virginia, see Stratford (near Montross in Westmoreland County), built for Thomas Lee in the later 1720's. The mansion's baroque manner emerges in its monumentality, and in details like the arched and clustered chimneys. (See Louis B. Wright, *et al.: The Arts in America. The Colonial Period* [New York, 1966], plate 29.)

Bisociative Tendencies in Colonial Minds

6. *Cotton Mather* (1663–1728) in 1727. Mezzotint by Peter Pelham.

Mather embodied and articulated several of the central themes in *People of Paradox*. Here is a brief passage from his *The Present State of New England* (Boston, 1690): "But if our God will wrest *America* out of the Hands of its old Land-Lord, *Satan*, and give these *utmost ends* of *the Earth* to our Lord Jesus, then our present conflicts will shortly be blown over, and something better than, *A Golden Age*, will arrive to this place, and this perhaps before all of our *First Planters* are fallen asleep. Now, Tis a dismal *Uncertainty* and *Ambiguity* that wee see ourselves placed in. Briefly, such is our case, *That something must be done out of hand*. And indeed, our *All is at the Stake;* we are beset with a Thousand perplexities and Entanglements." (P. 35. The italics are Mather's.)

7. *Benjamin Franklin* (1706–90) in 1778. Oil on canvas by Joseph Duplessis.

Franklin's "wise innocence," the savant as child of nature, is depicted here with a fur collar. Previously Jean Baptiste Nini, the sculptor, placed a Canadian fur cap on his famous bas-relief profile of Franklin; and in 1777 an engraving by Augustin de Saint Aubin also included the fur cap—symbol of simplicity, subtlety, and self-sufficiency.

Franklin will always remain elusive and intriguing because of his diligence and his indolence, his moralisms and his Machiavellianism, his sensitivity to his image in the eyes of others and yet his defiance as well.

Anomalies in Imperial Administration

8. *Edward Hyde, Lord Cornbury,* Governor of New York and New Jersey, 1702–8. Oil on canvas by an unidentified artist.

The grandson of Clarendon, lord chancellor under Charles II, and historian of the English Civil War, Cornbury was also a first cousin of Queen Anne. Because of financial difficulties, he pleaded for profitable offices in the colonies. A spendthrift, bigot, martinet, and generally foolish, his administrations in New York and New Jersey were complete failures.

On occasion, Cornbury appeared publicly in women's clothing. Some contemporaries said that he thought he resembled his cousin the Queen; and that by imitating her costume he would "represent" her literally as well as symbolically!

Cornbury's antics and administrations underscore a remark made in 1705 by his contemporary, Robert Beverley of Virginia: "Their [the colonies'] Distance makes 'em liable to be ill used by Men, that over-act Her Sacred Authority, and under-act Her Vertues." (See Beverley: *The History and Present State of Virginia*, ed. Louis B. Wright [Chapel Hill, 1947], 6.)

9. Cartoon *"Without,"* London *Evening Post, June 11, 1757.*

The caption reads as follows: "The introduction of the word WITHOUT is necessary to the Reader's Information. . . . 1. Supreme Majesty_____ Power. 2. Counsellors_____Abilities. 3. Bishops_____Religion. 4. Nobles_____Honour. 5. Senators_____Honesty. 6. Manufactories _____Trade. 7. Colonies_____Protection. 8. Seamen_____Encouragement. 9. Parading Fleets_____Fighting. 10. Great Armies_____Use. 11. The Common People_____Money. 12. The Poor_____Bread."

A visitor to New England at the close of the seventeenth century had used the same satirical device: "Many of the Leading *Puritans* may (without Injustice) be thus Characteris'd. They are *Saints* without *Religion*, *Traders* without *Honesty*, *Christians* without *Charity*, *Magistrates* without *Mercy*, *Subjects* without *Loyalty*, *Neighbours* without *Amity*, *Faithless Friends*, *Implacable Enemys*, and *Rich Men* without *Money*." (See Edward Ward: *A Trip to New-England with a Character of the Country and People* [London, 1699], 11.)

The Ambivalence of the Provincial Artist

10. *Boy with a Squirrel*, by John Singleton Copley, 1765. Oil on canvas.

A sea captain cajoled young Copley into finishing this picture of his half brother, Henry Pelham; then took it to London and gave it to Sir Joshua Reynolds for exhibition at the Society of Artists in 1766. Reynolds was delighted, and wrote to Boston that "in any collection of painting it will pass as an excellent picture, but considering the disadvantages you labored under, it is a very wonderful performance. . . . If you are capable of producing such a piece by the mere efforts of your own genius, with the advantages of example and instruction you would have in Europe you would be a valuable acquisition to the art and one of the first painters in the world, provided you could receive these aids before it was too late in life, and before your manner and taste were corrupted or fixed by working in your little way in Boston."

Copley's genius as a provincial painter lay in his unstudied combination of technical brilliance and gifted craftsmanship with the naïveté and stiffness characteristic of the so-called American primitives.

11. *Young Lady with a Bird and Dog*, by John Singleton Copley, 1767. Oil on canvas.

Copley anxiously absorbed the criticisms and suggestions sent to him from London, and tried to come to terms with them all in 1767 by painting Mary Warner. But he overwhelmed the little girl with too many too large objects: a spaniel, a broadly figured carpet, a chair, a parrot, a bright red curtain, and a thick marble column. The critics, including Benjamin West, conveyed harsh judgments this time; and were most critical on precisely those points where Copley had followed their earlier advice and had tried to please them.

In disgust he blamed his uncertainties upon the provincial environment: "a taste of painting is too much wanting to afford any kind of helps; and was it not for preserving the ressemblance of particular persons, painting would not be known in the place. The people generally regard it no more than any other useful trade, as they sometimes term it, like that of carpenter, tailor, or shoemaker, not as one of the most noble arts in the world, which is not a little mortifying to me. While the arts are so disregarded, I can hope for nothing either to encourage or assist me in my studies but what I receive from a Thousand leagues distance, and be my improvements what they will, I shall not be benefited by them in this country, neither in point of fortune or fame."

Ambiguities of the American Revolution

12. *The Golden Age*, by Benjamin West, 1776. Oil on canvas.

The painting depicts three generations of an Old Testament family. When exhibited in England in 1878, it bore the subtitle "Portrait of Mrs. West." But the political or psychological significance of the picture (and its title) in West's mind remain obscure. Born to Quaker parents in a village near Philadelphia, West's aptitude for art was recognized early. After living in Philadelphia and New York in the 1750's, he sailed for Italy in 1760 and his work there won acclaim. West then went to England in 1763, intending to make only a brief visit; but he remained there the rest of his life—fifty-seven years. By 1766 he had achieved immense popularity; he received the patronage of George III, became a charter member of the Royal Academy in 1768, and in 1772 was appointed historical painter to the King.

For most of his life, however, West felt a fond attachment for America and the Chester County of his origin. The imperial breach in 1776 must have been an extremely painful experience for him, and probably inspired him to paint *The Golden Age*. Perhaps the mother is Britannia, looking with detached affection at her offspring, wondering about its future prospects. In the background, meanwhile, their common ancestors lived and labored in sunnier, more certain times.

The Golden Age theme is a very ancient one, going back at least to Hesiod's *Works and Days:* "In the beginning, the immortals who have their homes on Olympos created the golden generation of mortal people. . . . They lived as if they were gods, their hearts free from all sorrow, by themselves, and without hard work or pain. . . . They took their pleasure in festivals, and lived without troubles. . . . Next after these the dwellers upon Olympos created a second generation, of silver, far worse than the

other. They were not like the golden ones either in shape or spirit. A child was a child for a hundred years, looked after and playing by his gracious mother, kept at home, a complete booby. But when it came time for them to grow up and gain full measure, they lived for only a poor short time; by their own foolishness they had troubles, for they were not able to keep away from reckless crime against each other, nor would they worship the gods, nor do sacrifice on the sacred altars of the blessed ones. . . ." (*Hesiod*, translated by Richmond Lattimore [Ann Arbor, 1959], 31–5.)

Nostalgia for a golden age is also the central theme in Cotton Mather's *Magnalia Christi Americana* (1702): "The first age [of Christianity] was the golden age; to return unto that will make a man a Protestant, and, I may add, a Puritan." (*Magnalia* [Hartford, 1855], 27.)

13. *A Society of Patriotic Ladies at Edenton in North Carolina, pledging to drink no more tea,* 1775. Engraving by Philip Dawe.

This satirical engraving was published in London by R. Sayer and J. Bennett. It seems to contrast the colonial posture of public rectitude with the personal decadence of private individuals—dissolute provincial ladies with hollow professions of political morality. The issues raised by this satire had considerable urgency in 1775 because the colonists believed that only a truly virtuous society could succeed at revolution and republicanism.

The statement reads: "We the Ladys of Edenton do hereby solemnly Engage not to Conform to that Pernicious custom of Drinking Tea, or that we the aforesaid Ladys will not promote the wear of any Manufacture from England untill such time that all Acts which tend to Enslave this our Native Country shall be Repealed."

Romantic Classicism in Republican Architecture

14. *Monticello*, in Albemarle County near Charlottesville, Virginia (c. 1769–1801), by Thomas Jefferson.

In designing, building, and continually rebuilding Monticello, Jefferson developed a new American architectural style, "romantic classicism." He adapted elements from the architectural treatises of Andrea Palladio, the sixteenth-century Italian who drew his designs from ancient Roman villas and surviving monuments. But Jefferson picked his site and drew his inspiration from the indigenous wilderness: "How sublime to look down into the workhouse of nature, to see her clouds, hail, snow, thunder, all fabricated at our feet! And the glorious sun when rising as if out of distant water, just gilding the tops of the mountains and giving life to all nature."

In planning his gardens, moreover, Jefferson followed the new landscape style then fashionable in England: irregular and rustic, romantic rather than classical, so that his landscape scheme would contrast sharply with his architectural design.

15. *The Alsop House*, Middletown, Connecticut (1838). Probably designed by Ithiel Town of New Haven.

The Alsop House was built by Richard Alsop, IV, son of the "Hartford Wit," for his widowed mother, later Mrs. Samuel Dana. Its design reflects the elegant grace sought in the 1830's and 1840's, yet does not follow the classical tradition too closely. The almost geometric severity of

the structure itself is countered by a porch supported by delicately scaled and detailed ironwork, and by a frieze of swags and simulated antique statues in niches. The interior of the house has even more *trompe l'oeil* figures, along with decorative motifs taken from Raphael and Piranesi. The *trompe l'oeil* statues on the façade are executed in oil on plaster, and are generally classical in inspiration. The central figure of the façade is taken from an engraving of Erato, the muse of Love Poetry, in the Vatican; the other two figures on the façade probably depict Juno and Victory. Alsop may have planned originally to have real statues, but found the cost too high and used the *trompe l'oeil* instead.

The Sociable Frontiersman

16. *Daniel Boone Escorting Settlers Through the Western Country*, by George Caleb Bingham, 1851–2. Oil on canvas.

Boone and his family are leading a procession of pioneers through the Cumberland Gap. The horse carries Boone's wife, Rebecca; behind her, white-shawled, is their daughter Jemima.

There are several popular (almost contradictory) images of Daniel Boone in American culture: Boone the solitary woodsman, the cultural primitivist, as well as Boone the harbinger of civilization. But as Clarence W. Alvord, a leading historian of the frontier, wrote in 1926: "Legend affirms that Boone was the agent who called the people across the mountains. The reverse is the truth. Boone was among the conjured, not the conjuror." ("Daniel Boone," *The American Mercury*, VIII [July 1926], 269.) In 1775, Boone led the first settlers into Transylvania. But months before his arrival in Kentucky, the frontiersmen of Virginia had founded Harrodsburg and several other settlements.

would be felt across the Atlantic in the seventeenth century. Irish history during the sixteenth had involved more than just a struggle by the English Crown to master a rebellious fief. Nor was it simply the domination of a native population by waves of English colonists. It was, rather, at certain times and places, mainly the one, or mainly the other. There were several trends to England's Irish policy. The first was to seek peaceful and effective "reformation." Doing so did not preclude the use of force, but relied mainly on administrative and legal reforms. The alternative required a thorough conquest prior to achieving any real changes in Ireland. Every part of the island would have to be coerced into submission, and thereafter English laws enforced without compromise. This second policy called for exploitation, and not merely pacification of the native population. Neither policy, of course, was pursued consistently; and that is just the point. When Englishmen turned their hands to North American plantations in the seventeenth century, the immediate precedents they might look to were profoundly ambiguous.[4]

To complicate matters, there had long been a fundamental ambivalence in European feelings toward nonwestern peoples. One paradoxical result in the seventeenth century would be that precisely while Europeans conquered the world, they also peopled a fictive universe with noble savages of superior insight and wisdom. Ideologues and utopians came to accept the moral integrity of native institutions. This view, the very antithesis of customary claims of European superiority, had existed earlier in the Mediterranean era. But then it had concerned imaginary peoples. "The Atlantic age," writes Henri Baudet, "was the first to apply the old antithesis to a political reality."[5]

There is an important distinction to be made, however, between utopianism (which was usually unrelated to reality)

4. David B. Quinn: "Ireland and Sixteenth Century European Expansion," in *Historical Studies*, I (London, 1958), 22–4.
5. Baudet: *Paradise on Earth. Some Thoughts on European Images of Non-European Man* (New Haven, 1965), 5–6, 23, 31–4.

and primitivism (which was directly related to the far-off lands recently discovered). The concepts of primitivism and utopianism reinforced each other, true enough. But poignant nostalgia for primitivism involved disconsolate awareness of an unattainable ideal lost forever. By contrast, utopianism encouraged hopes of achieving an ideal society if only certain requirements could be fulfilled. "Where primitivism thought on the whole in terms of 'no longer,' utopianism was mainly concerned with 'not yet'; if primitivism mourned the past, utopianism looked toward the future." [6]

There was, in addition, a subtle ambivalence inherent in the Christian understanding of heathenism. In one sense heathenism helped to define, by inversion, the proper Christian life. In another sense, however, the very existence of heathenism in the world implied a need to intensify one's Christian commitment. For Englishmen, certainly, the heathenism of blacks and Indians simultaneously provided a counter-image to their own religion as well as a summons to proselytize. The interaction of these two imperatives created problems. To act upon the felt need of converting colored peoples might ultimately eradicate familiar distinctions which made the world comprehensible. Yet not to act upon this necessity would constitute an immoral violation of their own faith. To anguish their consciences still more, there was also the Black Legend of Spanish wickedness incarnate in dealing with the Indians of New Spain since 1492. By 1603 the Black Legend had taken firm hold in England, and made anti-Spanish propaganda doubly virulent. [7]

6. Walter Hamond: *A Paradox. Prooving, That the Inhabitants of the Isle Called Madagascar . . . are the Happiest People in the World . . . With Most Probable Arguments of a Hopefull and Fit Plantation of a Colony There* (London, 1640), esp. F 4–5 (copy in the Folger Shakespeare Library, Washington, D.C.); Henry S. Bausum: "Edenic Images of the Western World," *South Atlantic Quarterly*, LXVII (1968), 683–4, 687.

7. Jordan: *White Over Black*, 21–3; W. S. Maltby: "The Black Legend in England, 1558–1660" (unpublished Ph.D. dissertation, Duke University, 1967).

Promotional literature designed to stimulate English colonization made manifest yet another transitional quality of the Tudor-Stuart period: its contradictory attitudes toward common people. If the tracts promised them instant wealth, outright possession of land, and the opportunity to stabilize their families, they were also filled with complaints about unruliness, lack of discipline, and want of practical sense. English fishermen along the Maine coast were said to be "worse than the very Savages, impudently and openly lying with their Women, teaching their Men to drinke drunke, to sweare and blaspheme the name of GOD, and in their drunken humour to fall together by the eares." [8]

Authors of promotional literature were inevitably caught between conflicting claims of authority and liberty. Except by creating a small, quasi-feudal military garrison and trading post supported by communal enterprise, there was no way to guarantee colonists adequate protection and sustenance. Since each settler looked forward to making his own private fortune, however, he chafed against the restraints of communal enterprise. The contradiction had very deep roots in Tudor-Stuart life; it appears in colonization literature from the outset, and was never logically resolved. Thus Sir George Peckham pleaded for the creation of a company to colonize Newfoundland, but also insisted that each investor retain complete freedom of trade. The abortive colonizing efforts of Sir Ferdinando Gorges in New England provide humorously tragic instances of the theoretical desirability, but practical failure, of the communal mode of colonizing.

Within many Englishmen who came to the colonies, certainly within every Puritan who migrated, and some who did not, there was a powerful psychological tension, an internalized debate. They perceived an ethical crisis that could not be dealt

8. See Howard M. Jones: "The Colonial Impulse; An Analysis of the 'Promotion' Literature of Colonization," *Proceedings of the American Philosophical Society*, XC (1946), 149–52; "Of Plantations," in James Spedding, ed.: *The Works of Francis Bacon* (London, 1870), VI, 457–9.

with satisfactorily in the context of English society as it was then structured and governed. To leave may have seemed cowardly, even treasonous; but there was no apparent way to make a go of it in England without violating God's precepts for human behavior. The only clear resolution for many was to get out, to migrate to America. Robert Cushman argued so. Others, such as John White and John Cotton, vacillated. For a significant period, Cotton's sermons offered both alternatives: let us break with the Church and be Separatists at home; and let us leave England altogether. Ultimately, Cotton elected to depart. The significant point to be made is that the Bible was not the only *vade mecum* brought by the first colonists. They also carried, and perhaps even closer to their hearts, the profoundest doubts about their emigration, about what they were leaving, and why.[9]

Such doubts ran deepest during the 1620's and 1630's. Many who left England did so in the certainty that God would destroy their homeland—a corrupt nation where few men honored their obligations to Him. Nevertheless, despite these forebodings of doom, despite their hostility, most colonists brought with them a great pride in being Englishmen. Even Separatists at Plymouth accepted without question the view that England was the birthplace of the Reformation. Indeed, they left Leyden out of fear that their children would become Dutch. "The New World," in Edmund S. Morgan's words, "offered a way of remaining English, with all that that meant, and yet of escaping the fury that God must surely loose against His backsliding favorites."[1]

Under these circumstances it can scarcely be surprising to find ambiguities and misunderstandings touching the nature of

9. See Alexander Whitaker: *Good Newes from Virginia* (London, 1613); John White: *The Planter's Plea* (London, 1630). I am indebted here to Alan Heimert's paper, "The Ethics of the Puritan Migration," presented to the Columbia University Faculty Seminar on Early American History and Culture, October 8, 1968.

1. Edward Winslow: *Hypocrisie Unmasked* (London, 1646), 89; Morgan: *Roger Williams. The Church and the State* (New York, 1967), 80–1.

"foreign plantations" and their place in the English constitution. "We must distinguish between corporations within England and corporations of but not within England," wrote John Winthrop. "The first are subject to the laws of England in general, yet not to every general law, as the city of London and other corporations have divers customs and by-laws differing from the common and statute laws of England. Again, though plantations be bodies corporate, (and so is every city and commonwealth,) yet they are also above the rank of an ordinary corporation." [2] Almost a masterpiece of equivocation; but then, Winthrop was a masterful casuist.

He had to be, for the political and administrative complexities of colonization were enormous. In 1629, for example, Winthrop's Massachusetts Bay Company was polarized between merchants and moderate Puritans who wanted the company proper to remain in England, and East Anglian zealots (hoping to emigrate) who were becoming more influential. By this time the Pilgrim colony at New Plymouth was nine years old; yet its government, which rested wholly on the highly dubious Pierce Patent, was precarious indeed. A new patent, obtained in 1630, granted no governmental powers, so that Plymouth's political institutions remained exceedingly tenuous. After 1660, when Whitehall and the Crown took a more direct interest in colonization, anomalies abounded. Just before the issuance of quasi-feudal charters to Carolina's proprietors and the Duke of York, the Privy Council approved extraordinarily liberal charters for Connecticut and Rhode Island.

Ambiguities were often most pronounced within particular colonizing ventures. The most impossible constitutional arrangements were envisioned for the Carolinas; but the most practical efforts were made to implement them. The proprietors, who were guided by schemes grossly ill-suited to the American scene, had nevertheless a fairly clear understanding of New World realities. They wished to make political power dependent upon baronial chunks of landed property; but they also expected to give away real estate on the most generous terms. Along with the proprietors of East and West New Jersey, they expected to make allowance both for divergencies of religious opinion among settlers, and for the desire by communities of like-minded men to use the full force of public authority to support their churches. Somehow the dual objectives of security and prosperity had to be looked after. So Lord Shaftesbury and his friends tried to shape their policies according to commercial considerations without losing sight of their initial design for a stable society.[3]

Nowhere was English colonization any more closely linked with the beginnings of biformity than in Pennsylvania. William Penn's concept of "an holy experiment"—a Utopia governed like a feudal régime—provides a perfect illustration of pragmatic idealism struggling to be resolved. Penn himself was a peculiar combination of faith and worldliness, idealism and practicality. A liberal by English standards, he seemed fiercely conservative to his provincial opponents. Perhaps this was because of a frequent disparity between his private views and his public pronouncements. Although Penn failed miserably in provincial politics, he was remarkably adroit in public affairs at home. His great colonizing scheme could not have been launched at a less auspicious moment, however, for the Crown in the 1680's was revoking charters rather than granting them. Penn's "absolute proprietary" was thus a real anomaly—the wrong sort of grant at a difficult moment for colonial settlements. There were an unusual number of contradictory tendencies involved in the establishment of Pennsylvania, and this volatile mixture of low politics and high ideals complicated Penn's relationship with both his settlers and the Crown for three decades.[4]

How else could it have been in Pennsylvania and the Jersies, given the circumstances of English Friends during the

3. See The Shaftesbury Papers; Collections of the South Carolina Historical Society (1897), V, 399.

4. See Joseph Illick: William Penn the Politician (Ithaca, 1965), 26–7, 40–4, 51–2, 68–9, 84, 87–8, 90–3, 96–9, 125, 245–6.

last quarter of the seventeenth century? By then—the second generation of Quakerism—individual illumination was being subordinated in many respects to the corporate sense of the Society of Friends. Authoritative expression was found through elders who were sound in their faith. Fellowship was still grounded in a common experience of spiritual life, yet agreement with approved practices and principles which had sprung from that experience was also essential. Quakerism was becoming a Church. It kept touch with the righteousness of life, but also began to ease its arch language about personal infallibility, and became conscious of the peculiar implications of enthusiasm. The unification of Quakers into a common witness and way of life had first been achieved through fellowship and worship. By the turn of the century, however, tradition became imposing. With the growth of organization, the acceptance of rules of conduct on Church authority became in many cases a substitute for living principles of truth in the heart. The Society now included members by birth and tradition as well as by inner persuasion.[5] In essence, the second generation of English Quakerism was burdened by inconsistencies of growth, and it was precisely during this period that the Quaker migration to America began.

"I'M NOT A BIRD-WATCHER or an Indian, Mr. Morton. I don't see the point of this outpost of England."

So speaks the Reverend Mr. Blackstone in Robert Lowell's *Endecott and the Red Cross*. The experience of emigration and settlement was fully charged with tensions of comparison: what had been left behind with what had been gained, if anything. Is it any wonder that enlightened Europeans would eventually admit their nescience of the New World and ask collectively, "Was America a Mistake?"[6]

5. W. C. Braithwaite: *The Second Period of Quakerism* (2nd ed., Cambridge, 1961), 247–50, 498–9.

6. See H. S. Commager and Elmo Giordanetti, eds.: *Was America a Mistake? An Eighteenth-Century Controversy* (Columbia, 1968).

It was not; but it was oppugnantly misunderstood, and has often been so since. In the lengthy chapter which follows, I shall try to indicate those areas in which processes of differentiation, tension, and biformity were taking place. There was no consistent pattern of Americanization at work in the colonies; nor was there a steady or uniform growth of Anglicization either. In some important respects the overseas provinces followed certain European trajectories; in others they became something else again. The processes were complex, always evolving, and constantly subject to change. Therein lies the compelling fascination of colonial America.

CHAPTER 6

CONTRADICTORY TENDENCIES
IN COLONIAL AMERICA

I. ENVIRONMENT, RESOURCES, AND REWARDS

> The people of the Plantation began to grow in their out-
> ward estates, by reason of the flowing of many people into the
> country. . . . By which means corn and cattle rose to a great
> price, by which many were much enriched and commodities
> grew plentiful. And yet in other regards this benefit turned to
> their hurt, and this accession of strength to their weakness.
>
> WILLIAM BRADFORD, *Of Plimoth Plantation*

One of our assumptions about life in early America has been
that the New World environment had peculiarly destructive
powers to alter human aspirations. Certainly the colonists
themselves did not consistently make such assumptions. In
1622, Captain Nathaniel Butler visited Virginia and "found
the Plantacons generally seated uppon meer Salt Marishes full
of infectious Boggs and muddy Creeks and Lakes, and therby
subiected to all those Inconvenyencies and diseases, which are
soe commonly found in the most unsound and most unhealthie
partes of England, wherof every Country and Clymate hath
some." For much more than a century to come, settlers would
observe, as did Gottlieb Mittelberger in 1756, "that oak tree
stumps are just as hard in America as they are in Germany."[1]

1. "The Unmasked Face of our Colony in Virginia," in Susan M.
Kingsbury, ed.: *The Records of the Virginia Company of London*

We now know that between the later sixteenth century and the close of the seventeenth, England suffered her coldest period during the past thousand years. Especially after the 1590's, again in the 1690's and 1740's, climatological effects were severe. Emigration to the New World, therefore, often meant entering an easier milieu, rather than a more menacing one.[2]

When we scratch beneath the panegyric pamphlets promoting colonization, and get behind the hyperbole of those opposed to emigration, we will find that impoverished dalesmen from the moors of England, as well as chapmen and peddlers from town and country, were commonly pleased with New World environments, which often seemed more malleable and generous than in the Old. In 1705, Robert Beverley criticized Virginians bitterly for their indolence: "they depend altogether upon the Liberality of Nature, without endeavouring to improve its Gifts, by Art or Industry. They spunge upon the Blessings of a warm Sun, and a fruitful Soil, and almost grutch the Pains of gathering in the Bounties of the Earth."[3]

An American trait seems to have resulted which I like to call resourceful wastefulness. Many illustrations may be found in William Byrd's engaging *Journey to the Land of Eden in the Year 1733*. Byrd led a party of men to survey lands which he had acquired along the Virginia border. Near their camp one autumn day, the group located "several large chestnut trees very full of chestnuts. Our men were too lazy to climb the trees for the sake of the fruit but . . . chose rather to cut them down, regardless of those that were to come after."[4]

(Washington, D. C., 1906), III, 374; Mittelberger: *Journey to Pennsylvania*, ed. Oscar Handlin and John Clive (Cambridge, Mass., 1960), 20.

2. See H. H. Lamb: "Britain's Changing Climate," *The Geographical Journal*, CXXXIII (1967), 445–68, and David M. Ludlam: *Early American Winters, 1604–1820* (Boston, 1966).

3. Louis B. Wright, ed.: *The History and Present State of Virginia* (Chapel Hill, 1947), 319.

4. Louis B. Wright, ed.: *The Prose Works of William Byrd of Westover* (Cambridge, Mass., 1966), 397, 409. For a more recent illustration, see Samuel P. Hays: *Conservation and the Gospel of Efficiency. The Progressive Conservation Movement, 1890–1920* (New York, 1969), 263.

James Fenimore Cooper would later perceive quite clearly the irony of resourceful wastefulness. In *The Pioneers* he satirized settlers who shot cannons into the sky in order to kill as many pigeons as possible, and who dredged lakes in order to net all available fish at once.

DESCRIPTIVE CONVENTIONS of Elizabethan English were not altogether applicable to the North American environment. Nevertheless, European explorers were obliged to use such tools as were available to them. There resulted a legacy of misinheritance for seventeenth-century settlers, who were really more concerned with developing the land than with describing it. By the eighteenth century, when familiarity and a growing sense of identity might have elicited depictive accuracy, colonial writers too often returned to intentional imitations of older English literary conventions.

Early visitors also brought with them environmental preconceptions conditioned by contradictory notions then circulating in Europe. The landscape was seen as an "Earthly Paradeis," but also as a "howling wilderness," depending upon social circumstances. Neither was an accurate characterization, of course, and "Earthly Paradeis" itself involved a theological contradiction in terms. Yet both were linked to divergent images (long held) of the non-European universe, and they would come into conflict later when Americans made the metaphors of "garden" and "wilderness" into actual ideals.[5]

In seventeenth-century New England and Virginia, "wilderness" implied both wasteland and refuge to the colonists, a land of darkness that might also prove to be a place of comfort. "Yet it pleased our mercifull God," wrote William Strachey, "to make even this hideous and hated place, both the place of our safetie, and meanes of our deliverance."[6] To publicists of col-

5. Peter A. Fritzell: "Landscapes of Anglo-America During Exploration and Early Settlement" (unpublished Ph.D. dissertation, Stanford University, 1966), 3–7, 69–70, 79, 183–5; *The Complete Writings of Roger Williams* (New York, 1963), I, 126.

6. Quoted in Leo Marx: *The Machine in the Garden* (New York, 1964), 44–5.

onization, such as Daniel Defoe, the plantations appeared as a kind of moral Purgatory where exiled convicts would be redeemed. Thus, by the early eighteenth century, America as reformatory jostled cheek by jowl with America as arboretum of primal innocence.

Like so many colonials, William Byrd felt ambivalent about the relative merits of civilized and primitive life. Throughout his *History of the Dividing Line*, Byrd complains about the discomforts of roughing it. Then suddenly, "we chose rather to lie in the open field, for fear of growing too tender. . . . The truth of it is, we took so much pleasure in that natural kind of lodging that I think at the foot of the account mankind are great losers by the luxury of feather beds and warm apartments." But later, "at the end of thirty good miles," apprehensions of guilt return. "We arrived in the evening at Colonel Bolling's, where first from a primitive course of life we began to relapse into luxury." The larger context of these tensions enveloped Byrd's ambiguity about his primitive paradise. "Thus, my Lord," he wrote to the Earl of Orrery in 1726, "we are very happy in our Canaans if we could but forget the onions and fleshpots of Egypt." [7]

Elsewhere, however, as Lewis Evans observed of the Pennslyvania "Dutch" in 1753: "It is pretty to behold our back settlements, where the barns are large as palaces, while the owners live in log huts; a sign, though, of thriving farmers." The great difficulty, and source of a network of anomalies, was that the colonial farmer was simultaneously canonized in formal literature of pastoral praise while being condemned in practical writings about American husbandry. Bucolic literature was of English derivation, and conventionally lyrical. When visitors and colonials themselves began to look directly at the American farmer, however, they were often irritated by what they saw. The land had vast potentialities, but the farmer seemed to neglect them. Indeed, accumulated evidence indicated the innocent swain to be seriously flawed. [8]

7. *Prose Works of William Byrd*, 19, 187, 319.
8. "A Brief Description of the Province of Pennsylvania, 1753,"

The English pastoral tradition had been enthusiastically accepted by aspiring colonial poets, who asserted that since the country was clean, natural, and beautiful, he who worked its earth inevitably absorbed its virtues. Nevertheless, there arose through the eighteenth century a spirited criticism of the American farmer. An anonymous essayist writing in 1758 for *The American Magazine and Monthly Chronicle* tells why:

> The inhabitants, who were confined to narrow farms in their native country, are many of them, insatiable in their desires after lands, and rather waste and impoverish, than improve them. Many have acquired a roving unsettled temper, and are grown impatient of labor and frugal industry; and having abused their farms, sell them, and move back to purchase new lands, on the borders of the *Indian* nations.

What a distance there was between Jefferson's paean to the sturdy yeoman and George Washington's contemporary critique: "The aim of the farmers in this country, if they can be called farmers, is, not to make the most they can from the land, which is, or has been cheap, but the most of the labour, which is dear; the consequence of which has been, much ground has been *scratched* over and none cultivated or improved as it ought to have been." [9]

The pastoral idyll stood in sharp contrast with agrarian wastefulness. Moreover, neither the hired laborer nor the slave, who did the same work as the yeoman (and perhaps more of it), shared the dignity and honor conferred by mythology on the yeoman. The employer of such labor might do little manual work himself, and yet enjoy the comforts of the myth all the same. [1]

The paradox of poverty amidst plenty came to haunt the

---

in L. H. Gipson: *Lewis Evans* (Philadelphia, 1939), 100–1; Richard Bridgman: "Jefferson's Farmer Before Jefferson," *American Quarterly*, XIV (1962), 577.

9. *American Magazine* (Feb. 1758), 235; Franklin Knight, ed.: *Letters on Agriculture* (Washington, D.C., 1847), 32.

1. See C. Vann Woodward: "The Southern Ethic in a Puritan World," *William and Mary Quarterly*, 3d series, XXV (1968), 359–60.

minds of many thoughtful colonials. "They have their Cloath-
ing of all sorts from England," wrote Robert Beverley in 1705.

> Yet Flax, and Hemp grow no where in the World, bet-
> ter than there; their Sheep yield a mighty Increase, and
> bear good Fleeces, but they shear them only to cool
> them. The Mulberry-Tree, whose Leaf is the proper
> Food of the Silk-Worm, grows there like a Weed, and
> Silk-Worms have been observ'd to thrive extreamly,
> and without any hazard. The very Furrs that their Hats
> are made of, perhaps go first from thence; and most of
> their Hides lie and rot, or are made use of, only for
> covering dry Goods, in a leaky House. . . . They are
> such abominable Ill-husbands, that tho' their Country
> be over-run with Wood, yet they have all their Wooden
> Ware from *England;* their Cabinets, Chairs, Tables,
> Stools, Chests, Boxes, Cart-Wheels, and all other
> things, even so much as their Bowls, and Birchen
> Brooms, to the Eternal Reproach of their Laziness.[2]

As an antidote to poverty amidst plenty, one also discovers
in colonial society sources of snobbish humanitarianism. In
Charleston, South Carolina, for example, individuals found
their cachet of nobility by competing feverishly with one another to perform charitable acts. Lavish philanthropy characterized the newly rich gentry. It satisfied both their human
sympathies and their desire to exceed others in making public
contributions. But then, Charleston was also at the very heart
of what Carl Bridenbaugh has called "the Carolina paradox:
the unacquisitive spending standards of an acquisitive society."
Men desperately sought to make their fortunes; but squandered
them with equally reckless abandon. "Every Tradesman is a
Merchant, every Merchant is a Gentleman, and every Gentleman one of the Noblesse. We are a Country of Gentry. . . .
The better Sort of Gentry, who can aim no higher, plunge
themselves into Debt and Dependance, to preserve their
Rank." [3]

2. Beverley: *History and Present State of Virginia,* 295.
3. See *Myths and Realities. Societies of the Colonial South* (Baton
Rouge, 1952), 76, 98, 115.

This same provincial, writing in the *South Carolina Gazette*, had located a consideration of great consequence. The upper reaches of society in colonial America formed a bourgeois aristocracy. Its origins were middle-class and its prime objective was the attainment of wealth and status. There were regional differences to be sure, and anomalies abounded within those differences. The New England colonies, which had been established in the interest of religion, became a laboratory of the capitalist spirit, while the southern colonies, which had been employed in the interest of business, eventually generated a milieu uncongenial to full-scale commerce. The Reverend Charles Turner, preaching at Plymouth in 1773, worried because he could not "point out a country, founded in oeconomy, industry, frugality and temperance, that has arrived to such a degree of luxury, in so short a time as ours." [4]

Nothing in Calvinism *per se* led automatically to capitalism. But in a society already becoming capitalistic, Reformed Protestantism reinforced the triumph of new values. Puritanism undermined obstacles which the more rigid customs of Catholicism had imposed. True enough, Puritan doctrines could often provide hindrances to purposeful and systematic economic behavior: the churches tended to regulate rather than stimulate business enterprise. Most often in colonial America, however, Calvinism and capitalism strained in yoked tension. John Hull, mintmaster of Massachusetts, had an unusual ability to keep the two in equilibrium. Like so many subsequent entrepreneurs in American history, he enjoyed the role of benevolent monopolist. In times of crisis he refused to reduce his fee as mintmaster; but at year's end he would make a fat contribution to the commonwealth's treasury.[5]

4. *Ibid.*, 12, 53, 115–16; Woodward: "Southern Ethic in a Puritan World," 355; Turner: *A Sermon, Preached at Plymouth.* . . . (Boston, 1774), 36.

5. See Christopher Hill: "Protestantism and the Rise of Capitalism," in *Essays in the Economic and Social History of Tudor and Stuart England*, ed. F. J. Fisher (Cambridge, 1961), 15–39; Samuel Eliot Morison: *Builders of the Bay Colony* (2nd ed., Boston, 1958), 151–3, 160–2, 165.

Given the Quaker merchants' diligence and wealth, it is not surprising that contemporaries became conscious of a conflict implicit in the Quaker ethic. On the one hand, Friends were encouraged to be industrious in their callings by the promise that God would bestow prosperity upon them. On the other, they were warned against permitting profits and luxuries to accumulate or make them worldly. John Woolman put it this way in his *Journal:* "the increase of business became my burthen, for though my natural inclination was towards merchandize, yet I believe Truth required me to live more free from outward cumbers. There was now a strife in my mind betwixt the two." [6]

Anthony Benezet, Quaker son of a Huguenot immigrant, became deeply concerned because the Philadelphia merchants —at least many of those he saw every First Day in meeting— equated labor and wealth with piety and grace. "Now, that such a person shall esteem himself, and be esteemed, a religious man, and perhaps be the more regarded, even by religious people, because he is rich and great, is a mere paradox; yet it is too often the case." Gradually more sensitive members of the Society of Friends despaired at the disparity between Quaker theory and practice, and over the anomaly of poverty amidst abundance. "The appellation of *Steward*," wrote Benezet in 1760,

> is what we often take upon ourselves, but indeed, in the mouth of many it is but a cant, unmeaning expression. What a paradox it is, that people should imagine themselves to act as such, or that they are indeed fulfilling the second command of loving their neighbour as themselves . . . and at the same time live in the utmost ease and plenty. [7]

Despite the good intentions of many, however, distribution of wealth became steadily less equitable. Ironically, most of

6. Frederick B. Tolles: *Meeting House and Counting House. The Quaker Merchants of Colonial Philadelphia, 1682–1763* (Chapel Hill, 1948), 43; Amelia M. Gummere, ed.: *The Journal and Essays of John Woolman* (New York, 1922), 183.

7. Tolles: *Meeting House and Counting House*, 63, 80, 81–4, 106.

the colonists before 1700 were relatively equal in their wealth and standing; but believing in a hierarchical society, thought they should be less equal. During the eighteenth century, they became relatively less equal in their holdings and statuses; but slowly acquiring a democratic ideology, thought they should be less differentiated. *Damnosa hereditas!*

So Europeans came to America expecting to find an "Earthly Paradeis." Partially because of their resourceful wastefulness here, they idealized the *rus in urbe* for their city-scapes. Conflicts between Calvinism and capitalism caught many in what they called "a beautifull abhomination." Understandably, tensions between social values and economic opportunities helped to produce both benevolent monopolists and avaricious philanthropists. Many achieved membership in locally entrenched bourgeois aristocracies, where only rarely were they troubled by the presence of poverty amidst plenty. A few practical visionaries eventually hoped that technological ingenuity might lead the way to a new utopia. They proved to be wrong in the long run, though their reasoning had much to recommend it.[8]

II. GOVERNMENT AND POLITICS

> Wee must Creep when wee cannot goe, and it is as Necessarie for us in the things of this life to be wise as to be Innocent.
>
> WILLIAM PENN

John Winthrop established his holy commonwealth on the interlocked bases of voluntarism and subordination, or as one scholar has put it: "compulsory voluntarism."[1] Winthrop's

8. See J. A. Etzler: *The Paradise Within the Reach of all Men Without Labor, by Powers of Nature and Machinery* (Pittsburgh, 1833); Charles H. Fitch: "The Rise of a Mechanical Ideal," *Magazine of American History*, XI (June 1884), 516.

1. Alfred de Grazia: *Public and Republic. Political Representation in America* (New York, 1951), 66–7.

best-known statement of the relationship between liberty and authority appeared in his speech "On Liberty," made before the General Court of Massachusetts on July 3, 1645.

> The great questions that have troubled the country, are about the authority of the magistrates and the liberty of the people. It is yourselves who have called us to this office, and being called by you, we have our authority from God, in way of an ordinance. . . . But when you call one to be a magistrate, he doth not profess nor undertake to have sufficient skill for that office, nor can you furnish him with gifts, etc., therefore you must run the hazard of his skill and ability. . . . For the other point concerning liberty, I observe a great mistake in the country about that. There is a twofold liberty, natural (I mean as our nature is now corrupt) and civil or federal. The first is common to man with beasts and other creatures. By this, man, as he stands in relation to man simply, hath liberty to do what he lists; it is a liberty to evil as well as to good. This liberty is incompatible and inconsistent with authority, and cannot endure the least restraint of the most just authority. . . . The other kind of liberty I call civil or federal. . . . This liberty is the proper end and object of authority, and cannot subsist without it; and it is a liberty to that only which is good, just, and honest. . . . This liberty is maintained and exercised in a way of subjection to authority; it is of the same kind of liberty wherewith Christ has made us free.[2]

Winthrop's sentiments are central to an understanding of the subsequent emphasis upon equilibrium and counterpoise in American political thought. His words would be rephrased in more secular contexts by Landon Carter in the eighteenth century (balancing off "Aristocracy and Popularity"), by William Graham Sumner in the nineteenth (balancing rights and duties in a moral political system), and by Carl Becker in the twentieth (balancing freedom and responsibility).[3]

2. Winthrop: *The History of New England* (Boston, 1853), II, 280–2.

3. See Jack P. Greene, ed.: *The Diary of Colonel Landon Carter of Sabine Hall, 1752–1778* (Charlottesville, 1965), I, 31–3; Robert G.

Public affairs in Rhode Island were characterized by this dualistic imperative from the very outset. At the first court of election, held at Portsmouth in 1647, an explicit "engagement" was embodied in the preamble to the code of laws: "Wee whose names are here underwritten, doe engage ourselves to the uttmost of our estates and strength *to maintayne the authority and to enjoy the Libertie* granted to us by our Charter." [4] Four decades later, William Penn sought to maintain the same delicate balance in the Preface to his first proprietary Frame of Government (1682):

> viz: to support power in reverence with the people, and to secure the people from the abuse of power; that they may be free by their just obedience, and the magistrates honourable for their just administration: *for liberty without obedience is confusion, and obedience without liberty is slavery.*[5]

The problem was made more complex, however, by a cluster of ambiguities concerning the nature of authority in colonial America, especially the fuzzy distinctions between private and public authority. Seventeenth-century colonists chose, for example, to adopt only that portion of the common law which concerned itself with the ordering of public affairs. Nonconstitutional and private segments of the laws of England tended to be disregarded. When the Puritans of New England were charged, from time to time, with constructing their own body of private, nonconstitutional laws, they simply ignored

McCloskey: *American Conservatism in the Age of Enterprise, 1865–1910* (Cambridge, Mass., 1951), 65–7; Becker: *Freedom and Responsibility in the American Way of Life* (New York, 1945).

4. John R. Bartlett, ed.: *Records of the Colony of Rhode Island* (Providence, 1856), I, 147, 156.

5. See Edwin B. Bronner: *William Penn's "Holy Experiment." The Founding of Pennsylvania, 1681–1701* (New York, 1962), 91; *Minutes of the Provincial Council of Pennsylvania* (Philadelphia, 1852), I, 31 (italics mine). Dr. William Douglass of Boston would recite Penn's exact words two generations later, adding that "to support a coercive Power over a giddy people, and to secure the People against the abuse of this Power, are difficult Problems."

the accusation![6] The code of *Lawes and Liberties* promulgated by Massachusetts in 1648 contained major ambiguities concerning local franchise requirements. Those ambiguities led to misunderstanding, controversy, and the complaint that several sections "seeme not well to consist together, the latter also repealing the former, and finding inconvenience in the execution of that." [7]

Although political institutions and the constitutional structure of the colonies were roughly similar to England's, they nevertheless functioned differently in the New World. In Georgian England the mixed and balanced constitution produced public harmony to an unusual degree; yet in America it had a different sort of effect. One reason was that the kinds of influence by which the executive in England disciplined dissent and maintained parliamentary supremacy were severely restricted in America. The informal arrangements which made England's formal, or "public" constitution work were much reduced overseas. "The paradoxical result," as Bernard Bailyn has perceived,

> was that while in important respects the colonial constitutions were archaic by eighteenth-century standards, in other respects they were radically reformed. The reduction of influence, of "corruption," that was so avidly sought by a succession of would-be reformers of the English constitution for a century after Walpole's time, had been achieved in the mainland colonies of North America at the beginning, almost insensibly, largely by the force of circumstance. The original characteristics of American politics were formed in the tensions of this paradox.[8]

6. Mark DeWolfe Howe: "The Sources and Nature of Law in Colonial Massachusetts," in *Law and Authority in Colonial America*, ed. George A. Billias (Barre, 1965), 10–11. See also xiii, 79, 92, 96, 107, 178–9.

7. Quoted in Timothy H. Breen: "Who Governs: The Town Franchise in 17th-century Massachusetts," *William and Mary Quarterly*, 3d series, XXVII (1970), 471.

8. *The Origins of American Politics* (New York, 1968), 63, 70–1.

By the close of the seventeenth century, imperial officials found themselves in the peculiar position of deploring colonial lapses from English institutional and legal norms, yet also criticizing the tendency of provincial assemblies to imitate the House of Commons too closely. Whitehall had begun to recognize a logical inconsistency between colonial self-government and proper dependence. Both centrifugal and centripetal forces had conditioned the evolution of America's place in the Empire. In one direction lay the integrative constitution shaped in England and conditioned by a period of direct rule under English officials. In another direction lay an autochthonous constitution formed locally and fashioned in periods of indirect rule by men sensitive to local usage and needs. No wonder conflicting loyalties obtained everywhere. No wonder political anglophobia began to chafe at being harnessed with cultural anglophilia.

Resistance slowly became apparent after 1670, and especially so between 1685 and 1690. By the opening years of the eighteenth century, when North American colonists were beginning to think in more expansive terms, they were also becoming ever more conscious of their continuing dependence upon England. Members of colonial councils were bound by oath to uphold the Crown or proprietary interest; but they were also driven by personal ambition and various local pressures in ways that could not always be reconciled. Lack of self-control in a figurative sense (political subordination) bred a lack of self-control in the most literal sense (outbursts of rebellion and protest); and both, quite obviously, stemmed from the quest for legitimacy and the problem of unstable pluralism.

Loyalties were difficult to define and align accordingly, in part because the structure of society was not quite congruent with the structure of politics—at least not in ways that seemed normative and satisfactory. At the very outset in Massachusetts and Connecticut, for example, this was not a pressing problem. Both places exhibited the anomaly of a "popular aristocracy" wherein the people elected their rulers, but the same men were continually rechosen. Elsewhere, however, and eventually everywhere, there were not enough figures of commanding authority and social presence to man the political bastions of shaky settlements. To make matters worse, the very process of emigration and resettlement tended to attract Europe's more restless, anti-authoritarian types. The experience of transplanting embraced both alienation and a new birth of freedom, both uprootedness and opportunity, by men who cherished security but constantly took risks in order to achieve it. By the close of the seventeenth century, divergence between political and social leadership at the highest levels of public life created the potential for permanent conflict.

By the middle of the eighteenth century, popular aristocracy had been subtly transmuted by the growth of pluralism into democratic élitism. "We must consider ourselves chosen by all the People," said John Randolph in 1736, when he was selected speaker of the Virginia House of Burgesses, "sent hither to represent them, to give their Consent in the weightiest of their Concerns. . . . It may be often impossible [however] to conform to their Sentiments, since, when we come to consider and compare them, we shall find them so various and irreconcileable." [9] Virginia, mind you, was one of the most homogeneous colonies. Imagine the difficulty where American pluralism was already much more in evidence: Pennsylvania, New York, and Rhode Island.

In addition to the colonial assembly, still another instrument of government—much less noticed by historians—reveals awkward inconsistencies in early American political life. The whole system of courts and the administration of justice were fraught with ambivalence. Was it the primary function of courts to protect or to prosecute the individual? To safeguard the accused or society? As one source of confusion, distinctions

9. H. R. McIlwaine, ed.: *Journals of the House of Burgesses of Virginia*, 1727–1740 (Richmond, 1910), 240. "Oligarchy was undergirded by democracy—the country democracy of all the landholders"; Merrill Peterson: *Thomas Jefferson and the New Nation* (New York, 1970), 37.

between criminal and civil law, between public and private offenses, between crimes and torts emerged slowly and not always distinctly. Judicial positions were associated with plural officeholding, and the courts—often regarded as instruments of the rich—were resented because of their expense. They were associated with oaths repugnant to certain religious minorities, and came to be regarded by many as political weapons in the hands of the privileged. Not surprisingly, colonial courts commonly became the focal point of movements of social protest.

A long history of judicial abuses prepared colonial society for actions taken during the revolutionary generation: closing courts during the Stamp Act crisis; seething at the court's decision after the Boston Massacre; and the courthouse confrontations of Shays' Rebellion. Just how it all began is hard to say; but before the seventeenth-century settlements were very old, men already conceived of courts as more often the violators of men's rights than the defenders of those rights. During the troubled years of the Dominion of New England, 1686–9, inchoate fears and resentment of courts acquired form and thrust. When Sir Edmund Andros arrived he established, as part of the Dominion, a new judicial system conformable to English practice and custom. Although the new system did not introduce any startling innovations in the substance of the law, it did alter administration of the law by eliminating many indigenous practices devised by colonists over decades in order to adjust English custom to their more immediate needs. Inevitably, the Puritans resented these changes. They bitterly opposed, for example, the illegality of trying cases outside of a county which concerned inhabitants or land within it.[1]

Between 1690 and 1700, several episodes and issues contributed to the growth of colonial concern over courts. At Salem in 1692, when witchcraft had the colony in a frenzy, it was not at all clear whether the court's primary role was to prosecute

1. For fierce counter-criticisms of court abuses by the insurgents, see Gershom Bulkeley: *Will and Doom, or The Miseries of Connecticut by and Under an Usurped and Arbitrary Power* (1692) in *Collections of the Connecticut Historical Society*, III (1895), 88, 141, 222–7, 256.

the guilty or protect the innocent. Ambivalence about judicial institutions reached still larger proportions. Then, when rioters wished to show their displeasure with New Jersey's proprietary régime in 1700, they repeatedly disrupted court proceedings with "soe high a Contempt and so Impudent Behavior to the Dignity and Authority of the Court, which may if not timely prevented turn to a convulsion in Government to the Ruine of the Collony." [2]

By mid-century there were desperate appeals for judicial reform in the colonies, to which responses came slowly where they came at all.[3] Court bills became ever more prominent in legislative politics, as in North Carolina in 1759 and South Carolina a decade later. Is it any wonder that many colonists felt fuller justice could be obtained *outside* of the courts? This was precisely Benjamin Franklin's point of view. His hilarious and poignant satire, printed in 1747 as the courtroom speech of a woman being prosecuted for the fifth time for bearing a bastard child, was the logical culmination of popular frustration with insensitive courts. Proceedings could be "so tedious and the Expence so high, that the Remedy, Justice, is worse than Injustice, the Disease." Hence Franklin's admiration for Andrew Hamilton, the canny Philadelphia attorney who so often was able to reconcile conflicts out of court.[4] This hostility toward courts would burgeon during the revolutionary era, as would the uncertainty of most Americans regarding the proper

2. William A. Whitehead, ed.: *Documents Relating to the Colonial History of the State of New Jersey* (Newark, 1880–6), II, 313–15, 333–4, VII, 216–17.

3. Isabel Ferguson: "County Court in Virginia, 1700–1830," *North Carolina Historical Review*, VIII (1931), 28–9; *The Letters and Papers of Cadwallader Colden*, IX, in *Collections of the New-York Historical Society for the Year 1935*, LXVIII, 257; Colden to Earl of Egremont, Sept. 14, 1763, in *ibid.* (1876), 231; William Livingston: *The Independent Reflector*, ed. Milton M. Klein (Cambridge, Mass., 1963), 250–6, 301–4.

4. See Max Hall: *Benjamin Franklin and Polly Baker. The History of a Literary Deception* (Chapel Hill, 1960), esp. ch. 8; Paul W. Conner: *Poor Richard's Politicks. Benjamin Franklin and His New American Order* (New York, 1965), 64–5.

way to achieve both justice and security in a rapidly growing society.

WHAT WOULD EVENTUALLY EMERGE from these tensions between liberty and authority, between society and its instruments of government? For one thing, a political style, a way of doing and viewing public affairs in which several sorts of biformities would be prevalent: pragmatic idealism, conservative liberalism, orderly violence, and moderate rebellion.

The first of these had its discernible genesis during John Winthrop's generation. Illustrations of "lawful expedience" and "holy pretence" are more numerous in Winthrop's career than I can adequately enumerate here. In his English Puritan predecessors, preservation of the common good had been important but subordinate nonetheless to imperatives of individual behavior. With Winthrop the godly state became all-important, so that Puritanism and *raison d'état* became inextricably bound together. To Winthrop, responsible as he was for the preservation of a fragile cluster of communities, "actions done in the fulfilment of the intentions of God became actions performed in the service of a state which is both secular and divine." Puritan leadership in early New England was essentially untroubled by the double morality implicit in manipulative *raison d'état*.[5]

The colonists had to be pragmatic idealists because in a wilderness things must be made to work, yet idealism is required to reinforce the courage to confront that wilderness: Calvinism combined with the frontier experience plus commercial expansion amidst rising capitalism. Perhaps pragmatic purposefulness would be better: the mission to make a viable New Jerusalem through workable ideas. In any event, this proclivity for both practicality and high idealism would later cause Tocqueville to observe of the American that "his ideas

5. See George L. Mosse: *The Holy Pretence* (Oxford, 1957), 93, 99, 106, 121–9, 151–2. See also Gary B. Nash: "The Framing of Government in Pennsylvania. Ideas in Contact with Reality," *William and Mary Quarterly*, 3d series, XXIII (1966), 183–4, 191–2, 204.

are all either extremely minute and clear, or extremely general and vague: what lies between is a void."

By the time one reaches the last thirty years of the eighteenth century, the most creative era in American political thought, one encounters what Peter Gay has called "pragmatic rationalism." The Founding Fathers had a Calvinist, Hobbesian pessimism about human passion and fallibility. Consequently, they sought an equilibrium among political and constitutional forces in order to achieve a proper balance between freedom and control. Nevertheless, they also had an optimistic inclination, based on the belief that America was a certain kind of experiment. If they were realistic, they were also hopeful; if they trusted institutions, they treated them as being provisional. Madison, Hamilton, and Jay, authors of *The Federalist Papers*, "distinguished between Utopian political blueprints and sensible political machines, but they never doubted that the state could be made into a successful mechanism promoting freedom while repressing the anarchy of passion." [6]

A related phenomenon might be called conservative liberalism. We find it in Connecticut and Rhode Island, colonies with utopian origins which were nevertheless the last to discard property qualifications for suffrage. We find it in John Wise of Ipswich, the wrestling minister who led local opposition to the Dominion of New England, and whose reverence for the past often clouded his perspective on ecclesiastical issues of his time, so that he has been appropriately described as a "conservative radical." We find it embedded amongst tendencies in the political thought of William Penn, who seemed to combine with his utopianism a nostalgic longing for the feudal past with its well-ordered society and "old time Nobility and Gentry." We shall find it in a great many Americans of the past

6. Gay: "The Enlightenment," in *The Comparative Approach to American History*, ed. C. Vann Woodward (New York, 1968), 43–4. For practical idealism in Progressive America, see Henry F. May: *The End of American Innocence. The First Years of Our Own Time, 1912–1917* (New York, 1959), 9–19.

two centuries, such as Eric Johnston, who just a few years back called us all "conservative liberals."[7]

Although American history in the seventeenth and eighteenth centuries was filled with movements of protest, very few were socially revolutionary. Most were outright struggles for political and economic power, and had an overlay of constitutional discussion; but the men involved shied away from "thorough." As the Leislerians of New York admitted in summarizing their grievances, "we are able to make appear, if thereunto Required, that never a Revolution was carried on and mannaged with more moderation in any part of the Christian World."[8]

A century later, Thomas Jefferson would convey his thoughts on insurrections to James Madison: "I hold it that a little rebellion now and then is a good thing, and as necessary in the political world as storms in the physical. . . . An observation of this truth should render honest republican governors so mild in their punishment of rebellions, as not to discourage them too much. It is a medicine necessary for the sound health of government." Learning of Shays' Rebellion in Massachusetts prompted Jefferson's remark to Abigail Adams: "The spirit of resistance to government is so valuable on certain occasions, that I wish it to be always kept alive. It will often be exercised when wrong, but better so than not to be exercised at all."[9]

7. John M. Ericson: "John Wise: Colonial Conservative" (unpublished Ph.D. dissertation, Stanford University, 1961); Nash: "Ideas in Contact with Reality," 192–3; Richard Polenberg, ed.: *America at War. The Home Front, 1941–1945* (Englewood Cliffs, 1968), 33; John G. Sproat: *"The Best Men": Liberal Reformers in the Gilded Age* (New York, 1968), 230.

8. Michael G. Hall, *et al.*, eds.: *The Glorious Revolution in America. Documents on the Colonial Crisis of 1689* (Chapel Hill, 1964), 39–40, 139. See the sermons of Jonathan Mayhew (1750) and Samuel West (1776), reprinted in Peter N. Carroll, ed.: *Religion and the Coming of the American Revolution* (Waltham, 1970), 40, 51, 155.

9. Julian P. Boyd, ed.: *The Papers of Thomas Jefferson* (Princeton, 1950–   ), XI, 93, 174, XII, 356.

So moderate rebellions, or what Increase Mather called "happy revolutions," became a positive good in the minds of many Americans. Others, however, terrified by lawlessness and anarchy, would learn to organize counter-violence of their own. The Regulator movement in South Carolina during the 1760's, for example, contained the seeds of its own destruction. A movement which originated to provide law and order became lawless and disorderly itself. A "Moderator" movement had to be formed to repress the Regulators! Ironic, true, but the beginnings nevertheless of a sustained tradition of ordered violence and illicit legality in American history: the vigilante movements, Klansmen, and Minutemen.[1]

III. THEOLOGY AND CHURCHES

> To see a Weak man Strong,
>   And strongest when most weak;
> To see the strong through weakness fall
>   And all their bones to break:
>   This is a *Mystery*
>   A Christian *Paradox;*
> And this ensuing little key
>   The Cabinet unlocks.
>
> MICHAEL WIGGLESWORTH, *Riddles Unriddled
>   or Christian Paradoxes* (1669)

Ecclesiastical life in the colonies deviated from English norms less than we have customarily assumed. Yet tensions which were both transplanted and indigenous did develop, almost from the outset. They polarized around theological issues, Church-State relations, and conflicts between changing social values and the vital need to preserve viable traditions and stability.

Calvinism was a dialectical faith, resting upon a scheme of

1. See Richard M. Brown: "Legal and Behavioral Perspectives on American Vigilantism," *Perspectives in American History*, V (1971), 95–144; Leonard L. Richards: *"Gentlemen of Property and Standing": Anti-Abolition Mobs in Jacksonian America* (New York, 1970).

counterpoised contentions. The saint thirsted for life, and yet hungered after death. The saint was not really of the world, yet he must live in it under a temporal régime of law which protected the civil rights of both the saved and the damned. The inner life of Puritanism turned on an axis between opposite poles of conflict and conciliation, anger and love, aggression and submission. In America, especially, Puritanism generated both respect for individual freedom and a need for external discipline, a sense of personal privacy as well as a system of public accountability, reliance on self-assertion as well as belief in erratic fate. The main dilemma of Puritanism throughout the early years in New England, perhaps, was to reconcile these discrepant sets of qualities.

Part of the problem rested in the Puritans' ambivalent conception of Divinity. "God sets up, and He pulls down," wrote Samuel Willard. Somehow they had to maintain the subordination of humanity to God without unduly denigrating human values, appreciate the powers of human intellect without losing their sense of divine transcendence. How could man understand God without depriving Him of His unpredictability? How could man justify God's ways without losing the sense of His absolute Divinity? [1]

A network of covenants collectively called the federal theology would help to rationalize some of these dilemmas, but also create others as well. The covenant of grace between man and God, and the church covenant among visible saints, were ideally to be as concentric rings in perfect juxtaposition. After the middle of the seventeenth century, however, the disjunctions between them increased. Ultimately, after three generations, New England society confessedly contained many hypocrites, albeit "sincere hypocrites" who were socially useful: they helped to praise and glorify God, thereby keeping the social covenant successfully intact. The consequence was an unusual tension in which hypocrisy unwittingly became a positive good. The strain bore heavily upon ministerial consciences,

1. Willard: *The Character of a Good Ruler* (Boston, 1694), 18.

for as Cotton Mather observed of the Lord's Supper: "It is a sin to come unworthily to, but it is also a sin to stay unworthily from, that Blessed Ordinance." In short, the sacraments presented an insoluble dilemma. Unless more men were persuaded to take communion, the churches would decay; yet those who took it without spiritual assurance would be undone. No wonder some men looked upon the covenant as a "giftless gift." [2]

Generations of colonists would read and reread the *Riddles Unriddled or Christian Paradoxes* of Michael Wigglesworth, which went through countless editions.

> Light in Darkness,
>   Sick mens Health,
> Strength in Weakness,
>   Poor mens Wealth.
> In Confinement,
>   Liberty,
> In Sollitude,
>   Good Company.
> Joy in Sorrow,
>   Life in Deaths,
> Heavenly Crowns for
>   Thorny Wreaths.
> Are presented to thy view,
>   In the Poems that ensue.

Eighteenth-century divines, such as Peter Thacher of Connecticut, drew heavily upon *Riddles Unriddled* for sermonic material, imitated their style, and simply plagiarized the more poignant paradoxes. Note John Adams's stricture upon his cousin Zabdiel, minister of the First Congregational Society of Lunenberg: "Zab's mind is taken up with . . . Questions, Paradoxes and Riddles." [3]

. . .

2. Perry Miller: *The New England Mind from Colony to Province* (Cambridge, Mass., 1953), 54, 71–3, 78, 80–1, 96, 224–5, 277.

3. I have used the Boston 1689 edition (Evans no. 500); see esp. 51–2, 60, 92, 100, 108, 111, 121. Thacher: *A Divine Riddle. He That is Weak is Strong.* . . . (New London, 1723), viii, 2, 5, 9, and *passim;* Adams: *Diary and Autobiography*, ed. L. H. Butterfield, *et al.* (Cambridge, Mass., 1961), I, 142.

IN THE MATTER OF ecclesiastical polity, some anomalies of early American history are well known. One of Perry Miller's earliest achievements involved clarification of the tension between those Pilgrims who wished to abandon the Church of England (Separatists) and Puritans who ostensibly hoped to reform it from within (Nonseparating Congregationalists). John Cotton caught the essence of the latter ambivalence in 1634: "Wee conceive the Lord hath guided us to walke with an even foote between two extreames; so that we neither defile ourselves with the remnant of pollutions in other Churches, nor doe wee for the remnant of pollutions renounce the churches themselves, nor the holy ordinances of God amongst them, which ourselves have found powerfull to our salvation." [4] The inconsistency confronted by most Puritans in Zion was that while professing their loyalty to the apostolic Church, they were actually establishing autonomous congregations.

Unexpected reversals occurred in the role of church government. The southern colonies, which had Anglican establishments, did not become properly hierarchical because a bishop was lacking, because vestry supervision was locally strong, and because the poorly populated parishes were elephantine. In the Chesapeake colonies, ad hoc congregationalism prevailed instead of the expected episcopal chain of control. In New England, quite the reverse occurred: ad hoc Presbyterianism took hold in congregational colonies where Presbyterianism was despised. How did it happen? In New England, through a curious biformity they called "consultative synods." As early as 1633, Bay Colony clergy began gathering once a fortnight to discuss questions of common interest. Their meetings were quite fruitful and eventually received legal sanction. Together the ministers became known as "the Reverend Elders." As Congregationalists they eschewed coercion, preferred persuasion and voluntarism. But because the times were so unsettled, heretical opinions simply had to be controlled. Hopefully a kind of dependent voluntarism could be achieved. If the elders re-

---

4. *A Letter of Mr. John Cotton's . . . to Mr. Williams* (London, 1643), 11.

jected coercion as a mode of ecclesiastical authority, they none-theless exercised a persuasive admonition which relied on the power of magistracy for sanctions.

The paradox of ad hoc Presbyterianism in a congregational system became manifest in 1648. In that year the General Court published the *Lawes and Liberties of Massachusetts*, confirming the ministers' right to associate just as the Cambridge Synod was reaffirming the congregational way and re-jecting Richard Mather's notion of consociation. New England thus had a system of "Christian Vigilantes" to keep ecclesiasti-cal order, a system that became more clearly formalized with the passage of generations.[5] Implicit within it were quite con-tradictory tendencies. Lacking a proper synod, congregational churches of New England had to get along with the ministerial convocation (which had no clearly defined authority), with imperfectly formed associations (which remained inchoate out-side the Connecticut Valley), with councils (which often created further dissensions), or else with "societies for improv-ing manners" (which could not reach those sectors of the community most in need of improvement).

Spiritual and secular authorities alike realized that one consequence of removing from England was to breed "the dis-sidence of dissent." This in itself would perpetrate a debili-tating irony and eventually require reformulation of relations between Church and State. Reverend Josiah Smith, a Presby-terian in South Carolina, put it this way in 1730: "Is it not shocking that the same people who left their native country to enjoy liberty of conscience should turn persecutors as soon as they were in power? Yet this is true of many who went to New England . . . to avoid persecution, and there persecuted the poor harmless Quakers merely for their opinions."[6]

For Roger Williams, who sought a balance between coer-

5. See Robert F. Scholz: "'The Reverend Elders.' Faith, Fellow-ship and Politics in the Ministerial Community of Massachusetts Bay, 1630–1710" (unpublished Ph.D. dissertation, University of Minnesota, 1966), 4–6, 103, 118, 123–4, 131, 137–8, 140, 148, 152, 154–7, 241–5.

6. *American Weekly Mercury*, June 18–25, 1730.

cion and liberty, the conventional wisdom was inadequate. He defined liberty of conscience as the right to be wrong, and established religious toleration in Rhode Island for reasons that can only be appraised as pragmatic idealism. Because he lived in "the most *unchristian Christendome*," because most men (despite baptism and church attendance) were "*unconverted Converts*," that is, "*one unturned turned: unholy holy*," enforced worship would be meaningless. The greatest irony is that the one idea which Williams insisted upon most strongly— liberty of conscience—was rejected by his contemporaries but subsequently adopted by a nation which he would have found more apostate than his own New England.[7]

THE POINTS AT WHICH traditional religious ideas and changing social values intersected were often the precise points which touched off the most serious controversies in colonial America. The central doctrine of Protestantism being justification by faith, insistence that each believer should look inward to his own heart gave Puritanism a fundamental stress upon individualism. Nevertheless, in new and insecure plantations there also had to be strong emphasis upon collectivism. Because the search for visible and effective agencies of authority appeared at the outset of American history, individualism and collectivism emerged as counterpoised tendencies from the outset. Few groups were so well prepared as the Quakers to preserve an equilibrium. For them, as Frederick Tolles suggested,

> the "social ethic" was held in a creative tension with the "Protestant ethic" of individualism. Here, in short, was a paradox that resolved the eternal problem of the one and the many, the individual and the group: in losing themselves in the pregnant silence of the worshipping community they found themselves most completely.[8]

7. Edmund S. Morgan: *Roger Williams. The Church and the State* (New York, 1967), 29, 114, 141; *Complete Writings of Roger Williams* (New York, 1963), III, 133–4, 184, IV, 442. Italics Williams's.

8. *Quakers and the Atlantic Culture* (New York, 1960), 22.

For Puritans the problem was more difficult. Anne Hutchinson's movement during the 1630's, and the clerical response to it, exposed the contradiction between Puritan ideals of social order and the need for a personally transforming spiritual experience. Roger Williams's banishment from Massachusetts served similarly as a dramatic illustration of the paradox that a Christian society could persecute the very men who most nearly imitated Christ's love, humility, and devotion.

Attempts in New England to create both a pure Church—one in which visible saints were nearly co-extensive with invisible—and an established Church made for an unstable if not impossible situation. From the very first, churches in the Bay Colony found room for the "certain" elect as well as hypocrites who had some measure of grace—usually termed "common grace" as opposed to saving grace.[9] The whole dilemma of keeping spiritual exclusiveness compatible with social inclusiveness reached the first of several crises in 1662 with the Half-Way Covenant. Here was an arrangement which enlarged the congregation at the cost of diminishing the power of the "true" church. The attempt to keep church and community co-extensive meant minimizing control by full members over the choice of ministers and the nature of their doctrines. The Half-Way Covenant provides yet another example of pragmatic idealism, for if it was a necessary expedient, it resulted also from the high principles of men unwilling to perjure themselves by professing an experience of conversion they had not fully felt.

There were two essential ingredients in seventeenth-century Puritanism: a mystical element of passion and one which demanded rational obedience to an external social code. During the halcyon days, Puritan scholastics achieved a fusion of intellect and emotion that would be virtually unattainable for their descendants. Even into the fourth generation, in the eighteenth century, such divines as Benjamin Colman would

9. See David Kobrin: "The Expansion of the Visible Church in New England: 1629–1650," *Church History*, XXXVI (1967), 189–209.

try to keep head and heart co-ordinated through "a vein of rational emotionalism, of what may well be called a sentimentalized piety." And even the growing community of Anglicans would seek a middle way defined as "practical moralism." [1]

Stirrings of awakened piety in the 1730's, however, began to tear apart finally any binding attachment between rationalism and pietism. In 1733, an election sermon warned men not to "break into parties and draw different ways, and one party as Industriously pull down what another builds up." Sermons on homiletics during these years suggest that many ministers already were debating the merits of emotional preaching as against "cold rationality." Soon the same debate would divide most of their congregations. After 1740 the Great Awakening split colonial society into two camps, each constituting a segment of Reformed Protestantism, each marking the fulfillment of strains that in Puritanism had been held in precarious balance; piety and reason. Even revivalists, such as Gilbert Tennent, cast theological issues in terms of opposites: "We may as easily reconcile Light and Darkness, Fire and Water, Life and Death, as Justification partly by Works, and partly by Grace." [2]

Although pietism achieved permanence as part of the American temper, inconsistencies surfaced early and often. Within pietism lay an inherent tension, a conflict, in Professor McLoughlin's words,

1. Robert Middlekauff: "Piety and Intellect in Puritanism," *William and Mary Quarterly*, 3d series, XXII (1965), 457–70; Miller: *New England Mind from Colony to Province*, 273, 363–5, 440–1; Gerald J. Goodwin: "The Anglican Middle Way in Early Eighteenth-Century America: Anglican Religious Thought in the American Colonies, 1702–1750" (unpublished Ph.D. dissertation, University of Wisconsin, 1965).

2. Richard Bushman: *From Puritan to Yankee: Character and the Social Order in Connecticut, 1690–1765* (Cambridge, Mass., 1967), 178, 180–2, 197; Alan Heimert: *Religion and the American Mind* (Cambridge, Mass., 1966), 3, 5, 8–9, 12, 22, 551–2. In the Federal era there were two well-known New England divines named Reverend John Murray: one a Calvinist in Newburyport, the other a Universalist in Boston. They were popularly distinguished as Damnation Murray and Salvation Murray.

between the conservative and the antinomian aspects of pietism—between those whose primary concern is to maintain perfect moral order and those whose primary concern is to attain perfect moral freedom. This tension was central to the attempt to found a nation dedicated to the proposition that the moral law of God and Nature is supreme, and that all men owe their first and fundamental allegiance to that law rather than to their families, their community or to the state.[3]

For considerable time the two aspects of American pietism remained in tension because of their opposing views of the proper Christian society. Conservative pietists insisted that a Christian state required some official recognition and support for churches. By contrast, Separatists and especially Baptists contended that for the state to support an established denomination infringed upon the freedom of individual conscience and of the other churches. It is important in understanding the difference between European and American civilizations to note that church disestablishment in the late colonies and new states was not demanded by libertarian atheists but by evangelical pietists concerned with freedom of religion. Disestablishment, as McLoughlin has put it, was "undertaken to free America *for* religion and not *from* religion." [4]

The religious beliefs of many Americans by the middle of the eighteenth century—Calvinist as well as liberal—have been aptly described as "supernatural rationalism." According to this hybrid persuasion, man's unassisted reason can establish the essentials of natural religion: the existence of God, the obligations of morality, a divine order of rewards and punishments. Unlike Deists, however, the supporters of supernatural rationalism insisted that natural religion be supplemented with a special revelation of God's will. Yet reason was entitled to examine the evidences of any revelation, such as Christian revelation, which purports to come from God. Supernatural

3. William G. McLoughlin: "Pietism and the American Character," *American Quarterly*, XVII (1965), 165.
4. *Ibid.*, 166, 178. See also H. Richard Niebuhr: *The Kingdom of God in America* (New York, 1937), 109.

rationalism—a theological position rather than a particular sect—was essentially a form of Christian apologetics framed in language appropriate to the physics of Newton and the epistemology of Locke.[5]

WHAT LEGACY, then, did the colonial era leave in the spheres of theology, ecclesiastical polity, and an American style of spirituality? At least four sorts of biformities come to mind, all of them suggesting that religion in America has meant both tedium and *Te Deum*, both sorrow and thanksgiving. As John Greenleaf Whittier put it in "The Preacher":

> With zeal wing-clipped and white-heat cool,
> Moved by the spirit in grooves of rule. . . .
> A non-conductor among the wires,
> With coat of asbestos proof to fires.[6]

There is an element of fatalistic optimism, a belief in predestination and God's omnipotence combined with hope in human striving, with the purposefulness of making a decision for Christ. There is also "the Grand Point of Practical Piety," in which religion becomes a useful instrument of social order and underpins a crusade for benevolence. When Americans found themselves overwrought with sectarianism, they used that abundance of piety to solve the problem of religious liberty. Puritan idealism wed with Yankee pragmatism, and the progeny—pragmatic piety—has been with us ever since.[7]

Religion in seventeenth-century America required an intensity of conduct and feeling greater than most men could sustain. Yet somehow this high-pitched fervor, this desire to hear and obey the Word, left behind a quality of faith that lingered, though ofttimes expressed in other forms. Barrett Wendell, the literary critic, called it "reverent unbelief." In

5. Conrad Wright: *The Liberal Christians. Essays on American Unitarian History* (Boston, 1970), ch. 1.

6. See Frederick B. Tolles: "Quietism Versus Enthusiasm: The Philadelphia Quakers and the Great Awakening," in *Quakers and the Atlantic Culture*, 102–3.

7. See Cotton Mather: *The Christian Cynick. A Brief Essay on a Merciful Saviour* (Boston, 1716).

Virginia, Landon Carter leaned to "practical godliness." Though he had little use for the formalities of religion, he was an intensely devout man.[8] "My faith is the greatest of faiths and the least of faiths," sang Walt Whitman in 1855.

As Reinhold Niebuhr has observed, we are "at once the most religious and the most secular of western nations. How shall we explain this paradox? Could it be that we are most religious partly in consequence of being the most secular culture?" Whence cometh our "Godly materialism"? Niebuhr asked. "Perhaps we are so religious because religion has two forms among us. One challenges the gospel of prosperity, success, and achievement of heaven on earth. The other claims to furnish religious instruments for the attainment of these objectives."[9]

IV. BIFARIOUS SOCIETIES

> Englishmen are distinguished by their traditions and ceremonials,
> And also by their affection for their colonies and their contempt for their colonials.
>
> OGDEN NASH, "England Expects"

Too little has been written about the origins of American society; and this complex subject has been made even more obscure by the ambivalent intentions of genealogists and filiopietists. On the one hand, to perpetuate the legend of America as a land of refuge and opportunity for the oppressed, their ancestors must have been humble men and sorely persecuted. On the other, however, to satisfy the desire for lofty lineage, their forefathers must also have been aristocrats, or gentlemen

8. See Jack P. Greene, ed.: *The Diary of Colonel Landon Carter* (Charlottesville, 1965), I, 26; Robert Beverley: *The History and Present State of Virginia*, ed. Louis B. Wright (Chapel Hill, 1947), 104.

9. Niebuhr: *Pious and Secular America* (New York, 1958), 1–2, 4, 6, 8, 10–11.

at the very least. Neither image is accurate, of course; not even both together. But we still have not got very far beyond Edward Ward's judgment at the close of the seventeenth century: "Bishops, Bailiffs, and Bastards, were the three Terrible Persecutions which chiefly drove our unhappy Brethren to seek their Fortunes in our Forreign Colonies." [1]

When Thomas Jefferson called the American plowman "Nature's Nobleman," he indulged more irony than he realized. Ever since the seventeenth century—when Samuel Maverick settled in Massachusetts as a misanthrope, went back to England for civilized companionship, then returned to Massachusetts as a royal commissioner—colonial frontiersmen had craved *both* isolation and sociability. The self-sufficient yeoman often turned out to be a gregarious fellow who disliked loneliness. Although the Puritans spoke often of being "knit together" in communities, they also were the first to make frontiersmen the avatars of American wilderness virtues. John Cotton caught part of the paradox in his comments upon the exile of Roger Williams.

> The Jurisdiction (whence a man is banished) is but small, and the Countrey round about it, large and fruitful: where a man may make his choice of variety of more pleasant, and profitable seats, than he leaveth behinde him. In which respect, *Banishment in this countrey, is not counted so much a confinement, as an enlargement.* [2]

William Bradford wept when Plymouth began to encourage men to move outward in order to bolster the colony with new settlements. When good farms north of Duxbury were allotted "to special persons that would promise to live" there, "this remedy proved worse than the disease; for within a few years those that had thus got footing there rent themselves

1. Ward: *A Trip to New-England with a Character of the Country and People* (London, 1699), 3.

2. "A Reply to Mr. Williams His Examination: and Answer of the Letters Sent to Him by John Cotton," *Publications of the Naragansett Club* (Providence, 1862), series 1, II, 19. Italics mine.

away," and formed the separate town of Marshfield. How were responsible leaders supposed to control the collective individualism of agricultural acquisitiveness? Neither Bradford knew, nor Cotton Mather in 1690 when he admitted that the insoluble problem was how "at once we may Advance our Husbandry, and yet Forbear our Dispersion." [3]

Elsewhere the contradictory tendencies of companionate misanthropy took more whimsical forms. On the south shore of Currituck Inlet, in North Carolina, there "dwelt a marooner that modestly called himself a hermit," says William Byrd, "though he forfeited that name by suffering a wanton female to cohabit with him." The community living just outside Germantown, Pennsylvania, on the Wissahickon River—known as the "Woman in the Wilderness" (1708–48)—consisted entirely of male hermits! And at the Ephrata Cloister near Lancaster, Pennsylvania, people associated with the celibate sect were permitted to live in "sinful wedlock." [4]

What ultimately mattered, however, was not the way men isolated themselves, but the ways they organized and perceived themselves in society. Over and over again, I find in all the colonies recognition that provincial élites were really what Jefferson called "tinsel-aristocracies." In the Chesapeake region, men with the best fortunes derived their success from entrepreneurial activities—land speculation, moneylending, manufacturing, and law practice—as much as from their operations as producers of tobacco. [5] When Dr. Benjamin Bullivant

3. Bradford: *Of Plymouth Plantation, 1620–1647*, ed. S. E. Morison (New York, 1953), 253–4; Miller: *New England Mind from Colony to Province*, 51. See also Peter Carroll: *Puritanism and the Wilderness* (New York, 1969), 2–4.

4. Louis B. Wright, ed.: *The Prose Works of William Byrd of Westover* (Cambridge, Mass., 1966), 179; Peter Brock: *Pacifism in the United States from the Colonial Era to the First World War* (Princeton, 1968), 177–8.

5. Jefferson to John Adams, October 28, 1813, in Lester J. Cappon, ed.: *The Adams-Jefferson Letters* (Chapel Hill, 1959), II, 389, 391; Aubrey C. Land: "Economic Base and Social Structure: The Northern Chesapeake in the 18th Century," *Journal of Economic History*, XXV (1965), 646–8.

visited New York in 1697, he remarked upon his host "whose entertainment is generous & like a Nobleman though a merchant by his profession." At times the "earthly gods" of New England, with their conflicting loyalties to town meeting (for its political and economic power) and parish (with its ecclesiastical jurisdiction), found it difficult to establish proper criteria for leadership in a bourgeois aristocracy. When Benjamin Pickman of Salem built his fine mansion in 1750, he had the stair risers and panels ornamented with carved and gilded codfish. How perfectly symbolic of what Samuel Eliot Morison has called New England's "codfish aristocracy." [6]

There was an element of contradiction also in the notion of a Quaker aristocracy. Nevertheless, Pennsylvania did have its "mercantile aristocrats," as Professor Tolles has shown. The situation in which these men found themselves, with great wealth and political power, accentuated the awkwardness of their position in colonial society. During the first generation in Pennsylvania, Quaker leaders, like other Englishmen, held a traditional view of the natural, hierarchical ordering of social classes. But while they assumed that certain men with particular qualities ought to enjoy political and religious leadership, they also refused to observe customary tokens of deference: uncovering the head, bowing, or using complimentary titles of address. Although the Quakers opposed social deference, they did not oppose a deferential society. They accepted the structure of society, but rejected its social conventions. Insofar as early Friends were equalitarian, they confined that belief to the equality of each individual in the sight of God and the ability of every man to find God within himself apart from scriptural revelation. [7]

. . .

6. Wayne Andrews, ed.: "A Glance at New York in 1697. The Travel Diary of Dr. Benjamin Bullivant," *New-York Historical Society Quarterly*, XL (1956), 11–12; Clifford K. Shipton: *Sibley's Harvard Graduates*, XIV (Boston, 1968), 485; Morison: *Maritime History of Massachusetts, 1783–1860* (Boston, 1921), 25.

7. Tolles: *Meeting House and Counting House*, 109, 114.

AFTER A BRIEF PERIOD of settlement in the coastal villages of Massachusetts, many immigrants moved inland to plant themselves permanently in communities like Andover. In the process they raised families which were extended in structure, closely knit, and relatively immobile. Fathers became virtual patriarchs, controlled their lands until death, and maintained influence over mature sons for extraordinary lengths of time. Kinship networks began to form which would bind communities together for more than a century to come. By the third generation, family structure in colonial New England had become remarkably complex, and a circumstance described below by Philip Greven had fully emerged—the extended-nuclear family:

> The characteristic family structure which emerged in Andover with the maturing of the second generation during the 1670's and 1680's was a combination of both the classical extended family and the nuclear family. This distinctive form of family structure is best described as a *modified extended family*—defined as a kinship group of two or more generations living within a single community in which the dependence of the children upon their parents continues after the children have married and are living under a separate roof. This family structure is a *modified* extended family because all members of the family are not "gathered into a single household," but it is still an *extended* family because the newly created conjugal unit of husband and wife live in separate households in close proximity to their parents and siblings and continue to be economically dependent in some respects upon their parents. And because of the continuing dependence of the second generation upon their first-generation fathers, who continue to own most of the family land throughout the better part of their lives, the family in seventeenth-century Andover was *patriarchal* as well.[8]

Why this should have occurred in the colonies is not entirely clear; but at least a partial explanation is possible. At

8. Greven: "Family Structure in 17th-century Andover, Massachusetts," *William and Mary Quarterly*, 3d series, XXIII (1966), 254–5.

the outset, early American society may have been even more "traditional" in character than English society itself. "The colonial setting," as Greven remarks, "may have proved hospitable, in many instances, to forms of familial and communal stability which presumably had once dominated the English countryside." The amount of physical mobility, once the first period of colonization had passed, may have been less than in comparable communities of England. Families in colonial towns were at first, perhaps, a little healthier and longer lived, more extended in structure, and maintained more effective parental authority over children. By the close of the seventeenth century, however, as population growth and social change in the colonies proceeded more rapidly than in England, traditional family structure may have been abruptly shaken by the need to accommodate to change. The result was a biformity in the basic unit of social organization.[9]

There being a connection between idleness, unproductivity, and immorality, and there being much to do and learn in a new society, men often seemed to pursue culture in a relentless, joyless way. Pragmatic behavior, thereby, became an article of faith. Thus John Smith, a Philadelphian, informed his diary in 1746 that "for my part, tho' I love a free social Conversation as well as anybody, Yet I would have it turn upon such subjects as are Improving at the same time they Entertain." Random reading was uncommon in the colonies, as Louis B. Wright has shown. Rather, "purposeful reading" provided the usual fare: Vaughan's *Directions for Health, both Naturall and Artificiall*, Dalton's *Country Justice*, Barriffe's *Military Discipline; or, The Young Artilleryman*, and *A Verie Perfect Discourse and Order How to Know the Age of a Horse*.[1] The quest for productive leisure would later burgeon in a nation hyper-

9. Although my emphasis here differs in certain respects from Greven's, I have been much influenced by his excellent book, *Four Generations: Population, Land, and Family in Colonial Andover, Massachusetts* (Ithaca, 1970), esp. ch. 8.

1. Tolles: *Meeting House and Counting House*, 138–9; Louis B. Wright: "The Purposeful Reading of Our Colonial Ancestors," *ELH. A Journal of English Literary History*, IV (1937), 90–2.

organized for recreation, from Little League to yoga classes.

To be sure, not every colonial abided by Poor Richard's proverb that "Leisure is a time for doing something useful." A very human quotient of mischief contributed to the quiddity of colonial life. In New England, not surprisingly, Calvinist conceptions of criminality and social deviance were ambiguous. On the one hand there was a deterministic attitude toward offenders. They could barely be held responsible for their misconduct, and were asked to accept punishment simply because universal logic so required. Nonetheless, every delinquent who came before the bench did so as a free agent, completely culpable for his actions. He could not plead that he had been forced into sinful impulses by divine decree. Yet ultimately, and ironically, he would be asked to endorse the conclusions of his court. "The people of the community," Kai Erikson remarks, "vaguely aware of the contradictions of their own doctrine, were somehow anxious for the condemned man to forgive them." [2]

The bifarious nature of colonial society was apparent to its members, I suspect, though some tensions were more obvious than others. Few were then aware that owing to the imperatives of rural economy, extended-nuclear families, sociable frontiersmen, and productive leisure had become benchmarks of American life. Rather more realized the pervasiveness of ordered violence and planned irresponsibility. And no one could ignore the ubiquity of a "democratical despotism" or a codfish aristocracy. As colonials tried to cope with these incongruities, tried to rationalize their lives, tried to define what it meant to be English outside of England, they inevitably fell into new and bisociative patterns of thought.

The ambiguities of political anglophobia, for example, relentlessly compounded the complexities of cultural anglophilia.[3]

2. See Erikson: *Wayward Puritans. A Study in the Sociology of Deviance* (New York, 1966), 63, 192, 195.
3. James Fenimore Cooper perceived this phenomenon superbly and made it a major theme of *Satanstoe* (1845), one of his finest historical novels.

Thus Benjamin Rush and Arthur Lee, both educated in Britain during the 1760's, loved the "home" culture but abhorred its policies. In America, meanwhile, disparate provincial and regional identities were emerging just when improved communications were drawing the colonies together. Noah Welles of Connecticut caught the essence of these dualisms in 1764, and tried valiantly to reconcile them. "If therefore a principle of self-love, prompts us to seek our own particular happiness, because it is ours, the same principle must induce us to love our country and seek its welfare, because our own is involved in it, and inseparably connected with it." [4]

As early as 1676, an English clergyman traveling in Virginia had remarked upon the "American Britain" in the colonies. Among the commonest pseudonyms used during the decades of controversy, the 1760's and 1770's, were "Britannus-Americanus," and "British American." Authors designated their homeland as "British America"; and their hybrid identities were symptomatic of their desire for both the benefits of being American and the privileges of being English. [5] After 1763 they took great pains to insist upon the immemorial rights of Englishmen; but by 1775–6 a number had begun to explicate the prerogatives of Americans. Such shifts tell much about changing colonial consciousness on the eve of Revolution.

Although Independence alone would resolve this bifarious quality in American thought, more than a decade before 1776 colonials seized upon a different device for co-ordinating contradictory tendencies. They satisfied both their cultural anglophilia and their political anglophobia by borrowing the "opposition" tradition from English political culture—modes of anti-authoritarian polemic developed by "commonwealthmen"

4. Welles: *Patriotism Described and Recommended.* . . . (New London, 1764), 8–10.
5. "The Life of Tho. Reade . . . Written by his Own Hand . . . 1692," manuscript in the Alderman Library, University of Virginia, p. 27; "Britannus-Americanus" in *The Boston Gazette*, July 23, 1764, Sept. 7, 1767; Oxenbridge Thacher: *Sentiments of a British American* (Boston, 1764).

since the early eighteenth century—and made of it a new and explosive ideological weapon.[6]

V. Minds, Manners, and Morals

"May not a man have several voices, Robin, as well as two complexions?"

Nathaniel Hawthorne, *My Kinsman, Major Molineux*

We have seen how ambivalent the colonists could be about their environment: it seemed alternately a "howling wilderness" and an "Earthly Paradeis." By the eighteenth century these feelings had been reconciled for some, and rationalized by others. Young John Dickinson wrote home from London in 1754 that "America is, to be sure, a wilderness, & yet that wilderness to me is more pleasing than this charming garden. . . . Tis rude, but it's innocent. Tis wild, but it's private. There life is a stream pure & unruffled, here an ocean briny & tempestuous. There we enjoy life, here we spend it."[1]

It took much longer, however, to reconcile the colonists' contradictory feelings about the first inhabitants of North America and concomitantly their uncertainty about their own natures. Mary Mungummory, the "traveling whore o' Dorset" in John Barth's *The Sot-Weed Factor*, poses the critical question: "Does essential savagery lurk beneath the skin of civilization, or does essential civilization lurk beneath the skin of savagery?"[2] Neither she nor the colonists could answer easily.

Throughout the sixteenth and well into the seventeenth century, Europeans had disagreed among themselves over the origin and nature of America's Indians. Several schools of

6. Bernard Bailyn: *The Origins of American Politics* (New York, 1968), 38–9, 53–4 ff.
1. "John Dickinson's London Letters," *Pa. Mag. Hist. & Biog.*, LXXXVI (1962), 275.
2. *The Sot-Weed Factor* (New York, 1960), 638.

thought emerged, each originating among Spanish theorists, each having adherents in England.[3] Even in the first generation of English colonization, it became clear that Englishmen were deeply troubled about the natives. Responses in London to news of the Virginia massacre in 1622 were characteristic: a desire to destroy the Indians entirely, coupled with a reluctant recognition that the white man's primary responsibility was to civilize them.[4]

There were, of course, such men as John Eliot, whose missionary work brought many Indians to conversion and tears— "so we parted greatly rejoycing for such sorrowing"—and Robert Beverley of Virginia, who liked to think of himself as a "white Indian" because of his forthrightness.[5] More characteristic, however, was the Puritans' sanctimonious sense of mission, best summed up perhaps by a story concerning the early settlers of Milford, Connecticut. (One fervently hopes that it is only apocryphal.) In 1640 the inhabitants held a town meeting to discuss the problem of dispossessed Indian lands. Their ultimate reasoning was purportedly inscribed in the minutes as follows:

1. The earth is the Lord's and the fullness thereof. Voted.
2. The Lord can dispose of the earth to his saints. Voted.
3. We are his saints. Voted.[6]

3. Lee E. Huddleston: *Origins of the American Indians: European Concepts, 1492–1729* (Austin, 1967), vii, 127.

4. Susan M. Kingsbury, ed.: *The Records of the Virginia Company of London* (Washington, D.C., 1933), III, 553–4; see also Richard Hakluyt's letter of April 15, 1609, printed in Edward D. Neill: *History of the Virginia Company of London* (Albany, 1869), 27–9.

5. Alden T. Vaughan: *New England Frontier. Puritans and Indians, 1620–1675* (Boston, 1965), 249; Louis B. Wright: *The First Gentlemen of Virginia. Intellectual Qualities of the Early Colonial Ruling Class* (Charlottesville, 1964), 286.

6. Wilcomb Washburn, ed.: *The Indian and the White Man* (Garden City, 1964), 177; Louis B. Wright: *Religion and Empire. The Alliance Between Piety and Commerce in English Expansion, 1558–1625* (Chapel Hill, 1943), 158.

A. J. Liebling caught the bitter irony of this English "right of discovery" over Indian lands in North America, and rephrased it as the principle of the "Pre-eminent Right of the First Trespasser." [7]

In 1660 a sturdy ship called the *Gilded Beaver* set sail from Amsterdam destined for New Netherland. The cargo in her hold consisted of "all kinds of war materials, etc., for the new colony, besides small psalm and prayer books." On the deck above these Bibles and bullets, two dominies gathered the crew and passengers twice each day for prayers and songs. Attitudes had scarcely altered a century later. John Bartram's casual remark was characteristic: "Unless we bang the Indians stoutly, and make them fear us, they will never love us, nor keep the peace long with us." [8] The very concept of the "noble savage" exposed deep-rooted feelings of ambivalence; and descriptions of the Indian in early American literature depict him simultaneously as an agent of Satan as well as a noble savage, an enemy to civilization and yet the tutor of civilized men.

Transactions in which Indians sold their lands to white men were anomalous because the Indians often retained nearly full use of the property being sold—at least for a time. The Indian might sell his land without losing control of it; yet just as often he lost control of the land anyway without ever selling it. William Penn treated the natives of his province as virtually sovereign owners of the land; nonetheless, he accepted Charles II's claim to rule the entire area!

Washington Irving would later capture the pitiful paradoxes of the Indians' position in American life: "Luxury spreads its ample board before their eyes; but they are excluded from the banquet. Plenty revels over the fields; but they are starving in the midst of its abundance: the whole

7. "The Lake of the Cui-ui Eaters," *The New Yorker* (Jan. 15, 1955), 36.

8. Ellis L. Raesly: *Portrait of New Netherland* (New York, 1945), 312–13; William Darlington: *Memorials of John Bartram and Humphrey Marshall* (Philadelphia, 1849), 256. Nathaniel Hawthorne so often portrayed his archetypal Puritan elder with a Bible in one hand and a sword in the other.

wilderness has blossomed into a garden; but they feel as reptiles that infest it." [9]

Shifting from the "Indian problem" to the "Negro problem," we first must recognize that Englishmen were as ambivalent in their attitudes toward black men as their colonial cousins were. Many of the remarks made by Americans, both for and against slavery, were commonplace in Georgian England. American anti-slavery writers borrowed readily from their British counterparts, and reformers on both sides of the Atlantic shared a common set of assumptions.

There were, however, certain questions concerning the nature of black men which arose from intimate daily experience with them; and because of these questions, the "Negro problem" took a peculiarly American form. Winthrop Jordan has put it this way:

> The American colonists had more reason than Europeans, for instance, to find ways to express the social distance between Negroes and themselves. Yet slavery, which created this need, also answered it, for slavery served admirably as a means of categorization. Americans showed less need than Europeans to place the Negro in an ordered creation because slavery firmly fixed his position in their own immediate social world. On the other hand, American colonials had greater reason to emphasize the physical differences between themselves and Negroes in order to confirm the validity of their social order. It is clear, certainly, that in regard to physical distinctions Americans far more than Europeans were subject to powerful stresses arising from their intimate social relationships with Negroes.[1]

The underlying moral and social contradictions inherent in slavery since antiquity were more manifest when the institution became closely linked with American colonization; for the opening up of a New World was seen by many as an opportunity for mankind to create a more perfect society. By the close

9. "Traits of Indian Character," in *The Sketch Book of Geoffrey Crayon* [1819–20] (New York, 1961), 351–2.

1. Jordan: *White Over Black. American Attitudes Toward the Negro, 1550–1812* (Chapel Hill, 1968), 255.

of the colonial period, we encounter the irony of slaveholders fighting for the natural rights of man. George Bancroft would have to concede that "while Virginia, by the concessions of a republican government, was constituted the asylum of liberty, by one of the strange contradictions in human affairs, it became the abode of hereditary bondsmen." Dr. Samuel Johnson had put the problem most succinctly: "How is it that we hear the loudest *yelps* for liberty among the drivers of negroes?" [2]

Conflicts between slavery and Christianity in America grew more severe with the passage of time. Those evangelicals who hoped to bring blacks to Christ realized early that the greatest barrier they faced was the slaveowner's fear that conversion would weaken his grip on his chattel. Accordingly, reformers were obliged to argue that Christianizing Negroes would make them more docile rather than less, better slaves rather than worse.[3] In 1710, Cotton Mather would comment that "when we have Slaves in our Houses, we are to treat them with *Humanity*, we are so to treat them that their *Slavery* may really be their *Happiness*." Thomas Jefferson, more than any other figure perhaps, embodied and articulated the American dilemma. He combined heartfelt hostility to slavery with a deep conviction of Negro inferiority. "We have the wolf by the ears," he wrote in 1820, "and can neither hold him, nor safely let him go. Justice is in the one scale, and self-preservation in the other." [4]

A paramount source of tension lay in the problem of sexual attitudes and relations. No white believed miscegenation desirable. Yet its practice was widespread and its consequences were highly visible. "English colonials," as Jordan observes,

> were caught in the push and pull of an irreconcilable conflict between desire and aversion for interracial sex-

2. David Brion Davis: *The Problem of Slavery in Western Culture* (Ithaca, 1966), ix, 3–4, 10, 12, 21–25.

3. Jordan: *White Over Black*, 179–80, 190–1.

4. Mather: *Theopolis Americana* (Boston, 1710), 22; Jefferson to John Holmes, April 22, 1820, in Paul L. Ford, ed.: *Writings of Thomas Jefferson* (New York, 1899), XII, 159.

ual union. The perceptual prerequisite for this conflict is so obvious as to be too easily overlooked: desire and aversion rested on the bedrock fact that white men perceived Negroes as being both *alike and different* from themselves. Without perception of similarity, no desire and no widespread gratification was possible. Without perception of difference, on the other hand, no aversion to miscegenation nor tension concerning it could have arisen.[5]

The colonists' inability to admit *free* Negroes to social privileges seemed even more flagrant in a country which by European standards lay wide open as a land of opportunity. Paradoxically, also, while chattel slavery stood as a demonstration of social subordination, it was applied only to people of color. Consequently, the formal status of slave became a model of what white Americans must never become. Moreover, the close bond between slavery and blackness meant that free black men would by definition be socially anomalous, contradictions in terms. They were not only a bad example to slaves, their mere existence undermined the rationalizations underpinning slavery as a social system. By the mid-eighteenth century, then, many settlers recognized that their colonies offered both a new freedom unknown in Europe and a new slavery whose deprivations had ceased to exist in like degree across the Atlantic.[6]

All of which affected whites and blacks alike in ways both complex and manifest still. After Josiah Quincy, Jr., visited South Carolina in 1773, the problem of slavery haunted his thoughts. Recognizing it as a "perfect misery," he noted the beginnings of a dominant but unremarked bisociation[7] in

5. Jordan: *White Over Black*, 137, 149.
6. *Ibid*, 134–5, 108; Louis Hartz: *The Founding of New Societies* (New York, 1964), 55.
7. Arthur Koestler performed a valuable service when he brought the concept of bisociation to bear on the study of cultural history. He found it a convenient descriptive term in referring to mental occurrences simultaneously associated with two contexts normally incompatible. Bisociation describes the circumstance when two unrelated modes of thought collide or intersect, and each is then viewed in the light of

American civilization: whites who unconsciously affect the dialect and behavior of blacks. "By reason of this slavery," Quincy wrote,

> the children are early impressed with infamous and destructive ideas, and become extremely vitiated in their manners; they contract a negroish kind of accent, pronunciation and dialect, as well as ridiculous kind of behaviour: even many of the grown people, and especially the women, are vastly infected with the same disorder. Parents instead of talking to their very young children in the unmeaning way with us, converse to them as though they were speaking to a new imported African.[8]

The Negro, needless to say, was affected even more profoundly. Under slavery, African forms of social organization, family life, religion, language, and even art were transformed, leaving the slave neither an African still nor fully an American, but rather a man suspended between two cultures, unable to participate fully in either. W. E. B. DuBois and others would later detail the implications of "this double-consciousness, this sense of always looking at oneself through the eyes of others, of measuring one's soul by the tape of a world that looks on in amused contempt and pity."[9]

Eventually white men, too, began reluctantly to recognize the paradoxical implications of chattel slavery. In 1772, Daniel Bliss composed for a black client an epitaph which was engraved on a tombstone in Concord, Massachusetts:

> Here lies the body of John Jack, a native of
>   Africa . . .
> Tho' born in a land of slavery
> He was born free.
> Tho' he lived in a land of liberty,

---

the other. See *Insight and Outlook. An Inquiry into the Common Foundations of Science, Art, and Social Ethics* (New York, 1949), esp. 36–7.

8. "Journal of Josiah Quincy, Junior, 1773," Massachusetts Historical Society *Proceedings*, XLIX (Boston, 1916), 456–7.

9. DuBois: *The Souls of Black Folk* (Chicago, 1903), 3.

> He lived a slave.
> Till by his honest, tho' stolen, labor,
> He acquired the source of slavery,
> Which gave him his freedom;
> Tho' not long before
> Death, the grand tyrant,
> Gave him his final emancipation,
> And set him on a footing with kings.
> Tho' a slave to vice,
> He practiced those virtues
> Without which kings are but slaves.[1]

In the nineteenth century this became the most famous epitaph in America, and was reprinted in English, French, German, and Scandinavian newspapers. It is more than fitting testimony to the "unthinking decision" made by English colonials back in the seventeenth century.

As WE HAVE RECENTLY BEEN SHOWN, the European Enlightenment was characterized by several sorts of tensions. The *philosophes'* experience, Peter Gay points out, "was a dialectical struggle for autonomy, an attempt to assimilate the two pasts they had inherited—Christian and pagan—and to pit them against one another and thus to secure their independence." The fascination with antiquity and the "tension with Christianity" constituted essential elements in the progression through which the scheme of *Aufklärung* ideas developed.[2]

The Enlightenment in America was also characterized by dualisms, but at a different level of social and intellectual intensity. Nonetheless, their overall pattern is significant, I think, in the emergence of an American style.

Ever since the Maypole of Merrymount, there existed in New England's psyche a pervasive opposition between spiritual inclinations and earthy humor. Throughout the seventeenth century (in England and America), men had faced the prob-

1. George Tolman: *John Jack, the Slave, and Daniel Bliss, the Tory* (Concord, 1902), 4.
2. Gay: *The Enlightenment: An Interpretation. The Rise of Modern Paganism* (New York, 1967), xi–xii.

lem of maintaining an equilibrium between reason and passion. Wit and morality, therefore, had been regarded as antithetical. By the first decades of the new century, however, Americans began to reconcile Christianity and levity in a way best described as sober mirth, or moralized wit. Benjamin Colman (1673–1747) pleaded for "sober mirth" in Boston. "A great deal of Pleasantry there is in the Town, and very graceful and charming it is so far as it is Innocent and Wise. Our Wit like our Air is clear, and Keen, and in very Many 'tis exalted by a Polite Education, meeting with good Natural Parts." Mock jeremiads became commonplace by the second decade of the eighteenth century, and John Wise would weld a popular alliance between gravity and facetiousness. James Franklin and his younger brother would do the same during the 1720's. The *Courant* called its attempts at social reform in Boston "Joco-Serious." If the element of burlesque was obvious, the attempt at seriousness ran equally deep.[3]

Benjamin Franklin eventually emerged as the prime exemplar of witty moralism in eighteenth-century America. In his earliest published work, Franklin took the pseudonym "Silence Dogood," thereby relying on his readers to realize that Cotton Mather, author of *Essays to Do Good*, was rarely silent. Franklin's famous *Autobiography* owed much, to be sure, to English tradition. His narrative of a young tradesman must be placed alongside those of Joseph Andrews, Robinson Crusoe, and John Bunyan's allegorical Pilgrim. Nonetheless, the *Autobiography* achieves an American mixture of naïve perfectionism and skeptical empiricism: "I balanc'd some time between Principle and Inclination." Franklin was ever the practical moralist, and part of his enduring fascination rests in the

3. *A Memorial Between Jest and Earnest, from Ignoramus the First* (Philadelphia, 1691); Colman: *The Government and Improvement of Mirth . . . In Three Sermons on Civil and Natural Mirth, Carnal and Vicious Mirth, and Spiritual and Holy Joy* (Boston, 1707), esp. A4; Miller: *New England Mind from Colony to Province*, 271–2, 292–3, 300–1, 332–3, 335, 340–2; Thomas Symmes: *Utile Dulci. Or, a Joco-Serious Dialogue, Concerning Regular Singing* (Boston, 1723).

tension between what the real Ben *did* and the advice he offered to young men.[4]

An Anglican through the greater part of his life, he rejected almost all of Anglican theology, yet kept strict Lents, probably took communion, edited the Book of Common Prayer, and urged liturgical devotions upon his family. Franklin was an eminently reasonable man who maintained a deep skepticism about the power of reason. A model of industriousness, he retired from his printing shop at the age of forty-two. A cautious and prudent man, he was also a revolutionary. And as Leslie Stephen remarked, Franklin had "the acuteness of the philosopher . . . curiously blended with the cunning of the trader." [5]

The American Enlightenment may best be understood in terms of the supposedly antithetical terms "pragmatic" and "idealistic." Franklin, Jefferson, and their contemporaries did not rigidly separate theory and experience. If they valued empiricism, they also cherished moral and ethical knowledge. The Baconian emphasis upon experimental naturalism achieved a new field of influence and means of dissemination when Franklin founded the American Philosophical Society in 1743. Nevertheless, in both morality and politics Franklin often took theory as a guide to action, with the explicit purpose of increasing man's understanding and improving his lot.[6]

By 1750, America had become simultaneously a paradigm of two very different European aspirations. Admirers of primitive simplicity, as Peter Gay points out, could cite the colonies

4. David Levin: "*The Autobiography of Benjamin Franklin:* The Puritan Experimenter in Life and Art," *In Defense of Historical Literature* (New York, 1967), 58–76; *The Autobiography* (New Haven, 1964), 87.

5. Alfred Owen Aldridge: *Benjamin Franklin and Nature's God* (Durham, 1967), 47–57, 271; Stephen: *History of English Thought* (New York, 1876), II, 300.

6. See Adrienne Koch: "Pragmatic Wisdom and the American Enlightenment," *William and Mary Quarterly*, 3d series, XVIII (1961), 313, 316–17, 321, 328–9.

as readily as those who admired the achievements of civilized man. "This duality was the secret of Benjamin Franklin's enormous success as a missionary of the American cause: he seemed to embody both the virtues of nature and the triumphs of civility; he was—or rather, in his shrewdness, enormously enjoyed playing—the savage as philosopher." [7]

Similarly, Jonathan Edwards, who so often has been regarded as Franklin's fraternal twin in the American Enlightenment—they came from the same New England womb but bore no resemblance—also chose the language of paradox to express his central ideas. "There came into my mind," he wrote in his *Personal Narrative*, "a sweet Sense of the glorious Majesty and Grace of GOD, that I know not how to express. I seemed to see them both in a sweet Conjunction: Majesty and Meekness join'd together: it was a sweet and gentle, and holy Majesty; and also a majestic Meekness; an awful Sweetness; a high, and great, and holy Gentleness." In his poignant sketch of Sarah Pierrepont, his bride-to-be, Edwards compared a justified soul to the "peacefulness and ravishment" of an opening flower. "The soul of a true Christian . . . appeared like such a little white flower as we see in the spring of the year; low and humble on the ground, opening its bosom to receive the pleasant beams of the sun's glory; rejoicing as it were in *a calm rapture*." [8]

Both Edwards and Franklin were conscious of a certain equipoise within themselves between pride and humility. "Even if I could conceive that I had compleatly overcome [pride]," Franklin wrote in his *Autobiography*, "I should probably be proud of my Humility." Many of the colonists cultivated humble pride and were usually the first to recognize it in themselves. "Lord, grant that I may always be right," prayed a Carolinian, "for thou knowest that I am hard to turn." John

7. Gay: "The Enlightenment," in *The Comparative Approach to American History*, ed. C. Vann Woodward (New York, 1968), 41.

8. Daniel B. Shea: *Spiritual Autobiography in Early America* (Princeton, 1968), 202–3; Clarence H. Faust, ed.: *Jonathan Edwards: Representative Selections* (New York, 1935), 56, 63.

Checkley, preaching in Massachusetts Bay in 1719, reminded his listeners that "there is none so *proud* as the *proud-humble* man, who is proud of his Humility!" In New York, Dr. Hamilton encountered "a face where there was so much effronterie under a pretended mask of modesty." And in Virginia, a Carter criticized a Randolph as a "rank Tory, a proud, humble parasite, a fawning sycophant to his patron." [9]

A particularized expression of humble pride took the form of ostentatious austerity. The Quakers brought this biformity to its most sublime attainment: the paradox of a Quaker aesthetic. Wives and daughters of the Philadelphia grandees compensated for their self-denial in color and ornamentation by having their clothing made only of the finest fabrics. John Reynell caught the essence of it in a letter to London in 1738. He requested two "Japan'd Black Corner Cubbords, with 2 Doors to each, no Red in 'em, *of the best Sort but Plain*." During the 1780's, Brissot de Warville, a French visitor, noticed that furniture in Quaker houses had "the appearance of simplicity; but in many instances it is certainly expensive." [1] In William Byrd's *History of the Dividing Line* he remarks, with some sardonic amusement, upon passing by "no less than two Quaker meetinghouses, one of which had an awkward ornament on the west end of it that seemed to ape a steeple. I must own I expected no such piece of foppery from a sect of so much outside simplicity." [2]

Alongside practical moralism, humble pride, and ostentatious austerity, we might also place prurient prudishness. Only in Boston, perhaps, could a madam keep a brothel near the

9. Franklin: *Autobiography*, 160; [Checkley]: *Choice Dialogues Between a Godly Minister and an Honest Countryman, Concerning Election and Predestination* (Boston, 1720), 18; Carl Bridenbaugh, ed.: *Gentleman's Progress. The Itinerarium of Dr. Alexander Hamilton*, 1744 (Chapel Hill, 1948), 84; Wright: *First Gentlemen of Virginia*, 58, 162, 253.

1. Frederick B. Tolles: *Quakers and the Atlantic Culture* (New York, 1960), 76-7, 79, 86-8; Gary B. Nash: *Quakers and Politics. Pennsylvania, 1681-1726* (Princeton, 1968), 325.

2. Louis B. Wright, ed.: *The Prose Works of William Byrd of Westover* (Cambridge, Mass., 1966), 193.

Old South Meetinghouse and be known throughout town as "the little Prude of Pleasure." [3] Dr. Alexander Hamilton's ambivalence (or self-deception) showed through at Newport, Rhode Island, where he spent an entire morning closeted with the works of a Dutch antiquarian, "from whom all our modern sallacious poets have borrowed their thoughts. I did not read this book upon account of its liquorice contents, but only because I knew it to be a piece of excellent good Latin." When Elbridge Gerry served in Congress, he remarked upon the variety of pretty young ladies with whom he craved "an innocent spell of puritanical phylandering." [4]

In William Byrd, II, the patriarchal aristocrat as perpetual adolescent, we find the most candid combination of prurience and prudishness in colonial America. Two girls visited his camp in Princess Anne County, "one of which was very handsome and the other very willing. However, we only saluted [kissed] them, and if we committed any sin at all, it was only in our hearts." In 1741, aged sixty-seven, Byrd recorded in his diary that he "played the fool with Sarah, God forgive me. However, I prayed and had coffee." In an autobiographical sketch, Byrd described himself thus in the third person:

> Love was born to him so long before Reason, that it has ever since slighted its rebukes, as much as old Fopps do the good sence of a young man. However this Frailty has never been without some check, For Diana threw such a Weight of Grace into the opposite scale, that the Ballance has commonly been held very even. And if the Love-scale has happen'd to be carry'd down sometimes, the Counterpoise has not fail'd to mount it up again very suddenly. [5]

The least likely American satyr of the eighteenth century may well have been John Adams. "The curses against fornica-

3. *New England Courant*, March 5, 1722.

4. Bridenbaugh: *Gentleman's Progress*, 138, 152–3, 164; Gerry to Rufus King, April 7, 1785, Gerry Papers, Library of Congress.

5. Wright: *Prose Works of William Byrd*, 6, 58, 256; Byrd: "INAMORATO L'Oiseaux," in *Another Secret Diary of William Byrd . . . With Letters & Literary Exercises, 1696–1726*, ed. Maude H. Woodfin (Richmond, 1942), 276, 279–80.

tion and adultery," he wrote, "and the prohibition of every wanton glance or libidinous ogle at a woman, I believe to be the only system that ever did or ever will preserve a republic in the world. There is a paradox for you. . . . I say then that national morality never was and never can be preserved without the utmost purity and chastity in women; and without national morality a republican government cannot be maintained."

Yet Adams had what one critic has called "a sensuous apprehension of experience," and his writing abounds with suitable vividness: kissed girls "glowing like furnaces"; that "small, spungy, muscular substance growing fast to the rock, in figure and feeling resembling a young girl's breast." Adams was, as he recorded in his autobiography, "of an amorous disposition, and very early, from ten or eleven years of age was very fond of the society of females." [6] He was torn, as Professor Bailyn has shown, "between ambition and integrity, between the desire to appear knowing and sophisticated and the inability to be so, between the longing to retreat into a sensitive inner world of feeling and the need for self-mastery and control over external reality." The tensions between these contradictory tendencies affected his life in profound degree. A handsome dinner was not simply a banquet to Adams. It was "a most sinfull feast," which he enjoyed immensely and felt guilty about thereafter! [7]

JOHN BARTH'S HISTORICAL NOVEL *The Sot-Weed Factor*, set largely in England and colonial Maryland, poses many of the same problems we have been examining—and perhaps provides no more resolutions. Its central story concerns the loss of Ebenezer Cooke's innocence and Henry Burlingame's quest for his identity and ancestry. The New World turns out

6. Adams to Benjamin Rush, Feb. 2, 1807, in John A. Schutz, ed.: *Dialogues of John Adams and Benjamin Rush, 1805–1813* (San Marino, 1966), 76; Bernard Bailyn: "Butterfield's Adams: Notes for a Sketch," *William and Mary Quarterly*, 3rd series, XIX (1962), 246–8.

7. Bailyn: "Butterfield's Adams," 249; L. H. Butterfield, ed.: *Diary and Autobiography of John Adams* (Cambridge, Mass., 1961), II, 127.

to be a place where all the evils of the Old World persist—and then some. Colonists in English America, like Burlingame, became emotional orphans, without motherland or fatherland. Burlingame may have undergone a passionate search for his identity; he may have cared who he really was; but barely anyone else did. In America, any and all of his varied aliases seemed perfectly acceptable. The bisexual Burlingame was attracted to his siblings, male and female; he wanted to have relations with them both—and simultaneously. Why not? He had already declared himself the "Suitor of Totality, Embracer of Contradictories." Barth never makes clear whether the Englishman actually found or lost his innocence in America. Perhaps both?

EPILOGISM
Some Comparisons

AFTER A CENTURY and a half of settlement, the English colonies were discernibly different from their neighbors north and south. Spaniards who had come to the "Indies" encountered complex civilizations and subordinated them—at first physically, but then culturally as well. Hispanized Indians were too useful economically to eradicate, and too much in need of Christianity to be neglected entirely. The French encountered less "advanced" Indian tribes, yet adapted to them much more readily, learning and absorbing many of their folkways. English settlers encountered some of the most vulnerable and —to European eyes—least "civilized" Indian cultures, and gradually (greedily) chose to obliterate them. In consequence, indigenous peoples may have had less direct impact upon the making of English-Americans than upon the creation of Spanish-American or French-American identities.

Environment, and natural resources generally, may have shaped the civilizations of New Spain and New France more profoundly at the outset than was the case in English America. Mineral wealth, a considerable supply of available labor, and the fur trade had more visible and *immediate* impact upon the shape of society in the Indies and along the St. Lawrence than did the major resource of Nova Britannia: land. But whereas

New Spain would eventually engender a superficial splendor drained of wealth and vitality, and New France would display natural magnificence without the substantive support of established communities, English America would gradually combine corporeal substance with community, wealth with a healthy demographic growth.[1]

But if environment and native peoples contributed somewhat less initially to the making of English-Americans, immediate cultural inheritance may have mattered more. The social and political crises of Stuart England obliged colonists, Cavalier as well as Puritan, to redefine their relationship with the home culture, and forced them to recognize, certainly by the 1660's, that they were not simply Englishmen living *outre mer*. By contrast, during the two formative generations in French and Spanish colonial history, there were no domestic crises so monumental and so emotionally wrenching as to require provincials to reconsider the precise nature of their national-colonial identities. The psychological implications of being a conquistador or Creole, seigneur or censitaire, emerged more slowly and obscurely.

By contrast, the imperatives of being a Puritan in Massachusetts Bay, a Quaker in Penn's woods, or a patrician in the tidewater were more compelling, more difficult to ignore, and quickly cried out for some sort of resolution, some allegiance to place, some new perspective upon the perils of changing identity. More so than the Spanish and French, however, English colonists were inclined to gauge their *personae* in terms of not becoming barbaric like the Indians. No theme runs more persistently or anxiously through the sermons, essays, and histories of colonial America than this one: Are we degenerating to the crudeness and paganism of the primeval inhabitants?

The English colonies must have been more susceptible to

1. See Woodrow Borah and Sherburne F. Cook: "Conquest and Population: A Demographic Approach to Mexican History," *Proceedings of the American Philosophical Society*, CXIII (1969), 177–83.

biformities than their neighbors because the composition of their settlements was more heterogeneous. Proportionately more Spaniards came to the Indies, and more Frenchmen to the St. Lawrence, than Englishmen to the mainland and Caribbean colonies. By 1770 the total population of George III's America was little more than 60 per cent English, thereby creating more—and more complex—problems of social accommodation, more possible combinations and conflicts among divergent institutions, ideas, and groups.

There was, moreover, during the formative decades of English colonization, greater sensitivity and flexibility in those very institutions and ideas than in their Spanish and French counterparts, which were manifestations of absolutist states. No Stuart king or court could compare with those of Charles V, Philip II, and Louis XIV for stringent hierarchical control from a majestic throne. The suppleness and relative diversity of life in "Jacobethan" England would be exported, lend themselves to compromise, and facilitate transformation.

From the outset, the governments of France and Spain took more of a direct controlling interest in their overseas plantations than England's could or did. Because the Indies and New France were more minutely supervised from home, complex and ambiguous circumstances were dealt with more promptly, before biformities could become institutionalized, embodied in folkways or formal thought. Because the apparatus of Spanish and French imperial administration was proportionately denser, the likelihood of innovation or deviance was better controlled.

Similarly, English and Dutch Protestantism (because New York began as New Netherland) lent themselves more readily to innovation and new ecclesiastical forms than did Spanish and French Catholicism. Protestantism comprised a greater number of internal variations and deviations; it could more comfortably accommodate mergers and mutability; it possessed more flexibility then and adapted better to aggressive agents of change than did Catholicism. Almost necessarily, therefore, the culture and conscious identities of colonists in New France and New Spain remained more nearly like those of the homeland than was true in English America.

The principal change in Canada was toward more individual independence, for the *habitants* were dispersed on the land and could not be easily controlled from Quebec. In the Spanish Indies, with significant urban centers of authority, the dominant tendency was more toward collectivism and hierarchy.[2] In the English colonies, however, which were "rurban," owing to the interdependence of substantial cities, outlying towns, and extensive hinterlands, there was a simultaneous thrust toward collectivism *and* individualism. Only in America were the misanthrope and the mass so much encouraged to flourish *pari passu*. Therefore a special tension developed between the two. "It would not require much development or shuffling of the elements," as R. W. B. Lewis suggests, "for that tension to assume the more impressive shape of the one distinctly American narrative theme: that of the solitary hero and his moral engagement with the alien tribe. Such was to be the enduring fable of the American Adam." [3]

IF ENGLAND'S COLONIES were more susceptible to contradictory tendencies than those of France and Spain, they accurately reflected the agonies of constitutional and intellectual conflict under the early Stuarts and Cromwell. Thereafter, though, two full generations of brutalizing antinomies left England emotionally exhausted by 1660, fed to the teeth with politics of irony and the paradoxes of poetasters. For a century to come, Englishmen would relentlessly cherish security and tranquillity, reconciliation and the golden mean. In 1748, when David Hume addressed himself to the problem of national

2. See Richard C. Harris: *The Seigneurial System in Early Canada. A Geographical Study* (Madison, 1966), 195; James Lockhart: *Spanish Peru, 1532–1560: A Colonial Society* (Madison, 1968), 225–7; Stuart B. Schwartz: "Magistracy and Society in Colonial Brazil," *Hispanic American Historical Review*, L (1970), 715–30.

3. *The American Adam. Innocence, Tragedy, and Tradition in the Nineteenth Century* (Chicago, 1955), 84–5.

character in general and England's in particular, he marveled at the cohesiveness, the unity born of diversity that he found. In a society diffuse and yet tolerant, national characteristics were scarcely perceptible:

> We may often remark a wonderful mixture of manners and characters in the same nation, speaking the same language, and subject to the same government: And in this particular the ENGLISH are the most remarkable of any people, that perhaps ever were in the world. Nor is this to be ascribed to the mutability and uncertainty of their climate, or to any other *physical* causes; since all these causes take place in the neighboring country of SCOTLAND, without having the same effect. Where the government of a nation is altogether republican, it is apt to beget a peculiar set of manners. Where it is altogether monarchical, it is more apt to have the same effect; the imitation of superiors spreading the national manners faster among the people. . . . But the ENG-LISH government is a mixture of monarchy, aristocracy, and democracy. The people in authority are composed of gentry and merchants. All sects of religion are to be found among them. And the great liberty and independency, which every man enjoys, allows him to display the manners peculiar to him. Hence the English, of any people in the universe, have the least of a national character; unless this very singularity may pass for such.[4]

To simply say with Hume, however, that Georgian England enjoyed stable pluralism (albeit of a fairly homogeneous sort) and a well-integrated functionalism would miss much of the subtlety required of a proper comparison. England between 1660 and 1760 was not without tensions and anomalies. No society is ever totally devoid of them. But it is not essential to describe them in order to understand Georgian England, whereas it is imperative to comprehend the biformities of eighteenth-century America in order to grasp the ensuing course of its civilization. Contradictory tendencies occasionally

4. Hume: "Of National Characters," in *Essays: Moral, Political, and Literary* (London, 1889), I, 251–2.

offered puzzles of personal identity to the Augustans, but did not challenge their sense of national self precisely because legitimacy and stability were secure and unproblematic.[5] In the colonies, by contrast, dualisms had much to do with dilemmas of national development, style, and identity.

Whereas the tensions and conflicts of early American life were noticed by acute contemporaries despite the absence of professional intellectuals and social critics, the incongruities of Georgian England were of a special sort, visible primarily to men of letters; and that is because—as Cleanth Brooks has shown—paradox is essential to great literature.[6] Augustan writing from Dryden to Dr. Johnson was often urban in setting while intimately connected to the life of the landed gentry; and it tended to assume the superiority of rural wholesomeness over urban corruption. Hence Prior's "The Country-Mouse and the City-Mouse." Hence their antiphonal of nature (meaning savagery) versus civilization (meaning sophistication). Hence the interplay between patriotism and cosmopolitanism, between local attachment and being a citizen of the world, so important to Bolingbroke and Oliver Goldsmith.[7]

Eighteenth-century English literature displayed something of a fondness for exploring multiple points of view, a fondness linked to a literary instinct for fructive antitheses. The pseudo-Georgic poetry of the Augustans celebrated the new counterpoise of forces established in 1689. Men spoke of order versus

5. See Paul Tedeschi: *Paradoxe de la Pensée Anglaise au XVIIIe Siècle, ou, L'Ambiguité du Sens Commun* (Paris, 1961), which concentrates upon Locke, Berkeley, Hume, Pope, and Bolingbroke.

6. Brooks: *The Well Wrought Urn. Studies in the Structure of Poetry* (New York, 1947), ch. 1, "The Language of Paradox."

7. See John Hardy: "Johnson's *London:* The Country Versus the City," in *Studies in the Eighteenth Century*, ed. R. F. Brissenden (Canberra, 1968), 251–68; Chauncey B. Tinker: *Nature's Simple Plan. A Phase of Radical Thought in the Mid-Eighteenth Century* (Princeton, 1922); Lois Whitney: *Primitivism and the Idea of Progress in English Popular Literature of the 18th Century* (Baltimore, 1934); A. D. McKillop: "Local Attachment and Cosmopolitanism—The 18th-Century Pattern," in *From Sensibility to Romanticism. Essays Presented to Frederick A. Pottle*, ed. F. W. Hilles (New York, 1965), 191–218.

energy, hierarchy versus mobility, wit versus sense, and the danger of "legal tyranny." [8] But these were the polarities of a comparatively stable society with well-defined boundaries, traditions, and expectations. The notable phrases of eighteenth-century English life—manners, propriety, civility, decorum, sense, reason, taste, elegance, improvement—were largely irrelevant to provincial life in America.

Order, reconciliation, balance, and moderation mattered most to the Augustans. In discussing the relationship between reason and passion, Alexander Pope relied upon the ancient idea that harmony arises from the tensions inherent in things: *concors discordia rerum.* Thus Pope, in *An Essay on Man* (1733–4), sought equilibrium in the golden mean:

> That REASON, PASSION, answer one great aim;
> That true SELF-LOVE and SOCIAL are the same;
> That VIRTUE only makes our Bliss below;
> And all our Knowledge is, OURSELVES TO KNOW. [9]

The Augustans wished to encompass in a system of basic agreement the whole "community of sense," and thereby avoid the excesses of the seventeenth century. [1]

Significantly, however, a few unresolved antonyms of eighteenth-century England would be transported to America with dramatic impact. Hungrily, the colonists read and swallowed the writings of English Whig-republican theorists *as well as* Tory (or "country party") opponents of Hanoverian ministries. This oddly juxtaposed combination had the power of a reciprocating engine because both were doctrines of op-

---

8. See Paul Fussell: "The New Irony and the Augustans," *Encounter,* XXXIV (1970), 68–75. Cf. Isaac Kramnick: *Bolingbroke and His Circle. The Politics of Nostalgia in the Age of Walpole* (Cambridge, Mass., 1968), ch. 9, "The Ambivalence of the Augustan Commonwealthman."

9. Epistle IV, lines 395–8.

1. See Martin Price: *To the Palace of Wisdom. Studies in Order and Energy from Dryden to Blake* (New York, 1964), 132, 140, 184, 263, 267, 271–3, 324, 327, 361; J. W. Johnson: *The Formation of English Neo-Classical Thought* (Princeton, 1967); A. R. Humphreys: *The Augustan World. Life and Letters in 18th-century England* (London, 1954).

pugnance and therefore potential ideologies of anti-authoritarianism, especially in an unstable polity.[2] This peculiar harnessing together of libertarian thought with the "country party" cause contributed much to the subsequent American penchant for conservative liberalism.

DURING THE GENERATIONS of British colonization, then, and especially the century 1660–1760, some English ideas and institutions were simply transplanted to North America (hence the many on-going similarities) while others were being transformed (hence the biformities). The two processes occurred simultaneously. Similarities persisted because New World circumstances could, in many cases, arrest or delay social change. Biformities occurred because conditions overseas, especially unstable pluralism, could also accelerate change, thereby demanding compromises and accommodations.

The relationship between similarity and biformity was very much a two-way process. Some dualisms (potential biformities) which were imported directly (nonseparating congregationalism, for example), especially before 1660, thus began as similarities. Consequently, they were simultaneously similarities *and* biformities. Other imported attributes began as Anglo-American similarities, and only later became biformities. Still others long remained simply as similarities. Hence the prismatic complexity of our *paradoxus magnus*.

2. For the Whig-republican tradition and its colonial impact, see Caroline Robbins: *The 18th-century Commonwealthman* (Cambridge, Mass., 1959); and Bernard Bailyn: *The Ideological Origins of the American Revolution* (Cambridge, Mass., 1967). For the "country party" and Tory tradition, see Perez Zagorin: *The Court and the Country. The Beginning of the English Revolution* (London, 1969); J. G. A. Pocock: "Machiavelli, Harrington, and English Political Ideologies in the 18th Century," *William and Mary Quarterly*, 3d series, XXII (1965), 549–83; and Robert M. Weir: " 'The Harmony We Were Famous For': An Interpretation of Pre-Revolutionary South Carolina Politics," *ibid.*, XXVI (1969), 473–501.

PART THREE

The Implications of Biformity

❧ · ❧

Well, the generalization spreads out in space, but how to get the wretched thing to move forward in time! The generalization, being timeless, will not move forward; and so the harassed historian, compelled to get on with the story, must return in some fashion to the individual, the concrete event, the "thin red line of heroes." Employing these two methods, the humane historian will do his best to prevent them from beating each other to death within the covers of his book. But the strain is great.

CARL L. BECKER

PROLEGOMENON

> I am ready to wish—vain wish! that nature would
> raise her everlasting bars between the new and old world;
> and make a voyage to Europe as impracticable as one to
> the moon. I confess indeed, that by our connections with
> Europe we have made most surprizing, I had almost said
> unnatural, advances towards the meridian of glory; But
> by those connections too, in all probability, our fall will
> be premature.
>
> DAVID RITTENHOUSE,
> *An Oration Delivered February 24, 1775*

DURING the formative years of American history, especially
the period 1640–1760 which has been the central concern of
my preceding chapters, the most important tensions derived
from relationships between liberty (which pluralism requires)
and authority (which requires legitimacy), between the individual and society, the growth of political democracy and
oscillations of economic opportunity. By the middle of the
eighteenth century, few of these tensions or their implications
had been resolved; indeed, most had been drawn more dramatically taut. The theory of government and the practice of
politics were increasingly out of phase with one another.

Elizabethans had brought to the New World a strong
sense of order in the universe, of the "great chain of being."
Yet they encountered a new-found chaos whose natural wealth
and natural men were there to be ordered. Sustained by mem-

ories of method and system, they sought both in their the-
ologies and polities. The Puritans, who feared social and moral
disorder, regarded spiritual grace as a reinvigoration of capaci-
ties already present in the unregenerate soul. "As in the ruins
of a palace," they liked to observe, "the materials still exist,
but the 'order' is taken away; grace re-establishes the order by
rebuilding with the same materials." [1] So, too, natural law
would prove popular both as an expression of the search for
order and of the quest for criteria of legitimacy greater even
than Magna Charta and King-in-Parliament. So Landon Carter
of Virginia considered the prime goals of government to be
"peace, order, and moderation."

But by the time of Carter's maturity, the mid-eighteenth
century, no one knew whether order and liberty could comfortably co-exist in the colonies; and the attendant ambivalence
has been with us ever since. Submission versus resistance to
magistrates and ministers, orderliness versus confusion: these
were the stated alternatives. In 1755, Moses Dickinson
summed up the contrary emotions of a society just claiming its
majority: "They are like a Pond that being weary of Confine-
ment, contends for Liberty with the Dam upon which it depends
for its very Existence." [2]

A decade later, Noah Hobart described the same dilemma
in the context of New England's troubled Church polity:

> The great Difficulty in civil and ecclesiastical policy is
> to fix the Balance between Authority and Liberty.
> Authority is apt to degenerate into Tyranny, and Lib-
> erty into Licentiousness and confusion. . . . The
> Constitution of the consociated churches in Connecti-

1. See Perry Miller: "The Marrow of Puritan Divinity," in *Errand
into the Wilderness* (Cambridge, Mass., 1956), 79. Many of Nathaniel
Hawthorne's historical tales are centrally concerned with antagonisms
between forces of order, stability, and tradition as against those of
libertarianism, misrule, and destructiveness.

2. *A Sermon Preached Before the General Assembly of the Colony
of Connecticut* (New London, 1755), 7.

cut is in my opinion the true medium between these Extreams.[3]

Elsewhere, in Pennsylvania for example, observers found the polity in "a kind of anarchy (or no government), there being perpetual jarrs betwixt the two parts of the legislature." Why should this have been so, especially in a colony built upon foundations of brotherly love? One British critic caught part of the answer in 1763. The Americans believed themselves entitled to "a greater measure of liberty than is enjoyed by the people of England, because of their quitting their native country to make settlements for the advantage of Great Britain. . . . Hence the perpetual struggle in every colony between privilege and prerogative."[4]

Still another part of the answer arose from that longstanding ambitendency between economic ambitions and traditional restraints. Injunctions of seventeenth-century social thought had perpetuated a certain discomfort about the perils of prosperity and ascetic advantages of adversity. Nevertheless, men sought fame and fortune despite the belief that both were illusory and ephemeral. As the colonial period drew to a close, however, opportunities for economic improvement seem to have been diminishing *despite* the broadening of political participation. A clearly differentiated class structure made itself ever more apparent, with less fluidity than had been available for several generations past.[5] The frustrations attendant upon this

3. *An Attempt to Illustrate and Confirm the Ecclesiastical Constitution of the Consociated Churches.* . . . (New Haven, 1765), 43.

4. Carl Bridenbaugh, ed.: *Gentleman's Progress. The Itinerarium of Dr. Alexander Hamilton, 1744* (Chapel Hill, 1948), 29; Thomas C. Barrow, ed.: "A Project for Imperial Reform: 'Hints Respecting the Settlement for Our American Provinces,' 1763," *William and Mary Quarterly*, 3d series, XXIV (1967), 117.

5. See James A. Henretta: "Economic Development and Social Structure in Colonial Boston," *ibid.*, XXII (1965), 75–92; James T. Lemon and Gary B. Nash: "The Distribution of Wealth in Eighteenth-Century America. A Century of Change in Chester County, Pennsylvania, 1693–1802," *Journal of Social History*, II (1968), 1–24; Charles S. Grant: *Democracy in the Connecticut Frontier Town of Kent*

discrepancy between political inclusiveness and economic exclusiveness would contribute to the reorientation of American
institutions during the final decades of the eighteenth century.

THE JUXTAPOSITION of apparently irreconcilable ideals has
long provided a favorite pastime for the American intelligent-
sia: liberty against order in the eighteenth century; equality
against liberty in the nineteenth; order against equality in our
own time. "Although humane lovers of the masses," Carl
Becker noted in 1932, "we are, on the other hand, highly
differentiated individuals who prize our liberties, including the
liberty of not belonging to the masses whom we love." [6] The
ironic shaft of Becker's cynicism penetrates to the core of our
collective individualism; for the pulling and tugging of both
wanting to belong and seeking to be free have conditioned
Americans to attempt a reconciliation between the needs of
social cohesion and the impulse to self-satisfaction. I suspect
that our collective individualism owes much to our antecedent
unstable pluralism. The latter offers greater opportunities for
personal self-realization because each individual develops his
personality and style through multiple patterns of association.

The problem, perhaps, is that to some Americans the ambiguous concept of democracy has held out the prospect of
perfect freedom, while to others it has implied perfect equality.
So often it seems as though those whose emphasis is upon
freedom have already achieved equality, while those seeking
equality are less concerned with the more philosophical aspects
of freedom. So it was between Fenimore Cooper and American
society in the 1830's; so it is between William F. Buckley and
low-income Americans today.

American democracy has been ambiguous ever since colonial times; and the ambiguities have fitted the cam shaft of

(New York, 1961), chs. 5–6; Aubrey C. Land: "The Tobacco Staple
and the Planter's Problems: Technology, Labor, and Crops," *Agricultural History*, XLIII (1969), 69–81.
    6. "Liberalism—A Way Station," in *Everyman His Own Historian.
Essays on History and Politics* (2nd ed., Chicago, 1966), 98.

American life, projecting from the spinning society and imparting variable motion to the body politic and its accessory institutions. Settlers of New England were by inheritance suspicious of power in the hands of kings, aristocrats, priests, and churches. But they were equally suspicious of power in the hands of the people. Thus Peter Bulkley, pastor in Concord, Massachusetts, warned against "the putting of too much liberty and power into the hands of the multitude, which they are too weak to manage, many growing conceited, proud, self-sufficient, as wanting nothing." [7] Colonists knew that "the way of liberty lay along an exceedingly narrow path between the abysses of restraint and anarchy." They were, by necessity, equilibrists. Thus a town meeting vote might have formal validity; but the precinct would not sanction its legitimacy unless it had broad acceptability, saying "We will not be governed by numbers but by reason and justice." [8]

What emerged, then, from New England's spiritual élitism (based upon tribalism and covenants) conjoined with the democratic dogma of the town meeting? In essence, an unselfconscious acceptance of democratic élitism. Suffrage and potential participation were widespread among adult white males, yet control was exerted by relatively small groups which were continuously re-elected to office. "Let it stand as a principle," wrote Jeremy Belknap of New Hampshire late in the eighteenth century, "that government originates from the people; but let the people be taught . . . that they are not able to govern themselves." [9] John P. Marquand hit the bull's-eye

7. Quoted in Sumner C. Powell: *Puritan Village. The Formation of a New England Town* (Middletown, 1963), 151.

8. H. Richard Niebuhr: *The Kingdom of God in America* (New York, 1937), 77, 95; Michael Zuckerman: "The Social Context of Democracy in Massachusetts," *William and Mary Quarterly*, 3rd series, XXV (1968), 543.

9. Quoted in Richard Hofstadter: *The American Political Tradition* (New York, 1948), 6–7. For the implication that representative government in America owes more to aristocratic liberalism than to advocates of popular democracy, see R. R. Palmer: *The Age of the Democratic Revolution. A Political History of Europe and America, 1760–1800* (Princeton, 1959), I, 124–5.

equally well a few years ago when he wrote that "Newburyport was an orderly place where every inhabitant knew instinctively where he belonged in relation to everyone else, and he knew also that he was as good as anyone else, no matter where he belonged." And so federal America would be filled with Gentlemen Democrats, like Elbridge Gerry; and local politicians ever since have had to play the role of "professional gentlemen democrats." [1]

The danger, of course, has always been that democratic élitism out of kilter would disintegrate into what General Gage called "a kind of Democratical Despotism" (referring to revolutionary Boston). In 1686, William Penn made an extraordinarily revealing remark about politics and social change in his proprietary. "The Great fault is, that those who are there, loose their authority, one way or other in the Spirits of the people and then they can do little with their outward powrs." [2] Leaders throughout the colonies would repeatedly agitate the populace and then eventually lose control. Once traditional bonds had been broken, customary forms of political power and leverage were weakened, though not destroyed. In consequence, political society in early America remained in a state of transition —and vacillation—through almost the entire eighteenth century. John Adams would remark in 1775 that "a democratical despotism is a contradiction in terms." Yet a democratical despotism is precisely what one finds in revolutionary America; and Alexis de Tocqueville would subsequently burn that brand into the hide of Jacksonian America.

Perhaps the old shibboleth really should endure. Perhaps the growth of democracy really was the central theme of early American history, and was, in a certain sense, inevitable. Not

1. Marquand: *Timothy Dexter Revisited* (Boston, 1953), 57; Samuel Eliot Morison: "Elbridge Gerry, Gentleman Democrat," in *By Land and by Sea. Essays and Addresses* (New York, 1953), 181–99; Sam Bass Warner, Jr.: *The Private City. Philadelphia in Three Periods of Its Growth* (Philadelphia, 1968), 80.

2. Gage to Lord Hillsborough, Oct. 31, 1768, CO 5/86, Public Record Office, London; Penn to Thomas Lloyd, Sept. 21, 1686, *Pa. Mag. Hist. & Biog.*, LXXX (1956), 243.

because it was a positive good, obvious to all; nor because of a strong ideological thrust either. But rather because power did devolve to the localities, because a proper centralization of power proved impossible, because men and women expected greater opportunities here and the very expectation helped to make it so for many.

Moreover, the presence of unstable pluralism and the absence of legitimacy in several spheres also made democracy suitable; for democracy provided a pragmatically doctrinaire way to invest authority in "the people" at a time when institutions lacked full legitimacy, as well as a way to weld unwieldy social groups into some sort of free-floating equilibrium—like a large Calder mobile—that might minimize the most clanging effects of unstable pluralism.

The conceptual coupling of legitimacy with democracy is a delicate one, and unfamiliar to Americans because we tend to associate the problem of legitimacy with popes and kings and Old World aristocracies. In actual fact, however, modes of legitimacy are even more important in a democracy than in a traditionally hierarchical society because they are less visible and cannot be taken for granted. Hence the importance of our having a written Constitution. There are indeed canons of legitimacy appropriate to a democratic society, and one of the central problems of eighteenth-century Americans (with inherited European assumptions) was to identify and institutionalize them.

The constantly pressing problem with democratic legitimacy is that the majority is right (by definition) even when it is wrong (by prejudice or ignorance). The majority stands officially for truth, justice, and wisdom even when its errors and iniquities are glaringly evident. So Thomas Jefferson, disillusioned by uncontrolled legislatures right after the Revolution, wrote that "an elective despotism was not the government we fought for." [3]

Democratic legitimacy depends upon a delicately contra-

3. *Notes on the State of Virginia*, ed. T. P. Abernethy (New York, 1964), 113.

puntal arrangement of majority and minority, the ability to command and the opportunity to oppose. Whatever the nature of the mechanism by which people express themselves, sovereignty (or legitimacy) cannot be identified exclusively with either the will of the majority or the will of the minority. Each is a part of the sovereign will; and it is impossible to suppress either without ultimately mutilating the sovereign will and causing the very ligaments of legitimacy to deteriorate. Government and opposition in a democracy constitute a dualism whose harmonious interaction facilitates the achievement of genuinely popular legitimacy.

Which leads me to wonder whether a great many American biformities are not *calculated* ambiguities resulting from an instinctive imperative for adjustment and compromise. The New England Puritans had a special affection for Peter Ramus, the sixteenth-century dialectician who classified arguments by dichotomy, or deliberate ambiguity. Throughout the seventeenth century, Harvard College theses were written in praise of dichotomy. And, consistent with this penchant, theological disparities could be neutralized by resorting to a device first utilized in reconciling John Cotton to his fellow ministers after the Antinomian controversy in 1636–7—that is, to declare an irreconcilable difference *adiaphoron:* a thing indifferent.[4]

In discussing the American Enlightenment, Henry May has suggested that those European ideas flourished in America that were particularly susceptible of compromise. "In philosophy, Americans accepted the ambiguities and contradictions of the Lockeian tradition . . . with even less difficulty than Europeans. The primacy of sensation and the centrality of the moral sense could flourish at once, as long as each of these theories . . . did not push too far." It also became clear to Jefferson's generation that republicanism, and political de-

---

4. Perry Miller: *The New England Mind. The Seventeenth Century* (Cambridge, Mass., 1954), 125–8; Darrett B. Rutman: *American Puritanism. Faith and Practice* (Philadelphia, 1970), 112; Larzer Ziff: *The Career of John Cotton. Puritanism and the American Experience* (Princeton, 1962), ch. 7, "The Middle Path."

mocracy too, "was compatible with property rights and could even concede a special role to a cultural elite." [5]

Thus Alexander Hamilton, who wanted to avoid a "perpetual vibration between extremes of tyranny & anarchy," pleaded in *The Federalist*, Number 23: "Let us not attempt to reconcile contradictions, but firmly embrace a rational alternative." In writing *The Federalist Papers*, however, Hamilton, Madison, and Jay were very careful not to honor Hamilton's plea; for as John Mercer wrote in 1830, *The Federalist* "addresses different arguments to different classes of the American public, in the spirit of an able and skillful disputant before a mixed assembly. Thus from different numbers of this work, and sometimes from the same numbers, may be derived authorities for opposite principles and opinions." [6]

Relatively few Americans have ever accepted Hamilton's appeal to "embrace a rational alternative," and in so doing they have usually placed themselves outside the mainstream of national politics. This is precisely what John Randolph and the Quids did when they decided to oppose both the Federalists and the Republicans during the Jeffersonian era. The name they took, derived from *tertium quid*, means some third thing, something (left undefined) related in some way to two (definite or known) things, but distinct from both.

Compromise is the quintessential American way, then, and owes much to the reluctance, or inability, of most Americans to make hard choices and take clear-cut positions. But in another, less pejorative sense, compromise has meant co-operation and has been regarded by many as a positive virtue. Take, for example, Santayana's compelling essay on "English Liberty in America" (1920):

5. "The Problem of the American Enlightenment," *New Literary History*, I (1970), 207–8, 213. May concludes this essay with the observation that "ambivalent about change, given to accepting past Enlightenment as satisfactory, American thought has been a baffling mixture of conservatism and innovation."

6. Clinton Rossiter, ed.: *The Federalist Papers* (New York, 1961), 157; *Proceedings and Debates of the Virginia State Convention of 1829–1830* (Richmond, 1830), 187.

There is one gift or habit, native to England, that has
not only been preserved in America unchanged, but has
found there a more favorable atmosphere in which to
manifest its true nature—I mean the spirit of free co-
operation. . . . Far from being neutralised by American dash and bravura, or lost in the opposite instincts
of so many alien races, it seems to be adopted at once
in the most mixed circles and in the most novel predica-
ments. . . . Where individuality is so free, co-operation, when it is justified, can be all the more quick and
hearty. Everywhere co-operation is taken for granted,
as something that no one would be so mean or so short-
sighted as to refuse. . . . It was because life in
America was naturally more co-operative and more
plastic than in England that the spirit of English liberty, which demands co-operation and plasticity, could
appear there more boldly and universally than it ever
did at home.[7]

The kind of co-operation Santayana had in mind has everything
to do with collective individualism, as well as that anonymous
pluralism an American sociologist has labeled "the lonely
crowd."

WELL, IF THIS BE a proper prolegomenon, it will have to
provide direct passage, rather than a revolving door, to the
following chapter on ambiguities of the American Revolution.
But that is not difficult to do because the Revolution was
plastered with conservative liberalism and papered with pragmatic idealism. It was regarded as a moderate rebellion—a
constitutional revolution, not a social one. And paradoxically,
because it was so successful, self-satisfied Americans subsequently inculcated an anti-revolutionary hostility to radical
change. Their memories grew dimmer with the passage of
decades, and they convinced themselves—having become super-
legitimists—that a revolution, to be valid, must replicate the
moderation and constitutionalism of their own.

7. George Santayana: *Character and Opinion in the United States*
(New York, 1921), 193-9; See also Douglas L. Wilson, ed.: *The
Genteel Tradition; Nine Essays by George Santayana* (Cambridge,
Mass., 1967), 39-40.

During the century 1690–1790, economic change and political socialization brought three successive transformations in the nature and role of American government. Although these transformations have been partially perceived as discrete events, their sequential relationship has not been noticed despite the fact that each phase helped to make possible its immediate successor. Between about 1680 and 1720 an alteration in local government occurred, wherein town meetings picked up the baton of decision-making power from boards of selectmen. In consequence, a new generation of men gained greatly in political experience at the local level. Between about 1720 and 1760, provincial legislatures achieved maturity in the management of public affairs. By the eve of Revolution no one could say, as a doctor in New Jersey had in 1744, that the assembly "was chiefly composed of mechanicks and ignorant wretches." The husbandmen of colonial times had acquired experience and modes of expression necessary for participation in still a larger arena. Finally, between 1765 and 1790 a series of national congresses would be created and help to expand the dimensions of domestic politics once again. Generation by generation, the horizons of American government had broadened in response to changing codes and constellations of colonial politics.[8]

By mid-eighteenth century, assemblies had undoubtedly become the pivotal institutions in provincial politics. Significantly, however, their position within the imperial constitution was extraordinarily ambivalent. The legislatures in New York and Maryland, for example, often claimed that their privileges paralleled those of the House of Commons, while simultane-

8. See Kenneth A. Lockridge and Alan Kreider: "The Evolution of Massachusetts Town Government, 1640–1740," *William and Mary Quarterly*, 3d series, XXIII (1966), 550, 563, 573; *Itinerarium of Dr. Alexander Hamilton*, 31; William Smith, Jr.: *The History of the Late Province of New-York, From Its Discovery, to the Appointment of Governor Colden, in 1762 (Collections of the New-York Historical Society for the Year 1829* [New York, 1829]), IV, 309; Jack P. Greene: *The Quest for Power. The Lower Houses of Assembly in the Southern Royal Colonies, 1689–1776* (Chapel Hill, 1963), *passim*.

ously denying any such parallel between the colonial council and the House of Lords, or between governor and King. Add to this indigenous dualism the inherited one intrinsic in the "mixed" system of government established and solidified in Stuart England. James Whitelock, a lawyer and Member of Parliament, explained the anomaly superbly in 1610, when English colonization was newborn. "The sovereign power is agreed to be in the King; but in the King is a twofold power; the one in Parliament, as he is assisted with the consent of the whole state; the other out of Parliament, as he is sole and singular, guided merely by his own will." [9]

The colonists lived with this dualistic assumption for a century and a half. Ultimately, however, it had to be shucked away. For a long time there had been growing divergence between imperial theory and colonial practice; but the divergence meant little so long as each avoided abrasive contact with the other. British policy after 1763 threatened to upset this arrangement by implementing old ideals long after the conditions that produced them had ceased to exist. In ironic essence, political traditions which had evolved in America were perceived by the colonists foursquare in terms of conventional English precedents and legal patterns; but in reality, they no longer coincided with the *new* English view of their own constitutional framework at home.[1]

By the 1760's, tensions between cultural anglophilia and political anglophobia became intolerable for many colonists. Only Independence could fully relieve or resolve such strains. They were compounded, moreover, by related anxieties which also seemed to surface most visibly after 1763. Men began to harbor doubts about the purposefulness of all the activity evident in colonial cities. "We are a set of the busiest, most bus-

9. Quoted in C. H. McIlwain: *Constitutionalism and the Changing World* (Cambridge, Mass., 1939), 77.

1. See H. V. S. Ogden: "The State of Nature and the Decline of Lockean Political Theory in England, 1760–1800," *American Historical Review*, XLVI (1940), 21–44.

tling, hurrying animals imaginable," wrote one Carolinian from Charleston in 1764, "and yet we really do not do much, but we must appear to be doing."[2] Within Virginia's ruling élite there was an "uneasy confidence" during the pre-revolutionary years, a manifestation of economic stress and social tension, of ambiguous relations between burgesses and their constituents, of ambivalent attitudes toward the representative process in government, and, most of all, of psychological uncertainty about present stability and future prospects.[3]

There was no singular moment of epiphany, no exclusive flash of recognition in 1763, or 1775, or 1787, when Americans suddenly saw themselves—without bifocal vision—in the clear, self-conscious light of honest reappraisal. There were many such moments, collective and personal, and they occurred with especial frequency and intensity during the 1770's. But before values and realities could become congruent, a great deal of hard thinking and fighting would transpire, and much disillusionment. During the passion of revolutionary fervor, Utopia itself appeared as a biformity, the "Christian Sparta" of Sam Adams's dreams: vigorous and tender, primitive and sophisticated, Christian and pagan, free yet bound to a moral mission. By 1780, Adams knew that it could not be.[4] The interlocking spheres that had held communities, colonies, and an empire together for six generations—and had thereby helped to defuse tensions—were now revolving independently, and attendant energies had been released. No one could foresee whether they would be recaptured, reunited, or rearranged.

As it happened, the oldest polarities in American life would remain the most problematic: liberty versus authority, rights versus duties, individual enterprise versus social welfare, equal-

2. Quoted in Michael Kraus: *The Atlantic Civilization. Eighteenth-Century Origins* (Ithaca, 1949), 264.

3. Cf. Jack P. Greene: "Search for Identity. An Interpretation of the Meaning of Selected Patterns of Social Response in 18th-century America," *Journal of Social History*, III (1970), 218–20.

4. Adams to John Scollay, Dec. 30, 1780, in Harry A. Cushing, ed.: *The Writings of Samuel Adams* (New York, 1908), IV, 238.

ity versus achievement, populism versus élitism. For as Cleanth Brooks has remarked with taut eloquence: "The kite properly loaded, tension maintained along the kite string, [it] rises steadily *against* the thrust of the wind." [5]

5. "Irony as a Principle of Structure," in *Literary Opinion in America*, ed. M. D. Zabel (New York, 1951), 741.

CHAPTER 7

AMBIGUITIES OF THE AMERICAN REVOLUTION

> You will see a strange Oscillation between love and
> hatred, between War and Peace—Preparations for War
> and Negociations for Peace.
>
> JOHN ADAMS (1775)

WHY HAVE HISTORIANS of the American Revolution
offered such conflicting interpretations of that pivotal event?
They have regarded it as both radical and conservative, a
struggle for home rule and also one to decide who would rule
at home, a product as well as a cause of rising nationalism. Was
the Revolution in fact the work of demagogues or of statesmen?
Was it completed in 1776 (as one participant claimed), or
scarcely begun by 1787 (as still another insisted)? Did the
Revolution demonstrate that causes could also be consequences,
that new governments could grow from old imperatives, that
insurrectionists can be moderate while conservatives can be
innovators? To most patriots the prospect of Independence was
simultaneously frightening and exhilarating. Once it had been
achieved, they were torn "between a desire to reinstitute traditional political forms and the possibility of introducing striking
political and social innovations." [1]

1. See Edmund S. Morgan: "The Puritan Ethic and the American
Revolution," *William and Mary Quarterly*, 3d series, XXIV (1967),

What we call the era of the American Revolution, the final third of the eighteenth century, was perhaps the most complicated epoch in American history. A great many of the dualisms of the preceding colonial period fed the Revolution—and were swallowed up by it as well. Many others were in turn released and became accents of the American style and scene in the nineteenth century.

In this chapter I want to examine some relationships— particularly political and psychological ones—between Britain and the origins of our Revolution. Then we shall look more closely at ambiguities in the American ideology and at the tortured ambivalence of particular persons involved. Finally, let us turn to the manifold meanings of the Revolution, and its legacies for the military, the courts, the churches, and, most of all, for the institutional structure of American government.

DURING DECADES of intermittent international warfare, 1739– 63, a prolonged debate took place in England concerning her strategic relationship to the continent on the one hand and to her overseas plantations on the other. The debate devolved upon various issues: What were the objects for which a war was worth fighting? And what was the most effective way to fight a war against France and Spain? Several policies were envisioned. There were isolationists and interventionists; and the dispute was never clearly resolved. But its mere existence exposed the fact that England at mid-century lacked a clearly formulated policy touching her colonies. No one could be certain what relationship Whitehall perceived between colonies and the continent. The absence of policy invited ambivalence and worse—misunderstanding.

After the French and Indian War ended in 1763, England maintained a sizable military establishment in America; and in order to patch up inadequacies in colonial military administration, Whitehall decided to continue the wartime office of commander in chief. These decisions to keep an army in the

---

3; Jack P. Greene, ed.: *The Ambiguity of the American Revolution* (New York, 1968), 6, 13–14.

colonies, to centralize its control under a military officer, and to separate its administration from colonial politics, made the relationships between colonial governors and army commanders highly problematic. Military men were appointed as governors over East and West Florida, newly acquired West Indian islands, and Quebec; but all four of these figures ended their régimes under a cloud of some sort because the commissions of the commander in chief and of the diminished royal governors were simply incompatible. In essence, without fully considering the implications, Whitehall had imposed a centralized military organization on a decentralized political system. This decision would create numerous difficulties during the decade prior to 1776.[2]

By the mid-1760's, England's imperial intentions were seen by many as being incompatible with important aims of the colonists; and each side had constitutional arguments to bolster its position. Americans based their apologias on realities of the imperial system as it had operated in the past. Therefore, any change in established relationships seemed illicit if enacted without the consent of both sides. In effect, as one historian has suggested, "the English claims were based on the theory of the past and the colonial arguments on the reality." This confrontation between the "empire of theory" and the "empire of fact" produced critical tensions which strained the Anglo-American system severely.[3] Men in England responsible for colonial administration vacillated between policies emphasizing imperialist considerations and decisions oriented toward a more traditional mercantilism. Hence the appearance of am-

2. John Shy: *Toward Lexington. The Role of the British Army in the Coming of the American Revolution* (Princeton, 1965), 148–63; see also Frederick B. Wiener: *Civilians Under Military Justice: The British Practice Since 1689, Especially in North America* (Chicago, 1967), 78–85.

3. Thomas C. Barrow: *Trade and Empire. The British Customs Service in Colonial America, 1660–1775* (Cambridge, Mass., 1967), 211–12; see also Michael Kammen: "The American Colonies and the 'Seasons of Business' in Eighteenth-century Britain," in *Anciens Pays et Assemblées d'États*, LIII (Louvain, 1970), 245–59.

biguous and ofttimes contradictory acts and policies affecting the colonies.

Hence also the ebb and flow of colonial responses to these acts and policies. In 1754, Massachusetts Bay abandoned her traditional frugality in order to appropriate funds, fight for the Empire, and preserve autonomy. In 1765, the Bay Colony's General Court realized that only opposition to the Empire offered the hope of protecting her autonomy and preserving her frugality. Times and policies had changed so. Similarly, in 1766 a committee representing the inhabitants of Boston wrote to Massachusetts's agent in London that "the People universally opposed the [Stamp] Act but at the same time discovered the most zealous Attachment to his Majesty's Person & government & the strongest Affection to their fellow Subjects the People of Great Britain. This we know some of our Enemys have endeavored to represent as a Paradox." [4]

During the later 1760's and throughout the 1770's, colonials agonized and argued over tactics. What were the proper principles governing the use of power in provincial affairs? At what point should constitutional maneuvering give way to physical intimidation, to "measured violence," "trained mobs," "righteous riots," and "Mob-Law"? Were ostensibly legal forms of persuasion really more legitimate than flagrantly illicit ones? [5] The most astute colonials, even the most patriotic, perceived the peculiarity of their positions. "I have been informed," wrote William Hooper in 1774,

> that the Pamphlet entitled, *The friendly address to the Americans etc.* has thro a mistaken Zeal of the people been prevented from being publickly sold in this City; Strange Infatuation that while we contend with enthusiastic ardor for the liberty of the press ourselves that [sic] we should with such an intolerating spirit

4. Boston to Dennys De Berdt, Oct. 22, 1766, in Harry A. Cushing, ed.: *The Writings of Samuel Adams* (New York, 1904), I, 91.

5. See Donald C. Lord and Robert M. Calhoon: "The Removal of the Massachusetts General Court from Boston, 1769–1772," *Journal of American History*, LV (1969), 753; Hiller Zobel: *The Boston Massacre* (New York, 1970), 25, 28, 81, 87.

deny it to others. It is a strange freedom that is confined to one side of a Question! [6]

In 1775, the Continental Congress responded erratically to the pressure of external events. On May 26, it adopted a contradictory set of resolutions which reflected divergences of opinion among the delegates. The first two resolutions insisted that the colonies were menaced by the use of military force to implement illicit acts of Parliament, and that the commencement of conflict in Massachusetts required that "these colonies be immediately put into a state of defence." The third resolution, however, insisted that the colonies hoped for reconciliation and indicated that a "humble and dutiful" petition should be submitted to the King. The fourth resolution stated that negotiations for reconciliation should begin at once. By June of 1775, Congress was making fundamental commitments to prosecute a war for purposes as yet undeclared. [7]

Ambivalence within the Continental Congress simply reflected local realities. In Pennsylvania politics, the controversy over Independence helped stir up an "unstable, shifting, ambiguous system of political alignments." In 1774, James Wilson published a resounding condemnation of English tyranny. But instead of following his thoughts to their logical conclusion, he joined John Dickinson in manipulating congressional *opposition* to Independence! Between 1774 and 1776, a great many Pennsylvanians "remained firm in support of American liberty but equally firm in opposition to independence"—and held to this equivocation despite the beginning of actual war. [8]

6. Hooper to James Duane, Nov. 22, 1774, Duane MSS, New-York Historical Society.

7. See Merrill Jensen: *The Founding of a Nation. A History of the American Revolution, 1763–1776* (New York, 1968), 608–9, 613, 617.

8. See John M. Head: *A Time to Rend. An Essay on the Decision for American Independence* (Madison, 1968), 18, 33, 49, 56, 138, 145–6, 148, 170–2. There are numerous contradictions in Wilson's writings and career. Although devoted to popular democracy, his contemporaries regarded him as conservative. Outwardly dour, but sanguine within, he hoped to be rich and a great statesman; instead, he

Ultimately, ambiguities of the era appear most readily in the lives of individuals; for as Carl Becker observed in 1909, the Revolution was carried through by "boldly cautious spirits." Sir Egerton Leigh, judge of the Charleston Vice-Admiralty Court, attorney general of South Carolina, and a veteran of Anglo-American politics, captured the quintessential difficulty quite well: "We see so many persons in common life *halting*, *wavering* and *vibrating* between different opinions, with a mixture of so much *goodness* and so much *baseness*, and in general with such a compound of opposite *qualities*, *humours* and *inclinations*, that we are, all our lives long, at a loss to determine, with precision, what is such a man's predominant and ruling principle of action." [9]

Leigh literally exposed the rawest nerve ends of pre-revolutionary America. James Otis's famous tract on the *Rights of the British Colonies* (1764), which denied that Britain could tax America, was contradicted the following year by his *Vindication of the British Colonies*, which upheld Parliament's "just and equitable right, power and authority" to levy both internal and external taxes. In 1765, Otis suffered pangs of anxiety that Parliament would "charge the Colonies with presenting Petitions in one hand and a daggar in the other." Until the tensions of constitutional crisis drove Otis absolutely mad, he remained the great exponent of colonial rights while worshipping "the power, the majesty, and the order of the British empire." Is it any wonder that he was denounced as a "double-faced Jacobite-Whig"? [1]

Ebenezer Sparhawk, minister of the First Congregational Church of Templeton, Massachusetts, was called upon by a

lost both fame and wealth. See Robert G. McCloskey, ed.: *The Works of James Wilson* (Cambridge, Mass., 1967), I, 3, 4, 7, 15, 27, 46.

9. Becker: *The History of Political Parties in the Province of New York, 1760–1776* (Madison, 1909), 266; Leigh: *The Man Unmasked: or, The World Undeceived. . . .* (Charleston, 1769), 20.

1. John J. Waters, Jr.: *The Otis Family in Provincial and Revolutionary Massachusetts* (Chapel Hill, 1968), 132–3, 154, 157, 172–3, 177, 181; Ellen E. Brennan: "James Otis: Recreant and Patriot," *New England Quarterly*, XII (1939), 722.

town committee because he continued after 1775 to offer prayers on behalf of the King. Whereupon Sparhawk invited the members in and asked their advice:

> I find myself in a difficulty. You complained of me, and said a patriotic minister ought not to offer public prayers for King George III; and now I have received a circular from the American Congress, requesting all clergymen to offer prayers on the sabbath in behalf of the king and his government, and that the Almighty may help them to come to a better mind. What shall I do, brethren?

Peter Livingston of New York worried himself and his brother-in-law, William Smith, Jr. (the historian), into a nervous state. "Poor man," Smith remarked, "I compassionate the Agony of his Mind—Hedged on every Side he knows not what to do—Equally fearful of the Crown and the Congress—He has privately put up a few Necessaries to be ready to take Wing on the first Alarm." [2]

It all boiled down to the problem of keeping multiple allegiances co-ordinated. How in 1776 could a man possibly fulfill all of the emotional and political obligations he felt? How could he hope to remain simultaneously loyal to the Crown, his own colony, his region, and to the North American colonies collectively? [3] Men such as William Smith, Jr., appointed chief justice of New York at the crest of crisis, became "unwilling to take up my residence in a falling house. . . . I would list on neither side during the present troubles." As the war dragged on, Smith's attempt to achieve neutrality was interpreted variously and inconsistently: "To my old Whigg Friends of Rank I am represented as a Tory—But to the Lower Sort as favoring the popular Measures." [4]

2. George C. Groce, Jr.: "Benjamin Gale," *ibid.*, X (1937), 706, 711; Michael Kammen: "Intellectuals, Political Leadership, and Revolution," *ibid.*, XLI (1968), 587–8.

3. For one of the earliest statements of this dilemma during the revolutionary era, see Noah Welles: *Patriotism Described and Recommended. . . .* (New London, 1764), 8–10.

4. Quoted in L. F. S. Upton: *The Loyal Whig. William Smith of New York and Quebec* (Toronto, 1969), 99, 113, 116, 119.

For pacifist groups such as Quakers and Moravians, the beginning of bloodletting—which ironically commenced at a place called Concord—was a source of agonizing ambiguity. Although the Society of Friends discountenanced armed resistance to constituted authority, individual members, such as General Nathanael Greene, joined one side or the other out of personal conviction. Among those Quakers who did decide to fight, a majority joined the Continental Army or provincial militia rather than British forces. John Adams, writing in 1775 from Philadelphia, expressed amazement at seeing "whole companies of armed Quakers in uniform going through the manual." Moravians split fiercely over the justifiability of defensive measures. Some of the New York brethren, according to Bishop Spangenberg, "advised us to make no resistance to the barbarous enemy, but rather to come away from our settlements. Others, write us to stand upon our defence, and to oppose such wicked and abominable creatures." Anxious to remain faithful to their tenet of Christian noncombatancy, the Moravians also felt a deep responsibility to protect their families as well as the hundreds of non-Moravians who had sought refuge in their settlements.[5]

What men were compelled to do—at least those men who ultimately decided for Independence—was to argue simultaneously for rebellion *and* legitimacy. Most Americans, as Oscar Handlin has observed, considered revolution a way "not of destroying but of strengthening existing government. Their arguments and their thinking therefore were directed toward finding a conception of legitimacy that would simultaneously justify their disobedience to the Crown and establish the validity of the governments they were themselves forming."[6]

The colonists hoped to preserve their property from British threats. They hoped to return to the system and security they

5. Peter Brock: *Pacifism in the United States from the Colonial Era to the First World War* (Princeton, 1968), 188, 201–2, 296–8, 300, 304, 314.

6. Handlin: *The Dimensions of Liberty* (Cambridge, Mass., 1961), 31.

had known before 1763. They were indeed, most of them, reluctant rebels and "boldly cautious" liberals. After the war an extraordinary number of erstwhile radicals revealed themselves, like Sam Adams, to be covert conservatives. One of the most critical dilemmas of the American Revolution, therefore, rested in the question of how far the dogs of anti-authoritarianism should be unleashed. Abiel Leonard, chaplain of the Third Connecticut Regiment, saw all too clearly the delicate need for equilibrium: "He gave a Sensible and judicious discourse," George Washington wrote, "holding forth the Necessity of courage and bravery and at the same time of Obedience and Subordination to those in Command."[7]

Moreover, various strains of thought strategically used by the Americans—classical, common law, covenant theory, Enlightenment, and Old Whig—hardly blended into a comfortable or stable amalgam. There were among them, as Bernard Bailyn has demonstrated,

> striking incongruities and contradictions. The common lawyers the colonists cited, for example, sought to establish right by appeal to precedent and to an unbroken tradition evolving from time immemorial, and they assumed, if they did not argue, that the accumulation of the ages, the burden of inherited custom, contained within it a greater wisdom than any man or group of men could devise by the power of reason. Nothing could have been more alien to the Enlightenment rationalists whom the colonists also quoted—and with equal enthusiasm. These theorists felt that it was precisely the heavy crust of custom that was weighing down the spirit of man; they sought to throw it off and to create by the unfettered power of reason a framework of institutions superior to the accidental inheritance of the past. And the covenant theologians differed from both in continuing to assume the ultimate inability of man to improve his condition by his own powers and in deriving the principles of politics from divine intent

7. Washington to Jonathan Trumbull, Dec. 15, 1775, in John C. Fitzpatrick, ed.: *The Writings of George Washington* (Washington, D.C., 1931), IV, 164.

and from the network of obligations that bound redeemed man to his maker.[8]

Americans insisted all the while that they merely wished to
return to the *status quo ante* 1763. Nevertheless, they were
rushing into revolution, as Gordon Wood has remarked, "even
as they denied it, their progress both obscured and sustained by
a powerful revolutionary ideology—an ideology the radicalism
of which paradoxically flowed from the very heritage of the
English constitution they were rebelling against." [9] The heritage itself was biform, including even the traditional conception
of a constitution, "and so great was the pressure placed upon
it in the course of a decade of pounding debate that in the end
it was forced apart, along the seam of a basic ambiguity, to
form the two contrasting concepts of constitutionalism that
have remained characteristic of England and America ever
since." Even the oft-mentioned natural rights so dear to colonial
patriots were understood in a significantly ambiguous way: at
one and the same time the inalienable rights inherent in all
people, yet also the concrete specifications of English law.[1]

The concept of equality, increasingly important as the
Revolution unfolded, also contained an inherent dualism. For
some it meant equality of opportunity, which therefore implied
the existence of social distinctions. To others, however, it
meant equality of condition, thereby repudiating social differences. Yet the two meanings were inextricably intertwined
in the Americans' use of equality, and they would not be
separated. Men assumed that equality would underpin both
social harmony and public virtue. "It is this principle of
equality," wrote a Virginian in 1776, "which alone can inspire
and preserve the virtue of its members, by placing them in a
relation to the publick and to their fellow-citizens, which has a

8. Bailyn: *The Ideological Origins of the American Revolution*
(Cambridge, Mass., 1967), 33–4.

9. Wood: *The Creation of the American Republic 1776–1787*
(Chapel Hill, 1969), 13.

1. Bailyn: *Ideological Origins*, 67, 77, 177.

tendency to engage the heart and affections to both." What cherished dream could have been more admirable, or more elusive? [2]

Those Whigs who placed so much faith in equality

> assumed that Republican America would be a community where none would be too rich or too poor, and yet at the same time believed that men would readily accede to such distinctions as emerged as long as they were fairly earned. But ironically their ideal contained the sources of the very bitterness and envy it was designed to eliminate.

If the equality to which they aspired accorded all men equal status, regardless of wealth or rank, then the new society would certainly fail to eliminate disputes of the old. "Although few Americans could admit it in 1776, it was the very prevalence of this ambivalent attitude toward equality that had been at the root of much of their squabbling during the eighteenth century." What came swiftly to the surface during the 1770's and early 1780's was a "simultaneous hunger for and hatred of social pretension and distinction." New England lawyers and Virginia planters alike recorded in diaries and letters "their private struggles between the attractions and repulsions of the world of prestige and social refinement."

And so the paradoxical realization eventually emerged that the American people were both equal and unequal at the same time. Joel Barlow would sum it up in 1792:

> They all feel that nature has made them equal in respect to their rights; or rather that nature has given to them a common and equal right to liberty, to property, and to safety; to justice, government, laws, religion, and freedom. They all see that nature has made them very unequal in respect to their original powers, capacities, and talents. They become united in claiming and in preserving the equality, which nature has assigned to them; and in availing themselves of the bene-

2. This paragraph and the next are indebted to Wood: *Creation of the American Republic*, 70, 73–5.

fits, which are designed, and may be derived from the inequality, which nature has also established.[3]

Some revolutionaries realized, too, that somehow they would have to reconcile wealth with liberty, and accommodate prosperity to virtue. "Here then," wrote William Moore Smith in 1775, "is a sad dilemma in politics." If the people "exclude *wealth*, it must be by regulations intrenching too far upon civil *liberty*." "Is there no proper use of *wealth* and *civil happiness*, the genuine descendants of *civil liberty*, without abusing them to the nourishment of *luxury* and *corruption?*"[4] This, surely, had been an American dilemma since the very beginning: how to achieve prosperity without its attendant evils, and also without prejudice to the privileges of others? James Madison restated its ironic essence in 1792: "If the United States mean to obtain or deserve the full praise due to wise and just governments, they will equally respect the rights of property, and the property in rights."[5] Was an equilibrium really possible between the two? We still do not know.

The question became most urgent after 1775 when the success of republicanism seemed contingent upon the intrinsic integrity of Americans. From their inquiry into the problem, as Professor Wood has shown,

> flowed ambiguous and contradictory conclusions about the nature of their social character. On the one hand, they seemed to be a particularly virtuous people, and thus unusually suited for republican government; yet, on the other hand, amidst this prevalence of virtue were appearing dangerous signs of luxury and corruption that suggested their unpreparedness for republicanism.

How could the Americans' sense of their own identity have been more ambivalent? By European standards they seemed

3. *Advice to the Privileged Orders in the Several States of Europe Resulting from the Necessity and Property of a General Revolution in the Principles of Government* (Ithaca, 1956), 17.

4. [Philadelphia] *Pennsylvania Packet*, May 29, 1775.

5. Madison: "Property," *The National Gazette*, Mar. 29, 1792, in Gaillard Hunt, ed.: *The Writings of James Madison* (New York, 1906), VI, 103. I am obliged to Professor James M. Smith for this reference.

profoundly pure and uncorrupted. Yet a glance inward and about them exposed all the evils by which Enlightenment *philosophes* had said they were unencumbered. "Their society seemed strangely both equal and unequal, virtuous and vicious." [6]

By 1776 ambiguous ideological assumptions had evolved, under the pressure of events, into radical corollaries which seemed to threaten private property and established authority. Somehow, the American Whigs hoped to affirm both personal liberty and rights of possession. Consequently, conservative, liberal, and radical writers alike have subsequently perceived a cluster of fundamental tensions embodied within the Declaration of Independence. From one perspective, "the dilemmas of the Declaration of Independence are extraordinary, both with respect to the unity and plurality of the legal foundation of the Union and with respect to the far more complex question of the unity or plurality of the classes of men whose rights create any political community." [7] From another perspective (that of Staughton Lynd), however, "the latent tension within the natural rights philosophy of the Declaration of Independence between an outlook on society based on property and a contrasting perspective built on conscience, or on self-determining human activity, could not long be avoided." [8]

The coalition would not endure, and after the Revolution contradictions within it became ever more visible and had to be confronted. Americans would disagree about the nature of

---

6. Wood: *Creation of the American Republic*, 93, 123.

7. Harry V. Jaffa: *Equality and Liberty. Theory and Practice in American Politics* (New York, 1965), 138.

8. Lynd: *Intellectual Origins of American Radicalism* (New York, 1968), 8, 11, 67–8. See Alexander Hamilton's "Continentalist" essay of April 18, 1782: "There are some, who maintain, that trade will regulate itself, and is not to be benefitted by the encouragements, or restraints of government. Such persons will imagine, that there is no need of a common directing power. This is one of those wild speculative paradoxes which have grown into credit among us, contrary to the uniform practice and sense of the most enlightened nations." Harold C. Syrett, ed.: *The Papers of Alexander Hamilton* (New York, 1962), III, 76.

property and the essence of man. Colonists who could join together in opposition to a "crowned ruffian" would shortly divide into agrarian democrats and aggrandizing capitalists, laconic Jeffersonians and loquacious Hamiltonians. The conflicts generated by these impulses would eventually become endemic and systemic in American civilization.

THE IMPLICATIONS AND EFFECTS of the Revolution were almost as ambiguous as its ideologies and origins. We can find these contradictory tendencies clearly in the military, religious, judicial, and governmental institutions which took shape after the war. Most of all, we discover them in American attitudes toward the Revolution itself, toward Europe, the culture of the new nation and its heroes. In Washington and Jefferson, in the Federalists and Republicans of the young leviathan, are embodied many of the central paradoxes and biformities of the nineteenth century, and therefore the adolescent stages of American growth.[9]

The Revolution left a dual military legacy: pride in the citizen army alongside a rival tradition of the prowess in arms of American regular forces. George Washington created a professional army; and his best units were fully comparable to British regulars, as Maryland and Delaware Continentals demonstrated at Guilford Court House. For several years, Washington's maintenance of a body of continental regulars kept the Revolution alive. Nevertheless, traditional qualities of American militiamen had strategic value and were absorbed by the Continental Army. Militiamen did not fight in the ordered lines of European regulars, but rather in loose formations, "with an eye to any cover afforded by terrain." These tactics were important in skirmishing before a major attack, and in

9. See John Quincy Adams's retrospective assessment from the 1830's: "Freedom and order were also the elementary principles of the parties in the American Union, and as they respectively predominated, each party sympathized with one or the other of the combatants." *The Lives of James Madison and James Monroe* (Buffalo, 1850), 243–5.

reconnoitering the enemy; therefore, Washington's professionals continued to use them.

The point, as Russell Weigley has demonstrated, is that the United States drew from its War of Independence two conflicting military traditions. The Americans had attempted to create an orthodox professional force of their own; but they had also waged a national war with citizens in arms. The conflict

> had been fought by a mixture of both methods, but those who especially favored one method often saw little merit in the other. Therefore, the two military traditions born of the American Revolution came to be regarded as contradictory and rival traditions, and the struggle between their adherents was to become a dominant theme in the history of American military thought.[1]

Colonists had carried into the revolutionary era a fundamental ambiguity about the nature of law and the role of courts in society. In one sense they were strongly committed to the modern conception of statute law based upon legislative enactment, a commitment implicit in their reliance upon written charters. Even so, Americans would not happily acknowledge that constitutional obligation was solely contingent upon man-made law. Like James Otis, they continually held to the conviction that "righteousness should be the basis of law." Under these circumstances, there were "two Fountains of their Law," with all the attendant flexibility and confusion imaginable. Given the changing political context of the 1780's, this bifarious legal tradition posed a serious problem. In these thirteen new republics, more than ever before, laws would have to "be founded on the Principles of JUSTICE AND EQUITY." It became more apparent with every passing month, however, that legislatures were not always capable of equity. Nevertheless,

---

1. Weigley: *Towards an American Army. Military Thought from Washington to Marshall* (New York, 1962), ch. 1, "The Dual Military Legacy of the Revolution." See also Marcus Cunliffe: *Soldiers and Civilians. The Martial Spirit in America, 1775–1865* (Boston, 1968), 47.

judges could not be given overmuch discretion in setting statutory law aside. "This," Madison wrote in 1788, "makes the Judiciary Department paramount in fact to the Legislature, which was never intended and can never be proper." Somehow the Americans would have to reconcile "their abiding belief in the intrinsic equitableness of all law . . . with their commitment to legislative supremacy, without doing violence to either." [2]

Colonists also carried into the revolutionary era, *pari passu*, their highly ambivalent experience with courts as institutional sources of both protection and prosecution. Between the Stamp Act crisis and the Declaration of Independence, that ambivalence was profoundly reinforced by countless episodes—real and imagined—of intimidation by courts and judges: the use of writs of assistance in Massachusetts, the expanded power of vice-admiralty courts, "county court rings" notorious in North Carolina, the lack of local courts in South Carolina, the closing of courts in Virginia in 1774. No wonder several state constitutions written after 1775 included elaborate provisions for careful control of courts and the judiciary. "All courts shall be open," declared Pennsylvania's new Frame of Government, "and justice shall be impartially administered without corruption or unnecessary delay." [3]

But what relief did they actually gain? The number of court actions and the accumulation of court fees seemed worse than ever in the 1780's, and became a major factor in stimulating Shays' Rebellion. Look, for example, at the petition drafted by a popular convention in Worcester County, Massachusetts:

> The existence of the Courts of Common Pleas and Courts of General Sessions in their present mode has given general disgust; these courts are an amazing expence to the subject and . . . without the least advantage—not more than one action in forty brou't to

2. Wood: *Creation of the American Republic*, ch. 7, pt. 5, "The Ambiguity of American Law," esp. 292, 295–6, 300, 303–5.

3. S. E. Morison, ed.: *Sources and Documents Illustrating the American Revolution, 1764–1788* (Oxford, 1929), 152, 154–5, 171.

our lower courts is ever deigned for tryal, and in those cases that are disputable little dependance is placed on their decission.[4]

The Anti-Federalists could not concede that America, like Europe, needed the kind of strong central government promised by the Constitution.[5] But if not, how had the crisis and controversy of the 1780's ever reached the proportions it achieved by 1787? A number of contemporaries realized the incongruity of their situation. "In reality," said a South Carolinian, "though there never was a period in which calamity was so much talked of, I do not believe there ever was a period in which it was so little experienced by the people of this State. If we are undone, we are the most *splendidly ruined* of any nation in the universe." [6] Nevertheless, there *was* a crisis, though Americans who agreed upon its existence could not agree about how best to resolve it: by moral reform or by institutional innovations? The Anti-Federalists, as Mercy Otis Warren wrote, were "jealous of each ambiguity in law or Government, or the smallest circumstance that might have a tendency to curtail the republican system." [7]

What about proponents of the new régime? Ah, theirs were the most anomalous positions of all, for federalism emerged from a conception of authority in which two kinds of government co-existed, neither derived directly from the other, both built upon popular consent. This broadly based distribution of power would lead various delegates to exult that "We were

4. *Ibid.*, 208–12; see Forrest McDonald: *E Pluribus Unum. The Formation of the American Republic*, 1776–1790 (Boston, 1965), 137, 143–7, 149, 151–2.

5. They also complained about the ambiguity of the Constitution (which some persons have since argued is its greatest asset): "Most of the articles in this system," wrote "Brutus," "which convey powers of any considerable importance are conceived in general and indefinite terms which are either equivocal, ambiguous, or which require long definitions to unfold the extent of their meaning."

6. [Charleston] *S.C. Gazette and Public Advertiser*, May 18–21, 1785. Italics mine.

7. Warren: *History of the American Revolution* (Boston, 1805), III, 360.

partly national; partly federal" (Oliver Ellsworth of Connecticut), or "We were partly federal, partly national in our Union" (William R. Davie of North Carolina). In designing the mechanisms of a bicameral Congress, moreover, the Federalists created one of the most notable institutional biformities in American political culture: a double representation of the people in a reconceived Congress that would combine both actual *and* virtual representation. By the 1780's, it would seem logical for the people to elect two sets of agents who could speak for them simultaneously but in different ways, "by which means the Citizens of the States would be represented both individually & collectively" (William Pierce of Georgia at the Constitutional Convention). In this manner, one of the most fundamental ambiguities in colonial government—the relative roles of the two legislative houses—would be accommodated.[8]

Understood in these terms, the Constitution of 1787 was as much an experiment in bisociation as the state constitutions of 1776–80 had been. They had absorbed older aristocratic assumptions as well as incorporated the new democratic thrusts of American thought. The freshly created state senates, for example, were neither aristocratic nor wholly democratic in function and intent.[9] Similarly, the federal Constitution was designed to establish "a mixed regime," whose foundations could rest firmly if not comfortably upon differing ideas of justice, liberty, and the general welfare. The Founding Fathers, therefore,

> implanted two conflicting principles in the Constitution. . . . Democracy is a powerful principle. It must ever have great weight in a large and civilized society.

8. Charles C. Tansill, ed.: *Documents Illustrative of the Formation of the Union of the American States* (Washington, D.C., 1927), 164, 170, 304, 312; James Madison: *The Federalist*, Number 39, in *The Federalist Papers*, ed. Clinton Rossiter (New York, 1961), 244–6; Bernard Bailyn, ed.: *Pamphlets of the American Revolution, 1750–1776* (Cambridge, Mass., 1965), I, 298.

9. See Jackson Turner Main: *The Upper House in Revolutionary America, 1763–1788* (Madison, 1967), 235, 237.

But democracy is a principle which can lead to the tyranny of the many. If only for its own sake, democracy requires restraints, the restraints of a contrary principle, the principle of aristocracy.[1]

The Federalist mind tended toward bisociative patterns of thought, in part, because of the very nature of the problems faced after Independence. Localism versus centralism was a critical issue; and as Benjamin Rush reported, "half the people think the government too strong, and the other half too weak." John Adams felt compelled to reply that "in the hands of aristocrats it has been too strong without being sufficiently wise or just. In the hands of democrats it has been too strong without being either wise or just." A Connecticut contemporary could not decide whether to call his government an "elective despotism or rather an elective aristocracy." [2]

Because Federalists could not repudiate republicanism out of hand, they developed an élitist theory of democracy—what they liked to call "*a well regulated democracy.*" They adapted elements of democratic radicalism and rhetoric in their arguments, and they emphasized the popular character of the Constitution. Nevertheless, the kinds of polities they envisioned were self-consciously hybrids. Nathaniel Chipman called them "Democratic Republics," by which he meant "a Representative Democracy." Alexander Hamilton, too, said America would be "a *representative democracy*," and Thomas Paine presented the new government as "representation ingrafted upon democracy,"

1. Paul Eidelberg: *The Philosophy of the American Constitution* (New York, 1968), xiv, 260. Eidelberg's conclusion is worth quoting in this context. "What will be the effects of these principles on the American soul? Once again I say, that soul will be in tension. It will seek unity while praising diversity. It will desire change yet a sense of permanence. It will be acquisitive on the one hand, yet public-spirited on the other. It will love equality, yet aspire to excellence."

2. Adams to Rush, July 25, 1808, in John A. Schutz and Douglass Adair, eds.: *The Spur of Fame. Dialogues of John Adams and Benjamin Rush, 1805–1813* (San Marino, 1966), 112; Vernon L. Parrington, ed.: *The Connecticut Wits* (New York, 1926), xiii.

thereby creating "a system of government capable of embrac-
ing and confederating all the various interests and every extent
of territory and population." [3] No wonder James Lovell, con-
gressman from Massachusetts, would describe himself in 1803
as a "democratic-republican" in state politics and a "republican-
federalist" in national affairs.[4]

The new American government envisioned by Federalists
had to be—incongruous as it sounds—a "mixed" or "balanced
democracy." Such enlightened revolutionaries as Jefferson and
Adams could talk hopefully about the virtues of a "natural
aristocracy," one based upon talent and ability. But the only
aristocracy visible on the horizon was a bourgeois aristocracy,
or what one Bostonian designated as a "set of mushroom gentry." [5] Realistically, in fact, the demon to be contained was the
one Adams had termed "a democratick despotism," the same
one that Jefferson and Richard Henry Lee called "an elective
despotism." The aim of government, in James Iredell's words,
became necessarily twofold: to provide "for the security of
every individual, as well as a fluctuating majority of the people." [6]

WHAT HAD THE REVOLUTION meant to those who lived
through it? Different things at different times. When Samuel
Cooke of Arlington, Massachusetts, preached a sermon to com-
memorate the bloody beginning of Independence, he fulminated
with righteous indignation against the barbarous British.
Choosing as his text Isaiah 10: 1–13, he expressed the biblical
conviction "that Britain must have been the rod of God's anger
against the colonists for their moral failings." In another sermon, however, once Revolution and Independence were assured, he uttered the more popular conviction "that God in his

3. Wood: *Creation of the American Republic*, 517–18, 524, 562,
595.
4. Shipton: *Sibley's Harvard Graduates*, XIV, 45.
5. [Boston] *Independent Chronicle*, July 21, 1785.
6. Iredell: "To the Public" (1786) in Griffith J. McRee, ed.:
Life and Correspondence of James Iredell (New York: 1857–8), II,
146.

providence had great hopes for his Reformed people gathering as a new nation." [7]

American attitudes toward Europe changed ever more restlessly. By 1770, provincials were defining America in terms of what Europe was not, and in terms of those aspects of Old World life being rejected by colonials. American character came to be regarded as the obverse of whatever was recognizably English. By the later 1770's and 1780's, Republican writers expanded their conception of the American as a non-European, a new man unburdened by the heavy weight of Europe's past, a regenerate man whose identity stood in polar relation to his historical antecedents.[8] During the Constitutional Convention of 1787, Charles Pinckney expressed his belief in the British constitution as possibly "the best constitution in existence; but at the same time I am confident it is one that will not or can not be introduced into this Country, for many centuries." [9]

After the Revolution both David Ramsay, physician and historian from South Carolina, and Hector St. John de Crèvecoeur, the "American Farmer" from New York, asked essentially the same rhetorical question: "What, then, is the American, this new man?" Their answers could not have been more different. For Crèvecoeur, the American was a virtuous husbandman, simple and rustic, uncomplicated and honest, a compromise between nature and civilization: the Europeanized Indian, the civilized farmer. For Ramsay, by contrast, the new American was a clever, cultured sophisticate, easily the equal of his Old World peers. "When the War began," Ramsay argued, "the Americans were a mass of husbandmen, merchants, mechanics, and fishermen: but the necessities of the country gave a spring to the active powers of the inhabitants,

7. Quoted in George H. Williams: *Wilderness and Paradise in Christian Thought* (New York, 1962), 112.

8. See Frank Moore, ed.: *Songs and Ballads of the American Revolution* (New York, 1856), 90–1.

9. Max Farrand, ed.: *The Records of the Federal Convention of 1787* (New Haven, 1911), I, 398–9.

and set them on thinking, speaking, and acting, in a line far beyond that to which they had been accustomed." [1]

Whose American was truly the new American? Neither, or else both together; for the quintessential citizen of the young republic had a complex, bifarious character. He harbored ambitendencies. Thus in the first American comedy by a native playwright, *The Contrast* (1787), Royall Tyler could not decide whether his victorious Yankee character was a superbumpkin or a proper hero. Similarly, Washington Irving's treatment of Rip Van Winkle is highly ambiguous too, for he makes Rip at once the lazy, parasitic butt of a termagant wife and the townspeople as well as the wizened hero of an epic extravaganza. As artists, Tyler and Irving were torn between the attractions of reason and sentiment, between the desire to affirm the orderly world of the Enlightenment and the romantic desire to sing the sublime glories of a new nation.

The real heroes of young America were just as complex as their fictive imitations. George Washington, a republican whose highest goal was "the approbation and affections of a free people," had little faith, in fact, in that people's wisdom. Even so, and despite his toughness, Washington was intensely sensitive to public criticism. His rages were balanced by compassion, his moods of despair by optimism, while his frankness and generosity were sometimes marred by spite and lack of candor. More important, perhaps, when Washington looked back upon the revolutionary era, and then ahead to future prospects, he adumbrated beautifully the delicate balance required between liberty and order. Here is a critical passage from his letter to Lafayette in June 1792:

> We are however, anxious that the horrors of war may be avoided . . . and the rights of man so well understood and so permanently fixed, as while despotic oppression is avoided on the one hand, licentiousness may not be substituted for liberty nor confusion take [the] place of order on the other. [2]

1. Ramsay: *The History of the American Revolution* (2nd ed., London, 1793), II, 315.
2. Fitzpatrick, ed.: *Writings of George Washington*, XXXII, 54.

Thomas Jefferson, above all others, seems to have been the American nonesuch. It was not just his tortured ambivalence about the problem of slavery, nor simply his regard for the presidency as a "splendid misery." [3] It was because two predominant aspects of Jefferson's personality clashed so dramatically: his uncritical acceptance of established formulations, and his critical aggressiveness in the actual conduct of affairs. In Jefferson's case, as Bernard Bailyn has suggested,

> these strands or elements of personality were never tightly integrated; their configuration was mobile and unstable, shifting from time to time and from situation to situation. . . . At times it resulted in a syncopated response to problems and issues: an initial, instantaneous reaction, a reflex almost, in terms of one set of responses, subsequently qualified, even reversed, by another. . . . In his involvement in the early stages of the French Revolution, this weak integration of contrasting characteristics led to simultaneous but quite different responses at different levels of activity. At still other times, as in the negotiations of commercial arrangements, it led to an appearance of applying different principles to similar circumstances. It could easily result in apparent inconsistencies which animosity could construe as hypocrisy. [4]

Jefferson must have been aware of his own dualistic tendencies, his inclination to polarize the critical elements in an emotional or intellectual context. In October 1786, his letter to Mrs. Maria Cosway, cast as a "dialogue . . . between my Head and my Heart," pitted rationalism versus romanticism, and sentiment against science. "When nature assigned us the

3. Jefferson to Elbridge Gerry, May 13, 1797, in Paul L. Ford, ed.: *The Writings of Thomas Jefferson* (New York, 1896), VII, 120. In his speech on retrenchment and reform in 1828, John Randolph of Roanoke referred to the federal government in Washington as "this abode of splendid misery, of shabby splendor" (Henry Adams: *John Randolph* [Boston, 1882], 293). Lyndon B. Johnson adopted the "splendid misery" phrase in his first political speech on behalf of Hubert Humphrey (October 1968).

4. Bailyn: "Boyd's Jefferson: Notes for a Sketch," *New England Quarterly*, XXXIII (1960), 398–9.

same habitation," Heart declares, "she gave us over it a divided empire. To you she allotted the field of science, to me that of morals. . . . We have no rose without its thorn; no pleasure without alloy. It is the law of our existence; and we must acquiesce." [5]

Similarly, when Jefferson wrote the Marquis de Chastellux in 1785, he delineated with almost excessive precision the distinctions he then saw between northerners and southerners:

In the North they are	In the South they are
cool	fiery
sober	Voluptuary
laborious	indolent
persevering	unsteady
jealous of their own liberties, and just to those of others	zealous for their own liberties, but trampling on those of others
interested	generous
chicaning	candid
superstitious and hypocritical in their religion	without attachment or pretentions to any religion but that of the heart.[6]

Like Crèvecoeur, Jefferson was animated by opposing forces: reason and emotion, the ideal and the real, Enlightenment and Romanticism, Europe and America, civilization and wilderness, aristocracy and democracy, an educational meritocracy in a popular republic, peace and revolution. To both men nature seemed simultaneously predatory and benevolent; and for both, the leading attributes of European civilization—its cities and sophistication—posed the greatest threat to young America. How ironic that Jefferson, as President, accepted the very measures that turned the country toward manufacturing and industrialization.

As SUCCESSFUL REVOLUTIONARIES the Founding Fathers worked hard to conserve and consolidate the fruits of insurrec-

5. Jefferson to Maria Cosway, Oct. 12, 1786, in Julian P. Boyd, ed.: *The Papers of Thomas Jefferson* (Princeton, 1954), X, 450–1. Her reply appears on 494–5.
6. *Ibid.*, VIII, 468.

tion. They had been engaged for thirty years in what Professor Bailyn has called "this spirit of pragmatic idealism"—"the creative adjustment of ideas to reality." Through it all, the very meaning of provincialism and the implications of colonialism would be transformed. "What were once felt to be defects —isolation, institutional simplicity, primitiveness of manners, multiplicity of religions, weakness in the authority of the state —could now be seen as virtues, not only by Americans themselves but by enlightened spokesmen of reform, renewal, and hope wherever they might be." [7] The primary position of sovereignty in political society was relocated from the top to the bottom, from a monarch to his erstwhile subjects. In that ambiguous interplay of ideas which culminated in ratification of the Constitution, the ruled had become rulers.

In thinking about politics and society, however, the founders proceeded from paradoxical premises. They saw that men were greedy, corrupt, and self-interested by nature; and that therefore the science of politics consisted in creating a government strong enough to control such dangerous passions. But they also recognized that strong government was itself a threat to liberty, and that therefore the art of politics consisted in setting effective limits upon governmental authority.

The new man, the American, like the old one, was a mixture of discipline and dissipation. His political arrangements, however, were genuinely new—a mixture of consolidation and decentralization, confidence and distrust, exuberance and experimental hesitancy. They knew that only time would tell how well the new would do.

7. Bailyn: *Ideological Origins of American Revolution*, 160, 202, 232; see also Gerald Stourzh: "Reason and Power in Benjamin Franklin's Political Thought," *American Political Science Review*, XLVII (1953), 1092–1115.

CHAPTER 8

ENCRUSTATIONS OF SPACE AND TIME, CIRCA 1825–1925

"The idea that I was two persons, that my identity was double, began to fascinate me with its simple solution of my experience."

Julian West in EDWARD BELLAMY'S
Looking Backward (1888)

DURING the nineteenth century, America passed from adolescence to maturity. The generations between Jefferson and Jennings Bryan opened the frontier physically and then closed it psychologically. Theirs was truly the American century, when they were least involved with Europe and the wider world. Perhaps that disengagement permitted their penchant for ambi-tendencies to continue apace. In any case, nineteenth-century Americans nipped from the cookie jar and from the pickle barrel, the sweet and the sour. They built a Calvinistic Babylon: it could become so Babylonian because it had a Calvinistic creed, but desperately needed that creed precisely because it had become so Babylonian.[1]

Antinomies inherited from colonial times endured; but alongside them a new garden of dualisms blossomed. The re-

1. John P. Marquand once made the honest observation that "the spirit of Newburyport was made up of contradictory combinations of holier-than-thou right-living mingled with acquisitive materialism and heavy drinking." *Timothy Dexter Revisited* (Boston, 1953), 86.

currence and emergence of both sorts, treated topically, will be my first and last priorities in this chapter. In between, I want to discuss the dynamics of biformity chronologically— albeit sketchily—over four generations, roughly 1825–1925.

THE PROBLEMS OF LEGITIMACY and unstable pluralism be- came somewhat more manageable in the nineteenth century because guidelines and precedents—however subject to inter- pretation and violation—had been established by the Founding Fathers. Even so, the Hartford Convention in 1814 and South Carolina's attempt at nullification in 1828 provoked such major crises because both threatened the legitimacy of federal union. In 1814 the *New York Examiner* asked whether "the union and liberty are inseparable? Is it certain that they are compatible?" [2]

Between the Revolution and Civil War, two different con- ceptions of the nature of the union were often at odds. While some people asserted that the national polity had emerged organically from colonial times, others insisted that it was grounded in a conscious compact made after Independence. Both versions were vexed, however, by a basic ambiguity which reflected an uncertain historical notion of union. Confusion of terms commonly made "organic" and "compact" almost synony- mous, thereby allowing those who credited the states with in- divisible sovereignty to support nevertheless the idea of an organic union originating prior to 1787–8. [3]

Instability born of broadened heterogeneity also seemed to pose a threat to canons of legitimacy codified by the revolu- tionary generation. Anti-Masonic outcries in the later 1820's and 1830's, for example, were prompted by the belief that secret and élitist organizations had no place in a republican society. Shouldn't legitimacy flow from egalitarianism rather than from the older tap of élitism? Anti-Masons in Chautauqua County, New York, thought so, and were dedicated to achiev-

2. *Niles Weekly Register*, VI (Oct. 9, 1814), 306.
3. See Paul C. Nagel: *One Nation Indivisible. The Union in American Thought*, 1776–1861 (New York, 1964), 33.

ing equality and "supremacy of the law." [4] Yet many who discussed political and social issues in that era hoped to preserve a distinct American nationality, to which the more recent European immigration posed a grave threat. Hence the emergence of such groups as the Know-Nothings, who feared that American nationality would become diluted and lack strength. Similarly, most northerners during the 1830's and 1840's opposed abolitionism as "a doctrine which is . . . subversive of civil government, civil society and the legal rights of individual citizens—a species of moral treason against the government." [5]

Emergence of the first and second American party systems between 1790 and 1840, however, helped to provide new sources of both legitimacy and stability. Where traditional political institutions collapse, are relatively weak or new, the role of party may be enormously important as a source of authority and a release for potential restlessness. Where traditional political institutions are frail, in fact, the prerequisite of stability is at least one well-formed political party; and then the State commonly becomes the instrument of that party. So it was with the Republicans and the union after the demise of federalism.[6] Although fearful of faction, the Federalists had built a political party. Although supporters of national union, they developed a doctrine of state interposition and dared to consider secession. Although élitists, they borrowed the mechanisms of democratic politics in order to gain and hold political power. Their incongruities caused the Federalists to disintegrate into a rubble of contradictions, while the Republicans flourished through years of flexible adaptability and fluctuating cohesion.

Clearly, the liberal conservatism evident in colonial times

4. See Lee Benson: *The Concept of Jacksonian Democracy. New York as a Test Case* (Princeton, 1961), 17, 309.

5. See Joel H. Silbey: *The Transformation of American Politics, 1840–1860* (Englewood Cliffs, 1967), 55, 62–3; Howard M. Jones: *The Life of Moses Coit Tyler* (Ann Arbor, 1933), 31.

6. See Samuel P. Huntington: *Political Order in Changing Societies* (New Haven, 1968), 90–1; the fine review by Stephen G. Kurtz in *The William and Mary Quarterly*, 3d series, XXVII (1970), 480.

became permanently part of the American scene. Once the Revolution had been reduced to a maudlin memory, politics in the United States turned moderately conservative—accompanied, nevertheless, by a liberal, progressive, popular ideology. Despite our behavioral conservatism in public affairs, however, we have never developed a sound and substantial tradition of conservative thought. Here is the parallax of our political paradox: the intersection of actual inertia with an activist creed. Political scientists have found, in fact, that since the 1790's the greatest danger to democracy in America has come from the (socio-economically) lower portions of the population; that it has been the masses who have most often imperiled government of, by, and for the people. Hence the characteristic anxiety of William Ellery Channing's report from Boston in 1835: "The cry is, 'Property is insecure, law a rope of sand, and the mob sovereign.'" Democratic despotism again.[7]

Similarly, practical idealism also became a benchmark of republican culture, evidenced by orators, by popular denominations like the Baptists and Methodists, and embodied in the "pietistic pragmatism" of circuit-riding preachers and "practical mystics" like Senator William Peffer, leader of the Farmer's Alliance.[8] Morton White has labeled Thorstein Veblen an "amoral moralist" because he was indifferent to what he regarded as moral questions, wished to free economics from ethical assumptions, yet condemned human wastefulness and resented the failure of the leisure class to serve humanity well.[9]

Americans continued to prize what Wilberforce Nevin referred to in 1860 as "unlettered learning." Where men's minds

7. See Seymour M. Lipset and Earl Raab: *The Politics of Unreason: Right-wing Extremism in America, 1790–1970* (New York, 1970); *Memoir of William Ellery Channing, with Extracts from His Correspondence and Manuscripts* (London, 1848), II, 250.

8. See Richard Hofstadter: *Anti-intellectualism in American Life* (New York, 1966), 97; T. Scott Miyakawa: *Protestants and Pioneers. Individualism and Conformity on the American Frontier* (Chicago, 1964), 5.

9. Morton White: *Social Thought in America. The Revolt Against Formalism* (2nd ed., Boston, 1957), ch. 6, "The Amoral Moralist."

fed upon the common law, ballads, and unwritten customs, proper colleges were deemed aristocratic and formal education was regarded as an obstacle to success in commerce. Many frontier communities vocalized their faith in education; yet teachers faced indifference, suspicion, and derision, and books were scarce.[1] Tocqueville could not imagine that "there is a country in the world where, in proportion to the population, there are so few ignorant and at the same time so few learned individuals." In 1853, one well-known clergyman complained that there was "an impression, somewhat general, that an intellectual clergyman is deficient in piety, and that an eminently pious minister is deficient in intellect."[2]

The moralized wit of earlier times gave way to the bitter, even sad humor of a middle-class and more secular society. "I have been over 20 years trying to kid the great American Public out of a few loose giggles," Will Rogers remarked. "Somebody had to act the fool, and I happened to be one of the many that picked out *that unfunny business of trying to be funny*."[3] Mark Twain did so too, for like Tocqueville he found the Americans "serious, and almost sad, even in their pleasures."

The bitter-sweet quality of our humor owes a great deal to American pluralism. Heterogeneity, as Jesse Bier contends, "has furnished our humor simultaneously with both its targets and weaponry." Ambiguity permeates the language as well as the psychology of our humor. To be "shrewd" or "smart" is to be admired and condemned at the same time, and "to be taken in" evokes equal portions of consolation and ridicule. Will Rogers contended that Americans "conceived many odd inven-

---

1. Nevin: *Unlettered Learning, or a Plea for the Study of Things* (Lancaster [1860]); Jennette Tandy: *Crackerbox Philosophers in American Humor and Satire* (New York, 1925), ch. 2, "The Unlettered Philosopher in the Thirties."

2. Tocqueville: *Democracy in America*, ed. Phillips Bradley (New York, 1957), I, 54; Bela Bates Edwards: "Influence of Eminent Piety on the Intellectual Powers," *Writings* (Boston, 1853), II, 472-3, 497-8.

3. Donald Day: *Will Rogers* (New York, 1962), 173. Italics Rogers's.

tions for getting somewhere, but could think of nothing to do when they got there." And a characteristic bit of frontier doggerel, found on a hotel placard in Texas, ran this way:

> Come to Van Horn to live
> The climate is so healthy
> We had to shoot a man
> To start our graveyard.

Wit in the Wild West, as in the rest of America, had to be boastful, skeptical, cruel, and derogatory. It provides, perhaps, "a means of perspective between exaltation and destruction. Its prime function is antithetical." [4]

Nor was it any simpler for Americans to define a singular cultural style (and nomenclature) appropriate to the frontier. Again and again, mythic heroes of the trans-Allegheny west identified themselves in terms of biformities. As Davy Crockett and the popular *Hunters of Kentucky* proclaimed:

> If a daring foe annoys . . .
> We'll show him that Kentucky boys
> Are "alligator-horses."

What did it mean to be an alligator-horse? The Kentuckians and Mississippi River keelboatmen who appropriated this grotesque creature to themselves meant that they embodied both brute force and animal cunning, barbaric individualism in the child of nature stripped of his *a priori* endowment of natural virtue. [5]

Certainly Americans were of several minds about the Indian as they pushed him steadily westward. They pitied his condition but regarded it as inevitable. They hoped to "civilize" him but recognized that doing so would "ruin" the red man.

4. Bier: *The Rise and Fall of American Humor* (New York, 1968), 1–3, 10, 14–15, 24–5, 29–30; Mody C. Boatright: *Folk Laughter on the American Frontier* (New York, 1949), 83.

5. Arthur K. Moore: *The Frontier Mind. A Cultural Analysis of the Kentucky Frontiersman* (Lexington, Ky., 1957), 107, 114, 116. For an essay on the cowboy's "strange, paradoxical code of personal honor," see Henry King: "Over Sunday in New Sharon," *Scribner's*, XIX (1880), 771.

Primitivists continued to regard the Indian as a noble savage who embodied all that good men should be. Anti-primitivists, meanwhile, had unfurled a counter-concept of savagism; and by the 1820's, these separate strains of thought had fused into a double image of the Indian, noble and yet ignoble.[6] Fenimore Cooper summed up this tendency in his Introduction to the revised edition of *The Last of the Mohicans* (1850): "Few men exhibit greater diversity, or, if we may so express it, greater antithesis of character, than the native warrior of North America. In war, he is daring, boastful, cunning, ruthless, self-denying, and self-devoted; in peace, just, generous, hospitable, revengeful, superstitious, modest, and commonly chaste."

The Indian's incongruous position subsequently led to a different sort of ambiguity: mixed status as both citizen and also ward of the government. By contrast, the Negro was neither fully a citizen nor anyone's ward. John Brown, the mad martyr of Harper's Ferry, hoped to launch a massive slave rebellion. Yet he had no black deputies, took almost no advice from Negroes, "and most paradoxical of all, he completely concealed his intended insurrection from the Negroes who were expected to support it." Historically, as David Potter has shown, there was an anomalous relationship between Negro slaves and their would-be benefactors. Abolitionists assumed that black people were on the verge of insurrection; yet they rarely consulted any for corroboration, and conducted their activities with patent disregard for the aspirations and sentiments of Negroes. Abolitionists in ante-bellum America harbored profoundly ambivalent feelings about people of color, and most of their countrymen continued to do so long after the Civil War and Reconstruction.[7]

6. Roy Harvey Pearce: *Savagism and Civilization. A Study of the Indian and the American Mind* (2nd ed., Baltimore, 1965), 64, 66, 76, 136–8, 151, 199, 203; Reginald Horsman: *Expansion and American Indian Policy, 1783–1812* (East Lansing, 1967), 4, 70, 86, 105–6, 110, 114, 116, 165.
7. Potter: "John Brown and the Paradox of Leadership Among American Negroes," in *The South and the Sectional Conflict* (Baton Rouge, 1968), 203–4, 214; William H. and Jane H. Pease: "Anti-

That war and its long prelude perpetuated the dualistic military heritage of the American Revolution: belief in both the militia and a professional army. Despite great outpourings of ritual praise for amateur warriors, the American militia was never put on a satisfactory footing. Nevertheless, the civilian-soldier, in the manner of George Washington, remained our beau ideal, praised in presidential war messages, and by Elihu Root at the dedication of the Army War College in 1908: "We are warlike enough, but not military." During the 1840's, General Edmund P. Gaines, one of the nation's senior soldiers, made a lecture tour accompanied by his wife. Myra Gaines addressed her audiences on "The Horrors of War," followed by the uniformed general, his sword jabbing at a large map, lecturing on railroad construction in relation to military preparedness. The uniformed candidate for public office was an equivocal figure, attractive to the electorate for his heroic qualities, yet vulnerable to the venerable charge of military despotism.[8]

Plowshares and swords somehow seemed inextricably bound up together in taming the vastness of America. The national conception of wilderness, for example, has continually blended a compound of attraction and repulsion. The solitude of wilderness, wrote Ralph Waldo Emerson, "is a sublime mistress, but an intolerable wife." [9] The painter Thomas Cole, Emerson's contemporary, constantly idealized a juxtaposition of the wild and the civilized. Take for example "The Oxbow," a view of the Connecticut River Valley from Mount Holyoke, painted by Cole in 1836. The left half of the picture depicts a rugged cliff with shattered tree trunks and dark, violent clouds which Cole used to symbolize untamed nature. On the right, however, along the far side of the river, appears a bucolic scene. Cultivated fields and tidy groves separate inviting homes

slavery Ambivalence: Immediatism, Expediency, Race," *American Quarterly*, XVII (1965), 682–95.

8. Marcus Cunliffe: *Soldiers and Civilians. The Martial Spirit in America*, 1775–1865 (Boston, 1968), 14, 22–5, 27, 29, 62, 73, 81, 86, 97, 119, 148, 170–1, 179–80, 203, 286, 401, 412.

9. William F. Badè: *The Life and Letters of John Muir* (Boston, 1923), I, 259–60.

bathed in warm sunlight. Cole's schizoid canvas exactly conveys Thoreau's belief that man's best environment combined wildness and civilization, either by alternation, or, better still, through permanent residence in "partially cultivated country." [1]

Again and again Thoreau's contemporaries praised this faith in "amalgamation." Orestes Brownson's utopian society would have merged "all the individual freedom of the savage state with all the order and social harmony of the highest degree of civilization." Francis Parkman delighted in Fenimore Cooper's Leatherstocking, finding "something admirably felicitous in the conception of this hybrid offspring of civilization and barbarism." Charles Lane, a minor transcendentalist, would write in 1844

> that the experiment of a true wilderness life by a white person must . . . be very rare. He is not born for it; he is not natured for it. . . . Some amalgamation may, however, be possible; and to unite the advantages of the two modes has doubtless been the aim of many. . . . To view all things as male and female is a favorite habit of many acute minds; and to such it may appear, that the forest and civilized lives are the male and female, from whose marriage an offspring shall result more conducive to human bliss.[2]

Beyond wilderness lay the behemoth West. To some Americans it seemed a place in which to be saved from sin by the civilizing influence of agricultural pursuits. To others, however, it appeared as an unsullied refuge from society. The West would simultaneously mean regression and progress in nineteenth-century thought. Only gradually would equally persistent ironies become obvious: that limitation and deprivation —as to water and soil, for example—are watchwords of the reputedly limitless West; and that the West—because of mov-

1. Roderick Nash: *Wilderness and the American Mind* (New Haven, 1967), 81, 93, 102.
2. *Ibid.*, 77, 94; Lane: "Life in the Woods," *The Dial* (April 1844), reprinted with Thoreau: *Walden*, ed. Sherman Paul (Boston, 1957), 236–8.

ies, television, and "westerns"—is a place where life may often be seen copying art.[3]

It is ironic that the very traits required to survive in the wilderness and on the frontier were so often inappropriate to the civilization that rapidly ensued. Thus, attributes we idealize in folklore and fiction—cunning, resourcefulness, and ruthless individualism—are not necessarily the attributes we need most in our own time.

THE DYNAMICS OF BIFORMITY appear most readily when observed in the context of change, when seen through the central concerns of successive generations. Let's begin with the Jacksonian era, when democracy is traditionally believed to have come into its own in this country. What most struck Carl Becker about that period was the "peculiar union of strength & futility, of efficiency & vulgarity, of idealism and fustian demagogery, which is so characteristic of the 30's & 40's." [4]

Jacksonian democracy had two different, albeit related meanings: one realistic and the other romantic. Realistic democracy involved patterns of political behavior, caucuses and logrolling, struggles for office and sectional differences. Romantic democracy consisted of a cluster of assumptions and ideas about the goodness of man and his natural rights, all of which

3. See Charles L. Sanford: *The Quest for Paradise. Europe and the American Moral Imagination* (Urbana, 1961), 108, 177; Wallace Stegner: *The Sound of Mountain Water* (New York, 1969), 10, 20. In 1965, Congress asked the Public Land Law Review Commission for advice on what to do about the 755 million acres that are federally owned (about one-third of the nation's real estate). Should the government keep the land, or dispose of it? And if so, how? After five years, Congress received a 342-page report filled with contradictions and compromises, summarized as follows by *The New York Times*, June 25, 1970, 26: "Get rid of some of the land, but keep most of it. Give commercial interests, like the huge mining, timber, and farming industries, more leeway to make money from the public domain, but make them pay the Government more in doing so. Cut the tax-shy and land-shy states and localities in on more of the public-land benefits, but reserve a goodly amount for outdoor museums and parks."

4. Becker to William E. Dodd, 1915, copy in the Becker Papers, Cornell University Library.

taken together comprised a national faith. It had come to pass that the romanticism of those highly intellectual anti-intellectuals, the transcendentalists, merged with the nationalism of Daniel Webster and Justice Story to form a flamboyantly romantic nationalism.

Perhaps Ralph Waldo Emerson embodies best the polarities of nineteenth-century America. The United States has never had a more representative pundit; and James Russell Lowell was exactly on target when he called Emerson "A Plotinus-Montaigne, where the Egyptian's gold mist/ And the Gascon's shrewd wit cheek-by-jowl coexist." Emerson was both a seer and a Yankee. Like Montaigne, he was a superb essayist, a gentleman-scholar, skeptical, and inquiring. But like Plotinus, the third-century philosopher, Emerson's blend of western and oriental ideas could be elusive, as could his quest after Mind and Soul. Emerson harbored within himself both an enthusiasm for technological progress and a romantic yearning for nature. He knew all too well that conflict between them was inevitable because equilibrium was impossible.[5]

Emerson expounded endlessly upon the dualisms confronted by man in society. "All the universe over," he wrote in his journal (1842), "there is just one thing, this old double." He referred there to the ideal and the actual. A decade earlier he had already insisted upon "the distinction of the outer and the inner self—of the double consciousness. . . . There are two selfs . . . within this erring passionate mortal self, sits a supreme calm immortal mind." Emerson had emerged from Unitarianism, that distinctively American composite of Enlightenment optimism and Puritan asceticism, and he would comfortably teach what Stephen Whicher called "the fantastic paradox"—"that purity and strict conscience are *more natural* than the dreary years of routine and of sin that are the common lot." Emerson's rebellion against Puritanism had to be puritanical. As a man of the new republic he valued freedom. As a latter-day Puritan he prized purity. His faith in the Soul prom-

5. See Leo Marx: *The Machine in the Garden. Technology and the Pastoral Ideal in America* (New York, 1964), 178, 232–5, 263.

ised him both, but could not make them coincide. Throughout Emerson's life he relentlessly pursued both a monistic dualism and a dualistic monism.[6]

The Jacksonians both admired and feared self-reliant men. Hence the ambiguous press "King Andrew" received during his own day, but also the fact that Jackson's enemies shared an anxiety about the reign of "King Mob." What Americans required was some assurance that the self-reliant man was on the side of society, and not opposed to it or above it. They knew they would have to steer between the shoals of "elective despotism" and the reefs of "elective monarchy," as Jefferson had phrased it.[7]

Marvin Meyers has cogently defined a central paradox of the Jacksonian, whom he labels a "venturous conservative":

> the fact that the movement which helped to clear the path for laissez-faire capitalism and its culture in America, and the public which in its daily life eagerly entered on that path, held nevertheless in their political conscience an ideal of a chaste republican order, resisting the seductions of risk and novelty, greed and extravagance, rapid motion and complex dealings.

Moreover, the Jacksonians were uncomfortable about the blessings of prosperity. The surprising growth and distribution of wealth caused men to reconsider the relationship between material progress and America's spiritual duty to remain true

6. Whicher: *Freedom and Fate. An Inner Life of Ralph Waldo Emerson* (Philadelphia, 1953), vii, 7, 22, 29–33, 43, 49.

7. John William Ward: *Andrew Jackson. Symbol for an Age* (New York, 1962), 200–1; Jefferson to Madison, Dec. 20, 1787, in Julian P. Boyd, ed.: *The Papers of Thomas Jefferson* (Princeton, 1955), XII, 440–1. James Parton wrote in 1859 that Jackson was "a patriot and a traitor. He was one of the greatest of generals, and wholly ignorant of the art of war. A writer brilliant, elegant, eloquent, without being able to compose a correct sentence, or spell words of four syllables. The first of statesmen, he never devised, he never framed a measure. He was the most candid of men, and was capable of the profoundest dissimulation. A most law-defying, law-obeying citizen. A stickler for discipline, he never hesitated to disobey his superior. A democratic autocrat. An atrocious saint." *Life of Andrew Jackson* (New York, 1860), I, vii.

to its founding principles. Would success make men forget the foundations of their national origin? Prosperity without moral sustenance might cost the American experiment its exemplary and missionary character.[8]

No single issue more fully dramatized the tension between morality and prosperity than slavery. "Our great western republic," wrote William James two generations later, "had from its origins been a singular anomaly. A land of freedom, boastfully so-called, with human slavery enthroned at the heart of it, and at last dictating terms of unconditional surrender to every other organ of its life, what was it but a thing of falsehood and horrible self-contradiction?" Rapid settlement of the trans-Allegheny region after 1790 would quickly expose a critical dualism in the traditional American concept of agrarianism. Expansion of the plantation system into the deep south, stimulated by world markets for cotton, helped to create a slave society which was agricultural but very different from the free northwest. By 1830 there were two agrarianisms, not one; and each expressed itself in imaginative and symbolic terms: the south in a pastoral literature of the plantation, and the northwest in a myth of the garden of the world, with the idealized yeoman as a heroic figure.[9]

The very structure of bi-racial southern society obliged men to think in dualistic terms, in terms of "distant intimacy" between blacks and whites. Southern legislatures and courts never did settle the question of whether a slave was a person or merely property, an indecision which led to complex ambiguities concerning the legitimacy of slavery.[1] No wonder Daniel

8. Meyers: *The Jacksonian Persuasion. Politics and Belief* (New York, 1960), 12, and see 142–3; Fred Somkin: *Unquiet Eagle. Memory and Desire in the Idea of American Freedom, 1815–1860* (Ithaca, 1967), 17–18, 20, 32–4.

9. James: *Memories and Studies* (London, 1912), 42–3; Timothy L. Smith: "Christian Liberty and Human Bondage: The Paradox of Slavery," in *Revivalism and Social Reform in Mid-Nineteenth-Century America* (Nashville, 1957), 178–203.

1. See Daniel R. Goodloe: *The Southern Platform: or, Manual of Southern Sentiment on the Subject of Slavery* (Boston, 1858), 91.

Hundley, an Alabama lawyer, in writing his *Social Relations in Our Southern States* (1860), would devote a lengthy chapter to the case of the *"Southern Yankee,"* and especially his most detestable embodiment, the slave trader.

Steadily throughout the first half of the nineteenth century, as the "Reactionary Enlightenment" spawned a generation of southern conservative ideologues, Jefferson's belief in states' rights was emphasized at the expense of his belief in natural rights. In actual fact, the "democratic" and "aristocratic" themes have both been strong in southern history. The region has been marked by both plebeian and patrician impulses, as well as by an almost obsessive need to be at once at odds with the rest of the nation and yet a part of it. There is even a peculiar sense in which the south at secession was more radical than the north, for it demanded the right of revolution as the last resort of those who felt that the purposes of the original compact had been subverted.[2]

There has been an especially American ambiguity about whether limits upon government derived from the written text of constitutions or from an antecedent body of unwritten natural law. If the latter obtained, then discontented men might appeal to a higher authority against the Constitution. Because of this ambiguity, we have never been altogether clear about the "right" of revolution. During the 1840's and 1850's, for example, Abraham Lincoln believed in the right of revolution because it helped nations to achieve independence and spread democratic practices of government. Even in his first inaugural address, incredibly, Lincoln stated that "this country, with its institutions, belongs to the people who inhabit it. Whenever they shall grow weary of the existing government, they can exercise their constitutional right of amending it, or their revolutionary right to dismember or overthrow it." Nevertheless, Lincoln held yet another set of attitudes—revealed in his con-

---

2. David Potter: "The Enigma of the South," in *The South and the Sectional Conflict*, 3–16; Allen Guttmann: "The Paradox of Southern Liberalism," in *The Conservative Tradition in America* (New York, 1967), 32–46.

cern over certain domestic problems—and emphasized the
necessity of preserving the fabric of a plural society, and of
maintaining the law-abiding, nonviolent, and nonrevolutionary
practices which were part of that fabric. "I hold it to be a paramount duty of us in the free states," he wrote in 1845, "due to
the Union of the states, and perhaps to liberty itself (paradox
though it may seem) to let the slavery of the other states
alone." By 1858, however, he had come to believe that the
nation could not endure half slave and half free, and so he
sought to preserve the divided union, even at great human
cost.[3]

Skeptics and pessimists writing later in the century would
be equally ambivalent in their central concerns. To Henry
Adams, the Virgin of tradition battled to withstand the Dynamo
of modernity. Adams called himself "a conservative anarchist."
Toward the end of his life he further admitted to being "a Unitarian mystic." He organized reality by means of a scheme of
bipolar symbols: cold versus heat, town versus country, force
versus freedom, summer versus winter, theory versus practice,
the Middle Ages versus the twentieth century. The central
artistic problem of *The Education of Henry Adams* concerns
the interplay of these irreconcilable opposites. And to Adams
they were, indeed, peculiarly American, for as he wrote of himself, "no European spring had shown him the same intermix-
ture of delicate grace and passionate depravity that marked the
Maryland May." [4]

Again and again, the best minds of that generation were
caught between their desires and their declarations. Their
equivocal feelings about the Horatio Alger myth were manifest

3. Thomas J. Pressly: "Bullets and Ballots: Lincoln and the
'Right of Revolution,'" *American Historical Review*, LXVII (1962),
647–62; Lincoln to Williamson Durley, Oct. 3, 1845, in Roy Basler,
ed.: *The Collected Works of Abraham Lincoln* (New Brunswick,
1953), I, 348.

4. Henry Adams to John Hay, Jan. 16, 1894, in Harold Dean
Cater, ed.: *Henry Adams and His Friends* (Boston, 1947), 304; Ernest
Samuels: *Henry Adams: The Major Phase* (Cambridge, Mass., 1964),
262–3, 372–3, 559.

in their wish to succeed, but also in their wish to change the criteria for success. In Brooks Adams, Henry's younger brother, aristocratic disdain conflicted with his desire to join the hurly-burly. Ignatius Donnelly envied the successful while sharing the pathos of the oppressed. "Progress" thus seemed to be a very mixed blessing indeed. Consequently, many Americans in the 1880's and 1890's could not decide whether rapid social change was the prelude to development or disintegration. Many of the anarchists, who were so much feared then, displayed a proud disdain for democratic politics and the wider society it represented. There was in the American anarchist mentality—Albert Jay Nock, Max Eastman, and Emma Goldman provide prime examples—a "simultaneous commitment to the mass of mankind and to a peculiar kind of elitism." [5]

Meanwhile, an agrarian revolt had been fermenting since the 1870's, catalyzed by the contrast between image and fact, the ideal and the actual, hope and consummation in the lives of farmers. Richard Hofstadter astutely stated that the American yeoman has a dual character, "and one way of understanding our agrarian movements is to observe which aspect of the farmer's double personality is uppermost at a given time." The "soft" side of American agrarianism—its utopianism and social radicalism, its nostalgia for the yeoman tradition—is more than balanced by its "hard" side: agricultural improvement, business methods, and pressure politics. Populism, for example, had its hard side, especially in the early days of the Farmers' Alliance and the Populist Party; but this aspect became less important as the depression of the 1890's deepened and other issues were displaced by the silver panacea. The Populist farmer had developed the acquisitive goals and speculative

5. Frederic C. Jaher: *Doubters and Dissenters. Cataclysmic Thought in America, 1885–1918* (Glencoe, 1964), 7, 15, 17, 20; Michael Wreszin: "Albert Jay Nock and the Anarchist Elitist Tradition in America," *American Quarterly*, XXI (1969), 166–7. See also Olive Logan: "Saratoga's Attraction," *New York Times*, July 17, 1880, p. 2: "It is easy to account for the popularity of Saratoga as a summer resort, for it is at once fashionable or democratic, retired or demonstrative, as the occasion might require."

mind of the businessman, but he was still practicing the competitive individualism that more advanced sectors of industry and finance had outgrown. The Populist had much to learn about marketing devices, strategies of combination, and self-advancement through lobbying in Washington. "His dual identity itself was not yet resolved. He entered the twentieth century still affected by his yeoman inheritance but with a growing awareness of the businesslike character of his future." [6]

By 1900, tensions between the business community and the rest of American society seemed to preoccupy the minds of many. A newer and an older value system had come into conflict. Society seemed ready to polarize or disintegrate. Governmental authority would have to serve as counterpoise to the power of private business; and social critics began to appraise their physical and intellectual environments in bisociative metaphors. Thus Robert A. Woods, looking at urban slum conditions in 1898, wrote a devastating book entitled *The City Wilderness;* and William James decried in 1906 "the moral flabbiness born of the exclusive worship of the *bitch-goddess* SUCCESS. That—with the squalid cash interpretation put on the word success—is our national disease." Americans idolized a goddess who was also a bitch: the national mermaid was neither fish nor foul because she was both.[7]

For Progressive reformers, then, it became their special responsibility to sustain the emerging organizational nexus of American life while still preserving older social values. Given such a dual task, the nature of their response is almost predictable. Social philosophers of progressivism tried to reconcile within themselves an ethic of communal responsibility with one of unrestrained individualism. They could postulate almost total freedom accompanied by uniformity as the basis for a new co-operative commonwealth. They were simultaneously committed to liberty and regulation, freedom and authority,

6. Hofstadter: *The Age of Reform from Bryan to F.D.R.* (New York, 1956), 47, 59.
7. See Washington Allston, *et al.: The Bitch-Goddess Success: Variations on an American Theme* (New York, 1968), 13, 41, 73.

savagery and civilization, science and faith. Although they insisted that man was a creature of society, they nevertheless held to the belief that he could transcend history. They were ambivalent, once again, about the social implications of prosperity; for prosperity had diminished the prospect of class conflict, though the forces contributing to affluence were themselves of dubious virtue. The coin of prosperity clanked harshly upon the counters of reform.[8]

Progressivism, with its adaptation of Populist discontent to urban conditions, with its traditionalist and modernist wings, provides a prime example of "moderate rebellion." Why? Because middle-class discontent was rising in precisely that period when the middle class was growing both larger and richer. The movement subsumed forces of illiberalism as well as reform. Theodore Roosevelt's deepest impulses were quite conservative. He might not have been a Progressive at all had it not been for the necessity of fending off more radical threats to established ways of doing things. And in Virginia, for example, the reform impulse sprang from reactionary currents which ran deep within the local culture. "Progressive" legislation in Virginia simply returned the state to a stable system capable of resisting innovation. Even the most radical fringes of American progressivism were profoundly ambivalent in their social thought. Those who believed that sexual relationships should be free and unfettered also contended that the state should regulate marriage and the family for eugenic purposes![9]

During the later years of progressivism, many of these anomalies became especially obvious to contemporary observers. A new Democratic coalition emerged between 1910 and

8. See David W. Noble: *The Paradox of Progressive Thought* (Minneapolis, 1958), esp. 1–54, 246–53; and recall Hofstadter's observation about William Graham Sumner: "We may wonder whether, in the entire history of thought, there was ever a conservatism so utterly progressive as this."

9. Raymond H. Pulley: *Old Virginia Restored: An Interpretation of the Progressive Impulse, 1870–1930* (Charlottesville, 1968); Henry F. May: *The End of American Innocence. A Study of the First Years of Our Own Time, 1912–1917* (New York, 1959), 309.

1916 which combined the solid south, heavily agricultural, with dependable urban machines in the north. What a bifurcated base for a national political party. "To 'do good' and to preserve the *status quo;* to make the lion and the lamb, the Garys and Gomperses . . . lie down together—such, in brief, was the hope of more than one Progressive as 1912 drew nigh." So wrote John Chamberlain in his *Farewell to Reform.* "The dualism of Mr. [Henry] Ford was the dualism of America—and of the 'Progressive' forces: he wished to 'do good,' yet he wished to preserve the *status quo*—exactly the dualism of the trust-busting Roosevelt." [1]

Then came prohibition and the 1920's, a decade of sharp contrasts, of Babbitts and bohemians, of internationalism and isolationism, of extravagance and temperance. Will Rogers best summarized the paradoxes of prohibition. "If you think this country ain't Dry, you just watch 'em vote; and if you think this country ain't Wet, you just watch 'em drink." Until quite recently, Mississippi was a dry state with an indirect tax on liquor. Mississippi's 1908 Prohibition Law remained on the books for fifty-eight years even though officials taxed and regulated the flow of liquor after 1944. It was E. B. White who slyly proposed in the 1920's that the federal government nationalize speakeasies: "In that manner the citizenry would be assured liquor of a uniformly high quality, and the enormous cost of dry enforcement could be met by the profits from the sale of drinks." [2]

As a graduate student in empirical psychology late in the 1890's, Gertrude Stein became convinced that human nature fundamentally fell into basic types, which she called "independent-dependent" and "dependent-independent." When she left Johns Hopkins for Paris, Gertrude applied herself dili-

1. Chamberlain: *Farewell to Reform. The Rise, Life and Decay of the Progressive Mind in America* (1932: Chicago, 1965), 222–3.

2. Elizabeth Stevenson: *Babbitts and Bohemians: The American 1920's* (New York, 1967), 88; Handlin: *Al Smith and His America* (Boston, 1958), 125–6; William E. Leuchtenburg: *The Perils of Prosperity, 1914–1932* (Chicago, 1958), 215.

gently to a literary exposition of these convictions. The result, after many years, was a 1,000-page "novel" entitled *The Making of Americans. Being a History of a Family's Progress* (1925). It spanned three generations, described "the old people in the new world," "the new people made out of the old," and ultimately her two kinds of humanity: the attacking type and the resisting type. In subsequent writings about the United States, Miss Stein was inclined to fuse together the polarities she saw. On her triumphal visit to America in 1934, she "saw it and felt it and it had a tenderness and a horror too." In *Four in America*, published posthumously in 1947, she came close to capturing the essence of our collective individualism: "They act as if *they all go together one by one* and so any one is not leading." [3]

Collective individualism. What dualism in the American experience is more central to an understanding of our nature? Some of the most awkward contradictions in American civilization during the nineteenth century certainly derived from men's desire to retain a family brotherhood within a social framework based upon freedom of contract. They needed to strike a balance between the absence of restraint and the ability to belong. One result was that being "anti," or against something, often brought membership or belonging: in the Anti-Masons, the Know-Nothings, or the Klan, for example. Anti-party men in the 1820's who were frustrated by the Republicans organized an anti-party party, a party to end all parties. [4]

Similarly, the communitarian experiments of the 1840's and after were essentially anti-institutional institutions; and they veered erratically between extremes of anarchism and collectivism as they sought some way to eliminate social friction without using coercion. Henry Demarest Lloyd observed in

3. See Donald Sutherland: *Gertrude Stein. A Biography of Her Work* (New Haven, 1951), 53; John Malcolm Brinin: *The Third Rose. Gertrude Stein and Her World* (Boston, 1959), 339; Stein: *Four in America* (New Haven, 1947), viii, xvii.

4. See Michael Wallace: "Changing Concepts of Party in the United States: New York, 1815–1828," *American Historical Review*, LXXIV (1968), 480–1.

1894 that "we can become individual only by submitting to be bound to others. We extend our freedom only by finding new laws to obey. . . . The isolated man is a mere rudiment of an individual. But he who has become citizen, neighbor, friend, brother, son, husband, father, fellow-member, in one is just so many times individualized." [5]

In the later nineteenth century, conflicts between communalism and privatism, between social democracy and individual economic aspirations were severe. For a while the traditional ideal of philanthropic stewardship co-existed with the ethos of competitive acquisitiveness. But by the first decades of the twentieth century, two countervailing sorts of liberalism had begun to be polarized in parties and elections: laissez-faire liberalism versus welfare state liberalism.

Thus Tocqueville's classic volumes attest to the clarity of his vision, for they continued to provide the primary description of democratic man being pulled toward opposing goals of isolation and community. "If we have any such thing as an American culture," wrote Aldo Leopold in 1925, "its distinguishing marks are a certan vigorous individualism combined with ability to organize, a certain intellectual curiosity bent to practical ends. . . . These, if anything, are the indigenous part of our Americanism, the qualities that set it apart as a new rather than an imitative contribution to civilization." [6]

Histories of dissenting sects on the moving frontier repeatedly reveal a blend of collectivistic and individualistic features. These Protestant pioneers were sociable nonconformists, notable for their joining instinct. The western Quakers, for example, had a scheme of democratic organization which allowed a maximum of individual freedom within "the restraints of corporate action, group custom and accumulated habit." [7] Because a persistent tension existed between the desire for a corporate

5. Lloyd: *Wealth Against Commonwealth* (Englewood Cliffs, 1963), 174, 178.
6. Leopold: "Wilderness as a Form of Land Use," *Journal of Land and Public Utility Economics*, I (1925), 401.
7. Miyakawa: *Protestants and Pioneers*, 8, 73.

Christian state and demands for a voluntaristic polity in Church and State, there emerged an American phenomenon known as "civil religion." Amidst an intensely patriotic-religious atmosphere, where no single sect or group could possibly dominate, public life acquired secular-religious appurtenances: a set of beliefs, symbols, and rituals; patriotic days of reverence on which public figures reminded their audience of the mission of "our AMERICAN ISRAEL." [8]

In so many ways, the alternately nascent and overt nationalism of the nineteenth century tightened those tensions which underpinned American culture like coiled bedsprings. Relationships between regionalism and nationalism, for example, were unclearly defined: witness the famous case of Robert E. Lee. And the tumescence of nationalism had equally ambiguous effects upon art and culture in young America. Though Francis Scott Key wrote words for the "Star-Spangled Banner," they were set to a familiar *English* tune, a tune beloved by the very enemy in that War of 1812! The need for public architecture and an indigenous style stimulated artists who felt constrained because the obvious forms and modes of monarchical Europe were off-limits in a republican society. Neoclassicism, consequently, provided "a halfway point between the crudities of barbarism and the vulgarities of overrefinement," and the Greek revival blended elements of provincialism and cosmopolitanism. "Romantic classicism" at Monticello, or the Alsop mansion in Middletown, Connecticut, set the tone for an era. [9]

The classical revival flourished for three full decades because it provided a style appropriate for both public buildings and private dwellings, city structures and rural residences, at a time when agricultural and urban life styles were still in national equilibrium. Many Americans felt perplexed about the proliferation of cities, however; and as the balance shifted, am-

8. Robert N. Bellah: "Civil Religion in America," in *Religion in America*, ed. William G. McLoughlin (Boston, 1968), 3–23.

9. See Neil Harris: *The Artist in American Society. The Formative Years, 1790–1860* (New York, 1966), 13, 25, 28, 38, 43, 56, 58, 73; Talbot Hamlin: *Greek Revival Architecture in America* (New York, 1944).

bivalence gave way to confusion, anxiety, and hostility. They became, in Morton White's phrase, "ambivalent urbanites." The tranquillity of nature, the unorganized space of uninhabited land, were admirable, to be sure. But was it not the mission of America to build up the New Jerusalem and make the covenanted land flourish? "Americans paid homage to the ancient gods of solitude, while at the same time they went right on laying out the town lots and bringing in the railroad." [1]

In 1844, Ralph Waldo Emerson confided to his journal: "I wish to have rural strength and religion for my children, and I wish city facility and polish. I find with chagrin that I cannot have both." That was why he had moved to Concord. "Whilst we want cities as the centers where the best things are to be found, cities degrade us by magnifying trifles." [2] Henry Adams would echo these sentiments a generation later, along with Josiah Strong: "Where men are most crowded together they are farthest apart." By the turn of the century, some Americans found the city wanting—not because it was too civilized, but because it was not civilized enough. Others, however, agreed with Mr. Dooley that "th' throuble about our farms is that they're too far fr'm our cities." [3]

IT SEEMS AS THOUGH America's years of youthful inexperience, her salad days, were drenched with a mix of oil and vinegar. In 1827, young Horace Bushnell, who became the leading native theologian of the nineteenth century, taught a student at Yale the proper technique for sharpening a razor, "drawing it from heel to point both ways," and thus making "the two cross frictions correct each other"—an excellent method, the student would discover, "for making the roughness of opposite sides contribute to a mutual fine edge."

1. Morton and Lucia White: The Intellectual Versus the City. From Thomas Jefferson to Frank Lloyd Wright (New York, 1964), 13, 29–30, 71, 102, 227; Somkin: Unquiet Eagle, 125–6.

2. Bliss Perry, ed.: The Heart of Emerson's Journals (Boston, 1937), 208; E. W. Emerson, ed.: The Complete Works of Ralph Waldo Emerson (Boston, 1903–4), VI, 153.

3. Strong: The New Era (New York, 1893), 187–8; American Magazine (Nov. 1908), 97.

CHAPTER 9

THE CONTRAPUNTAL CIVILIZATION

We have met the enemy and he is us.

POGO

IN THIS FINAL CHAPTER I intend to look briefly at contradictory tendencies within the past generation of American history, then reflect upon our own time, and more especially upon some dominant expressions of cultural cleavage. And in conclusion I want to attempt a summary assessment; for our inheritance has indeed been bitter-sweet, and our difficulty in assessing it just now arises from the fact that American institutions have had too many uncritical lovers and too many unloving critics. We have managed to graft pride onto guilt—guilt over social injustice and abuses of power—and find that pride and guilt do not neutralize each other, but make many decisions seem questionable, motives suspect, and consciences troubled.

Perhaps so many American shibboleths seem to generate their very opposites because they are often half-truths rather than the wholesome verities we believe them to be.[1] Perhaps

1. Franklin Roosevelt made a pertinent remark to Henry Morgenthau in 1942: "You know I am a juggler, and I never let my right hand know what my left hand does. . . . I may have one policy for Europe and one diametrically opposite for North and South America. I may be entirely inconsistent, and furthermore I am perfectly willing

273

we ought to recall Alice in Wonderland playing croquet against herself, "for this curious child was very fond of pretending to be two people. 'But it's no use now,' thought poor Alice, 'to pretend to be two people! Why, there's hardly enough of me left to make one respectable person!' "

FRANKLIN DELANO ROOSEVELT's administrations provide us with an overview of the 1930's. Roosevelt the politician managed to synthesize what Erik Erikson calls "this native polarity of aristocarcy and mobocracy." As Roosevelt increased the radicalism of his rhetoric, he also augmented the conservatism of his decisions. He candidly observed in 1936 that "I am that kind of conservative because I am that kind of liberal." [2] In crucial respects, the New Deal proved to be the salvation of American capitalism; it became Roosevelt's policy, as he put it, "to energize private enterprise." Nonetheless, the New Deal's emphasis upon social planning and welfare provided creative responses to critical situations. [3]

Roosevelt's associates and subordinates were tough-minded, "anti-utopian" realists who nevertheless harbored their own vision of a Heavenly City (the greenbelt town) and an ideal

---

to mislead and tell untruths if it will help win the war." John M. Blum: *From the Morgenthau Diaries. Years of War, 1941–1945* (Boston, 1967), III, 197. I am indebted for this reference to my colleague, Richard Polenberg.

2. Erikson: *Childhood and Society* (2nd ed., New York, 1963), 287; Samuel I. Rosenman, comp.: *The Public Papers and Addresses of Franklin D. Roosevelt* (New York, 1938), V, 390.

3. Even before becoming President, FDR recognized the ambiguous expectations held by American businessmen concerning their relationship to government regulation. "For while it has been American doctrine that the government must not go into business in competition with private enterprises, still it has been traditional particularly in Republican administrations for business urgently to ask the government to put at private disposal all kinds of government assistance. The same man who tells you that he does not want to see the government interfere in business—and he means it, and has plenty of good reasons for saying so—is the first to go to Washington and ask the government for a prohibitory tariff on his product." (Commonwealth Club Address, Sept. 1932.)

polity (what David Lilienthal liked to call the "decentralized administration of centralized authority").[4] Theirs was a pragmatic utopianism, based upon the assumption that the good life would emerge from sufficient social engineering to create the enviable environment. As one observer remarked of Harry Hopkins, Roosevelt's aide-de-camp, "he had the purity of St. Francis of Assisi combined with the sharp shrewdness of a race track tout."

More than any previous event in American history, the Depression of the 1930's dramatized the enormous paradox of poverty amidst abundance. To Will Rogers the country seemed to be going "to the poor-house in an automobile." No country ever had more, he cracked, "and no country ever had less. . . . Ten men in our Country could buy the World, and ten million can't buy enough to eat."[5] The irony of impoverishment in the midst of agricultural surpluses drove America's farmers to drastic action and ambivalent demands. They wanted subsidies while opposing price-fixing. They wanted to curtail production, but be paid for doing so. As one wag put it, the New Deal might solve the paradox of want in the midst of plenty by doing away with the plenty!

Americans who looked around them during the 1930's saw that the nation's magnificent productive plant was still intact, that its ability to produce was unimpaired. Scarcity, therefore, represented a queer phenomenon—the result of rich resources rather than the stinginess of nature. There were food and commodities in abundance; only purchasing power was lacking. The mass production economy had failed by succeeding too well, for

4. During the winter of 1969–70, a treatise (written by Republican William Safire) called "New Federalist Paper No. 1" was circulated among the government departments in Washington. "We like the blessings of central government," it stated, but "we also like the blessing of decentralization, or home rule. Many have spent the past year working out a synthesis of the most desirable in both central government and home rule. The purpose [of the new federalism] is to come to grips with a paradox: a need for both national unity and local diversity. The new federalists . . . are using an approach best described as 'national localism.' " *Time* (Jan. 26, 1970), 9.

5. Donald Day: *Will Rogers* (New York, 1962), 260, 265, 271.

as Christian Gauss commented, "the horn of plenty is too heavy upon our hands." [6]

The problem would persist, of course, and be "rediscovered" subsequently. A young aspirant for public office in 1946, John F. Kennedy, inscribed in his looseleaf notebook a brief quotation from Thomas Jefferson: "Widespread poverty and concentrated wealth cannot long endure side by side in a democracy." Seventeen years later Kennedy remarked in a letter to Lyndon Johnson that "poverty in the midst of plenty is a paradox that must not go unchallenged in this country." In our present age of affluence, economic abundance has reduced older norms of inequality but created new forms as well. By eliminating the traditional system of class distinctions, abundance has created a situation in which almost any social differentiation seems invidious.[7]

During the war years, with the world torn between polarized ideologies, liberalism seemed to thrive in circumstances which might well have overwhelmed it. On several occasions during the early 1940's, Carl Becker posed what then seemed to be the critical question for American democracy: How to achieve idealism without illusions and realism without cynicism. Writing in 1944, Becker enumerated the enduring dualisms of American civilization:

> Whether it has been a matter of clearing the forest or exterminating the redskins, organizing a government or exploiting it for private advantage, building railroads for the public good or rigging the market in order to milk them for private profit, establishing free schools by law or placing illegal restraints on the freedom of teaching, conferring on Negroes their God-given con-

6. Albert U. Romasco: *The Poverty of Abundance. Hoover, the Nation, the Depression* (New York, 1965), 3–9; Stuart Chase: *The Economy of Abundance* (New York, 1934); Ray F. Harvey: *Want in the Midst of Plenty. The Genesis of the Food Stamp Plan* (Washington, D.C., 1941).

7. Arthur M. Schlesinger, Jr.: *A Thousand Days. John F. Kennedy in the White House* (Boston, 1965), 105; Sidney Lens: *Poverty: America's Enduring Paradox. A History of the Richest Nation's Unwon War* (New York, 1969).

stitutional rights or making sure they do not vote, applauding the value of temperance or perceiving the convenience of bootlegging—whatever the immediate task may be, the short cut, the ready-made device for dealing with it, is apt to seem to us good enough so long as it gets the business done. Throughout our history ruthlessness and humane dealing, respect for law and right and disregard of them, have run side by side: in almost equal degree we have exhibited the temper of conformity and of revolt, the disposition to submit voluntarily to law and custom when they serve our purposes and to ignore them when they cease to do so.

Becker, and other Americans at that time, were particularly worried by "a profoundly disturbing paradox. We seem to be offered a choice between depression and mass unemployment as the price of peace, and total war as the price of expansion and general prosperity. . . . This paradox, unless it be resolved, will surely wreck our institutions and destroy our freedoms." [8] Their concern over this dilemma in 1945 proved to be unfounded. America was just then entering a long era of sustained prosperity without having to pay the price of war—at least, not a "hot" war.

A different sort of price, however, would indeed be paid. Affluence in America meant that indications of inequality would be less visible than in Europe. Social distinctions here are not normally supported by great disparities in wealth, education, speech, or dress. Physical differences have been largely eliminated, however, without also reducing the prejudicial and cultural barriers to mobility and homogeneity. We have consequently achieved a situation of "classless inequality." We breed expectations among the less privileged but fail to fulfill them, thereby creating social tensions and personal frustrations. [9] Despite American pluralism, our political society has

8. *Freedom and Responsibility in the American Way of Life* (New York, 1945), xlviii, 18–19.

9. See David M. Potter: *People of Plenty. Economic Abundance and the American Character* (Chicago, 1954), 98–103, 121; Michael Harrington: *The Other America. Poverty in the United States* (New York, 1962), 12, 52.

been unable to guarantee equal protection and opportunity to ethnic minorities. Yet we pay full lip service to our democratic dogmas.

The less privileged nevertheless have had access to the "lonely crowd"—David Riesman's apt phrase for America's swollen and faceless middle class—the physical embodiment of collective individualism. Changes in the nature of "neighboring" mean that we have become "familiar strangers": a neighbor is merely someone who lives in close geographic proximity.[1] Hence the vogue of Esalen, encounter groups, and the so-called "human potential movement"—whereby people converge upon artificial settings to become "intimate strangers" for a weekend or a timeless moment removed from the monotony of their existence.

IN THE YEARS SINCE World War II, America's relationship to the wider world has been especially burdened with biformities and incongruities. Carl and Shelley Mydans have described our involvement in international affairs during the past quarter century as the era of *Violent Peace;* and Dwight Eisenhower chose to call the second volume of his presidential autobiography, *Waging Peace, 1956–1961.*[2] We stockpile atomic weapons in order to prevent a conflagration, even though doing so may actually make conflict more likely. We envision schemes of world order which bear no realistic relationship to either our dangers or our duties. The United States is now less potent to utilize its vast strength than it was half a century ago.

The American Beauty Rose must be handled with care because of its treacherous thorns. Similarly with the appearance our civilization offers to the world. To other peoples our brand of democracy has seemed attainable but not especially desirable, while our abundance has seemed infinitely desirable but not very attainable. Hence their tendency to hold us in

1. See Robin Williams: *Strangers Next Door. Ethnic Relations in American Communities* (Englewood Cliffs, 1964), 212, 386.
2. Carl and Shelley Mydans: *The Violent Peace* (New York, 1968).

"respectful contempt." Our perception of America's mission has been distorted by our failure to appreciate what outsiders regard as most significant in our development. Moreover, Americans like to envision their role in world affairs as that of umpire rather than empire; yet Third World nations regard the United States not as a referee but as a "preferee," a seeker of preferred status.

The Bald Eagle on the green side of your one dollar bill holds a clutch of deadly arrows in one clenched claw, and an olive branch in the other. Americans like to remind themselves, and others, that the United States emerged from a Revolution, an act of colonial self-emancipation. Nevertheless, they also like to emphasize that they stand for stability and order, balanced growth, constitutional procedures, and legitimacy. Americans like to speak the language of power and "talk tough," all the while stressing the need for a language of community and harmony. A form of double-entry bookkeeping seems to account for our efforts at international misunderstanding. We stress the need for nations to behave as equals, and to subordinate particular interests to the common cause of peace. At the same time, however, we insist that our very disinterestedness and worldwide responsibilities entitle us to the privilege of interpreting and vouchsafing the common good. All of these dualisms emerge from the fact, as Stanley Hoffmann believes, "that the nation's values (and leaders) point simultaneously in opposite directions. There is, in the American style, a tension between the instinct of violence and the drive for harmony." [3] Ofttimes our leaders offer nectar and napalm in the same breath, as President Johnson did in his speech on Vietnam at Johns Hopkins University in April 1965.

I cannot accept the convention that America's identity simply developed and persisted in opposition to the evils and *persona* of Europe. The United States was born of Old World arrogance—perhaps it all began when Columbus persuaded

3. Stanley Hoffmann: *Gulliver's Troubles, Or the Setting of American Foreign Policy* (New York, 1968), 109, 112, 177–81, 185, 187–8, 190–1.

Ferdinand and Isabella that he could get East by sailing West
—but bred in New World isolation and ignorance. We owe to
Europe aspects of our religion, our common law, our ideal of
constitutionalism; but also our dread of aristocracy, feudalism,
monopoly, and communism. Consequently, we are both attracted to and wary of Europe, and subsequently suspicious of
the world at large beyond the shrunken Europe of today.[4]

This dualistic state of mind may be found also in the
domestic political values subscribed to by most Americans. We
are comfortable believing in both majority rule and minority
rights, in both consensus and freedom, federalism and centralization. It may be perfectly reasonable to support majority rule
with reservations, or minority rights with certain other reservations. But this has not been our method. Rather, we have
tended to hold contradictory ideas in suspension and ignore the
intellectual and behavioral consequences of such "doublethink."
The Congress, perhaps more than any other political institution, is a repository of American ambivalence. The founders
created a bicameral body so that it would expressly embrace
contradictions. The House was dedicated to the proposition of
majority rule, and the Senate to the sacredness of minority
rights.[5]

There is, certainly, a sense in which Americans are still
obsessed with legalism and legitimacy.[6] Few countries have
ever assigned to courts the powers we have given them: the
judge is a particularly respected citizen; and we venerate constitutions. How, then, explain the pervasive American penchant

4. Cf. Daniel Boorstin: *America and the Image of Europe. Reflections on American Thought* (Cleveland, 1960), 11–12, 36, 46.

5. See the brilliant essay by Robert G. McCloskey: "The American
Ideology," in *Continuing Crisis in American Politics*, ed. Marian D.
Irish (Englewood Cliffs, 1963), esp. 14–23.

6. In 1970, in a well-publicized memorandum to the President,
Daniel Patrick Moynihan said: "In one form or another, all of the major
domestic problems facing you derive from the erosion of the authority
of the institutions of American society. . . . All we know is that the
sense of institutions being legitimate—especially the institutions of
government—is the glue that holds societies together. When it weakens,
things come unstuck."

for lawlessness? In part because we legitimize our lawlessness. Citizens of the United States can understand and even condone what Tammany boss George Washington Plunkitt liked to call "honest graft." Plunkitt was referring to financial benefits which came to entrepreneurial hustlers at no extra cost to the public. Every city must buy insurance and deposit its funds in banks. The premiums charged or the interest paid are usually uniform. Often they are set by law. It makes no difference to the city, therefore, which company gets the business; but it makes an enormous difference to particular companies—so much so that they are willing to pay something extra to get it: either in the form of cash, or by putting a key politician on its board, or by hiring him as its "lawyer." [7]

There is both integrity and intrigue in American politics. That is why we believe that our government is weak, stupid, overbearing, dishonest, and inefficient, and also believe it to be the best in the world and would like to offer it to others. Cleveland, Ohio, has an air pollution code which is most commonly violated by the city's own municipal utilities, especially the electric and gas corporation. The author of *Rights in Conflict*, a report on violence in Chicago during the Democratic National Convention of 1968, became convinced of the occurrence of what could only be called a "police riot," or lawless law enforcement. The searching question raised by that report, moreover, asked how the United States can "keep peaceful assembly from becoming a contradiction in terms?" [8] Given the deterioration of respect for government and politics in the United States, is it any wonder that tactics of "planned irresponsibility" (sit-ins, etc.) have become standard fare since the 1960's?

Why should it be so? In part because of the ironies of American technology. Poor people are victimized by the very inventions and machines which improve standards of living for

7. James Q. Wilson: "Corruption Is Not Always Scandalous," *The New York Times Magazine*, April 28, 1968, 54–62; Oscar Handlin: *Al Smith and His America* (Boston, 1958), 22, 35.
8. *The New York Times*, Dec. 2, 1968, 38.

the rest of society. Traditional "Negro jobs" are being destroyed by automation, and unskilled middle-aged workers find themselves "too old to work, too young to retire." In rural America, mechanization has helped to increase the class of "property-owning poor." As larger units of production become ever more efficient and modern, small farmers fall farther and farther behind. In addition, the welfare state seems to benefit least those who need help most. The poorest farmers, for example, are excluded from parity programs. Union fringe benefits, such as pension systems, restrict the mobility so badly needed when an area or an industry become depressed. The basic paradox of the welfare state in America is that it is not designed for the desperate, but for those capable of helping themselves.[9]

The trouble with this society, insists a New York City taxi driver, is that "it's overdeveloped and undernourished. It can't afford itself." In part the difficulty lies in our industrial-consumer arrangement of "creative obsolescence"—Alfred Sloan's program for General Motors—a form of resourceful wastefulness. It is the deliberate and publicly proclaimed policy of most American manufacturers to change styles at frequent intervals.

Within industry and finance, recent changes have created more rather than fewer anomalies. Stock ownership, for example, has become less exclusive than it once was, but ironically this fact has thrust even more power into the hands of the few large stockholders. Then, too, as Ralph Nader suggests, our capitalist economy is rapidly acquiring the character of "corporate-socialism" because the great corporations seek governmental protection from competition (Penn Central applies for welfare; oil producers insist upon import quotas, etc.).

Among American regions, the south has been especially prone to self-contradiction. It is known for profuse hospitality, and notorious for hostility toward strangers. It manages to combine legacies of gentleness and violence, of Puritanism and

9. Harrington: *The Other America*, 16, 19, 21, 30, 33, 38–9, 47, 49, 60, 80, 157–8.

hedonism. C. Vann Woodward has located the southern identity in a covey of paradoxical circumstances: the experience of defeat and frustration in a country where success is taken for granted; the experience of guilt (because of the Negro) in a country with a cult of Adamic innocence; the experience of poverty in a country where sufficiency (if not abundance) is taken for granted. As one panel of specialists on southern history recently agreed, "the conflicts that have been so much a part of the southern experience have occurred, we insist, between Southerners and within Southerners, as much as between North and South." [1]

Which brings us, ineluctably, to matters of color in a biracial nation. Black Americans have certainly shared and felt many of the dualisms described in this book. But they have also had to cope with tensions uniquely their own. "One ever feels his twoness," wrote W. E. B. DuBois in 1903, "an American, a Negro; two souls, two thoughts, two unreconciled strivings; two warring ideals in one dark body." DuBois often spoke of the "double-consciousness" of Negro life in the United States.[2] It appears in the contradictory role of the black mother, at once permissive and punitive, at once given to both gratification and deprivation for her children. It appears in the anomalous role of the black man: an archetype of virility who cannot achieve his manhood because he has been castrated by white society. It appears in the experience of southern black families living in northern ghettos, trying to raise their city children with rural values. Two black psychiatrists have recently insisted that Negro survival in the United States depends

1. W. J. Cash: *The Mind of the South* (New York, 1956), 69; Woodward: *The Burden of Southern History* (Baton Rouge, 1960); Charles G. Sellers, Jr., ed.: *The Southerner as American* (Chapel Hill, 1960), v–vi.

2. W. E. B. DuBois: *The Souls of Black Folk* (New York, 1961), 16–17. J. Saunders Redding remarked that "the Negro lives constantly on two planes of awareness," and that "one receives two distinct impacts from certain experiences and one undergoes two distinct reactions." (*On Being Negro in America* [2nd ed., New York, 1962], 12, 98–9.)

upon achieving a "healthy cultural paranoia." Blacks must maintain their suspiciousness without allowing it to impair their grasp of reality.[3]

There is considerable diversity within the black community, ranging from the Negro middle class—whom militants derisively call "black Anglo-Saxons"[4]—to radical advocates of black power whose positions are often paradoxical. They require "white funds" (from the Ford Foundation, for example) for operating expenses while proclaiming their capacity to sustain the institutional nexus of an urban community. They insist that "separate but equal" epitomizes their aspirations—thereby overturning a century of efforts by and on behalf of black people.[5]

For the black intellectual in America, achieving an identity free of burdensome contradictions is difficult. Eldridge Cleaver has written with pride of his "Higher Uneducation," and with contempt of black writers "who have become their own opposites, taking on all of the behavior patterns of their enemy, vices and virtues, in an effort to aspire to alien standards." *The Amsterdam News*, newspaper of Harlem, the largest black community in the United States, contains a strange mixture of attributes. The paper is caught between bourgeois aspirations and ghetto realities. It aims part of its appeal at the middle class and part at the working class. Consequently, it seems to

3. William H. Grier and Price M. Cobbs: *Black Rage* (New York, 1968), 61–2, 87, 161; Claude Brown: *Manchild in the Promised Land* (London, 1965), 269, 275. Brown refers to provincial blacks who spend their lives confined to the ghetto as "big-city backwoods people" (391).

4. Nathan Hare: *The Black Anglo-Saxons* (New York, 1965), 18, 37, 57, 115.

5. Martin Kilson: "Black Power: Anatomy of a Paradox," *Harvard Journal of Negro Affairs*, II (1968), 30, 33; *Wall Street Journal*, Mar. 24, 1969, 15. Cf. Arnold Hano's description of Harry Edwards: "Edwards is moderate *and* militant; he is separatist *and* integrationist. He symbolizes the Black Power advocate who . . . shouts from the ghetto to friendly whites: 'Stay out!' even though he sometimes secretly means, 'come in.'" ("The Black Rebel Who 'Whitelists' the Olympics," *The New York Times Magazine*, May 12, 1968, 41, 44.)

straddle the issues, and contends alternately that black is beautiful and not so beautiful, that blacks are militant but also
moderate.[6]

Similarly, the managing editor of *Time* magazine defines
its underlying philosophy as "progressive conservatism." [7]
Why? Because in a society so marked by cultural pluralism, he
is trying to please several different constituencies at once. But
Americans like to speak the language of irony. Mayor Daley of
Chicago labels unacceptable arguments as "unreasonable reasoning." Politicians tell their constituents that "you have never
had it so good," but also refer longingly in the same speech to
"the good old days." Call that nostalgic presentism. And Americans like to regard themselves as "optimistic fatalists," a phrase
originated by H. G. Wells with particular reference to this
country.[8]

Religious movements in American history have ceaselessly
sought to bring into being the City of God, but with amazing
consistency have built instead cities of man with the wages of
sin. In this country we have a spiritualized state ("one nation,
under God") containing secularized churches whose self-per-
petuating vestrymen have the power to select ministers, raise
and disburse funds. Denominationalism, the central fact of
American church history, has produced a spirit of competition
accompanied by a mitigating spirit of co-operation.[9]

Billy Graham's Christian Crusade distributes a pamphlet
entitled *How to Be a Christian Without Being Religious*. A
sizable number of American men of letters, especially during

6. Cleaver: *Soul on Ice* (New York, 1968), 13–14, 18, 75–8, 99,
102–4; J. Kirk Sale: "The Amsterdam News: Black Is Beautiful-Ugly,
Comfortable-Sensational, Moderate-Militant," *The New York Times
Magazine*, Feb. 9, 1969, 30–1, 37–45.

7. Richard Pollak: "*Time:* After Luce," *Harper's* (July 1969), 46.

8. *The New York Times*, April 18, 1968, 83; Jan. 11, 1969, 67;
C. Vann Woodward: "The Future of the Past," *American Historical
Review*, LXXV (1970), 724.

9. William A. Clebsch: *From Sacred to Profane America: The
Role of Religion in American History* (New York, 1968), 3, 8, 10–14,
16–17, 26–9, 43, 63, 72, 99, 115, 167, 172.

the 1940's and 1950's, proclaimed themselves "Atheists for
Niebuhr." [1] And in Troy, Michigan, the Catholic Church is
experimenting with a "churchless parish." [2] The "death of God"
theologians whose vogue was so prominent during the 1960's
call for a "religionless Christianity" in such books as *The Gospel of Christian Atheism* by Thomas J. J. Altizer. Here and
there Altizer insists that "God is Satan," but elsewhere that
"God is Jesus." By any conventional logic, therefore, Jesus
must be Satan. [3]

Literary critics have observed that the most characteristic
American fiction has been shaped by the contradictions, not by
the unities in American civilization. Look at the grimness and
the gaiety in Faulkner, the sustained tension between creative
and destructive impulses, the strains between hopefulness and
tragic reality. Nor is American fiction simply a function of
patriotism—love of country or of place. "Love of country?"
John Cheever asks rhetorically; "We all love our country, and
hate it." [4]

In *Bullet Park*, his latest novel, Cheever divides the American psyche between his two main characters: Eliot Nailles and
Paul Hammer. Nailles is conventional, upper-middle-class,
stable, and hypocritical. Hammer is unconventional, illegiti-

1. Supreme Court Justice Felix Frankfurter particularly admired
theologian Reinhold Niebuhr. After listening to one sermon, the late
Justice said: "I liked what you said, Reinie, and I speak as a believing
unbeliever." "I'm glad you did," the clergyman replied, "for I spoke as
an unbelieving believer."

2. *The New York Times*, Mar. 29, 1969, 71. At one of President
Nixon's White House worship services, the Reverend Dr. Richard C.
Halverson, pastor of a Presbyterian church in Bethesda, Maryland, re-
marked that "when we kneel to God, we stand tall."

3. *The Gospel of Christian Atheism* (Philadelphia, 1966), 15, 31,
101, 113; Richard Rubenstein: *After Auschwitz. Radical Theology and
Contemporary Judaism* (Indianapolis, 1966). Experimental forms of
worship, called "the no-service service," have been tried at Hillel Foundations on various campuses. (*The New York Times*, Dec. 22, 1968,
31.)

4. See R. W. B. Lewis: *The Picaresque Saint. Representative
Figures in Contemporary Fiction* (Philadelphia, 1959), 186, 190, 195,
205; *The New York Times*, July 11, 1969, 43.

mate, unstable, and brutally honest. Nailles is oversexed, provincial, respectable, and fond of the status quo, while Hammer
is undersexed, cosmopolitan, shady, and searching for change.
Nailles is first and foremost a father, raises an overprotected
child, loves his son, and finds friendship an important part of
his life, whereas Hammer is essentially a son, a neglected child,
unloved by his parents, and incapable of friendship. Nailles
has too much ancestry, his life is too routine, but ultimately he
affirms life. Hammer has no ancestry he can claim, is incapable
of permanency, and finally suffers from a death wish. Cheever
seems ultimately to affirm the bland and much-faulted sub-
urban gentry. He is sensitive to its failings, but suggests that
its predictability is accompanied by stability of personal affection and values. *Bullet Park* represents the latest and one of
the better attempts by a contemporary novelist to see the
American personality whole by dividing it in half.[5]

Among modern poets, Robert Frost and John Crowe Ran-
som have also pursued the same purpose. Frost's "divided
consciousness" and sensitivity to the paradoxes of American
history is distilled in what has become his best-known poem,
"The Gift Outright."

> The land was ours before we were the land's.
> She was our land more than a hundred years
> Before we were her people. She was ours
> In Massachusetts, in Virginia,
> But we were England's, still colonials,
> Possessing what we still were unpossessed by,
> Possessed by what we no more possessed.
> Something we were withholding made us weak
> Until we found out that it was ourselves
> We were withholding from our land of living,
> And forthwith found salvation in surrender.
> Such as we were we gave ourselves outright
> (The deed of gift was many deeds of war)
> To the land vaguely realizing westward,

5. Nailles, "in his experience with trains, learned something about
the mysterious polarities that moved him." *Bullet Park*, 56–7, 239.

But still unstoried, artless, unenhanced,
Such as she was, such as she would become.[6]

What about the arts in America? A major exhibition of
contemporary American art which toured the country in 1968
was entitled "The Articulate Subconscious." Ben Shahn and
others of his circle combined social criticism with surrealism,
and through their special talents made a success of social surrealism: a blend of European traditionalism, American realism,
and the ash can school. The avant garde in art circles today are
torn between fine art and applied art, between traditional tech-
niques on the one hand, and synthetics (e.g., plastics) on the
other. Wishing to inhabit both worlds—the world of the studio
and the world of the industrial designer—they have not successfully come to grips with either, thus far.[7]

As for popular culture, the trend seems to be toward
"studied casualness." Fashion designers from California have
decreed "formal informality" as the new vogue, while Henri
Bendel is accenting "respectable poverty" for "rich little poor
girls." The tendency toward flamboyant styles and bright colors
in men's clothes has caused Russell Lynes to label this generation "the mass-produced eccentrics." With regard to his clothing, the American male "wants to be different but not really
different. He wants to express his personality as he sees it, but
he does not want to give himself away. He wants to be in
fashion but he shudders at the idea of being fashionable. The
truth is that he wants neither to be mass produced nor lonely,
so he seeks his solace in being some of both."[8]

George Plimpton has earned the sobriquet to which many
American men aspire: "the professional amateur." The Broad-
way and Hollywood gossip column, because it synthesizes ex-
citement and ennui, has been designated "a thrilling bore."

6. *Complete Poems of Robert Frost* (New York, 1949), 467.

7. Hilton Kramer: " 'Plastic as Plastic': Divided Loyalties, Para-
doxical Ambitions," *The New York Times*, Dec. 1, 1968, D39; Barry
Ulanov: *The Two Worlds of American Art: The Private and the
Popular* (New York, 1965).

8. *The New York Times*, July 13, 1968, 14; Feb. 26, 1969, 42C;
Russell Lynes: *A Surfeit of Honey* (New York, 1957), esp. 71, 85.

And the essence of American humor continues to be what Hawthorne referred to as "the tragic power of laughter." For Woody Allen, "comedy is deadly serious business." Mark Van Doren, the poet and critic, is also given to this earnestly satirical outlook. "Humorists are serious," he remarks, "they're the only people who are." "Happiness is a very solemn, serious thing," Van Doren insists. "Joy is the most solemn thing on earth. You express it with tears." [9]

Among the youth culture, with its unstable mixture of precocity and dependency, there are "domestic expatriates," "native aliens," "Hell's Angels" on the road and "Unmarried Marrieds" on the campus. They love the music of "hip hicks" and "country slickers," hybrid stylists like Johnny Cash who blend pop with country music and a touch of rock.

For a considerable period of time now, middle-class children in America have been pulled by conflicting forces within the Protestant ethos: to obey moral rules and precepts of brotherhood while adjusting to forces of social mobility pushing children to compete strenuously against their playmates and peers. Many of the "cynical young idealists" who face difficult decisions about professional careers condemn what Kenneth Keniston labels "the failure of success." The world lies before them, but they reject it. Torn between the passionless mind of the formal curriculum and the sometimes mindless passion of student rebellion, they seek realistic alternatives. When Justice Abe Fortas addressed the "pious lawbreakers" in 1968, he asked "how, then, can I reconcile my profound belief in obedience to law and my equally basic need to disobey particular laws?" [1] There are no easy answers, and this quest looms as one of the largest dilemmas posed by the 1970's.

THROUGHOUT THIS INQUIRY, I have intermingled paradoxical qualities which seem particularly indigenous cheek by

9. *The New York Times*, Feb. 14, 1969, 26, 35; June 13, 1969, 45.

1. W. Lloyd Warner: *American Life: Dream and Reality* (Chicago, 1953), 88–9; *The New York Times*, Dec. 26, 1968, 33; *The New York Times Magazine*, May 12, 1968, 29.

jowl with cases from the American context which happen to be universal circumstances of the human condition. Perry Miller once invoked the phrase "nationality within universality," and I too would like to do so. Americans being a species of humanity, their characteristics are inevitably human and recurring. It is the particular configuration of those characteristics, and their consequences, which can be called peculiarly our own. Besides, the native who daily confronts a variety of institutional, intellectual, and circumstantial biformities does not bother to sort them into pigeonholes marked *U.S.A.* and *Universal.* He copes with them all, as a cluster, as best he can.

Americans have managed to be both puritanical and hedonistic, idealistic and materialistic, peace-loving and war-mongering, isolationist and interventionist, conformist and individualist, consensus-minded and conflict-prone. "We recognize the American," wrote Gunnar Myrdal in 1944, "wherever we meet him, as a practical idealist." [2]

Throughout our history we find, all too often, ironic contrasts between noble purposes and sordid results. One need only look at Reconstruction after the Civil War, or at World War I. Americans have experienced many disappointments because prospects for realizing national purposes have presented themselves but have often gone unfulfilled. There is a profound contradiction in the American ethos which commands men to seek worldly goods while warning them that the search will corrupt their souls. Those who aspire to middle-class membership will be thrifty on the way up and then extravagant upon arrival. The co-ordinate of Yankee ingenuity is resourceful wastefulness. We seek efficiency through labor-saving devices and then squander the savings through thoughtless exploitation.

The American passion for movement and change has been matched by an equally strong sense of nostalgia and inertia. Our garden has produced abundance but not fulfillment. Our cities have produced slum tenements as well as sanitary hos-

2. Myrdal: *An American Dilemma. The Negro Problem and Modern Democracy* (New York, 1944), I, xlii–iv.

pitals, ideas, music, and culture in addition to filth, disease, and misery. The National Commission on the Causes and Prevention of Violence reported in 1969 that "paradoxically, we have been both a tumultuous people and a relatively stable republic." Hannah Arendt has suggested that America is more likely to erupt into violence "than most other civilized countries. And yet there are very few countries where respect for law is so deeply rooted." [3] Perhaps the explanation is partially historical, for in the colonial era law had to be built everywhere as a bulwark against lawlessness, a process repeated on the moving frontier in the nineteenth century and the urban frontier of the twentieth. Even our anti-militarists have become violent about their pacifism.

Americans expect their heroes to be Everyman and Superman simultaneously. I once overheard on an airplane the following fragment of conversation: "He has none of the virtues I respect, and none of the vices I admire." We cherish the humanity of our past leaders: George Washington's false teeth and whimsical orthography, Benjamin Franklin's lechery and cunning. The quintessential American hero wears both a halo *and* horns.

Because our society is so pluralistic, the American politician must be all things to all people. Dwight Eisenhower represented the most advanced industrial nation, but his chief appeal rested in a naïve simplicity which recalled our pre-industrial past. Robert Frost once advised President Kennedy to be as much an Irishman as a Harvard man: "You have to have both the pragmatism and the idealism." The ambivalent American is ambitious and ambidextrous; but the appearance of ambidexterity—to some, at least—suggests the danger of double-dealing and deceit. The story is told of a U. S. senator meeting the press one Sunday afternoon. "How do you stand on conservation, Senator?" asked one panelist. The senator squirmed. "Well, I'll tell you," he said. "Some of my constituents are for

3. *The New York Times*, June 6, 1968, 32; June 6, 1969, 23; "Is America By Nature a Violent Society?" *The New York Times Magazine*, April 28, 1968, 24–5, 111–14.

conservation, and some of my constituents are against conservation, and I stand foursquare behind my constituents."

Raymond Aron, the French sociologist, has remarked that a "dialectic of plurality and conformism lies at the core of American life, making for the originality of the social structure, and raising the most contradictory evaluations." Americans have repeatedly reaffirmed the social philosophy of individualism, even making it the basis of their political thought. Yet they have been a nation of joiners and have developed the largest associations and corporations the world has ever known. Nor has American respect for the abstract "individual" always guaranteed respect for particular persons.[4]

There is a persistent tension between authoritarianism and individualism in American history. The genius of American institutions at their best has been to find a place and a use for both innovators and consolidators, rebellious dreamers and realistic adjudicators. "America has been built on a mixture of discipline and rebellion," writes Christopher Jencks, "but the balance between them has constantly shifted over the years." Our individualism, therefore, has been of a particular sort, a collective individualism. Individuality is not synonymous in the United States with singularity. When Americans develop an oddity they make a fad of it so that they may be comfortable among familiar oddities. Their unity, as Emerson wrote in his essay on the New England Reformers, "is only perfect when all the uniters are isolated."[5]

How then can we adequately summarize the buried historical roots of our paradoxes, tensions, and biformities? The incongruities in American life are not merely fortuitous, and their stimuli appear from the very beginning. "America was always promises," as Archibald MacLeish has put it. "From the

4. Aron in *As Others See Us. The United States Through Foreign Eyes*, ed. F. M. Joseph (Princeton, 1959), 59–60; Robert N. Beck: *The Meaning of Americanism. An Essay on the Religious and Philosophic Basis of the American Mind* (New York, 1956), 140–1.

5. Jencks: "Is It all Dr. Spock's Fault?" *The New York Times Magazine*, Mar. 3, 1968, 27, 76; Ralph Barton Perry: *Characteristically American* (New York, 1949), 9, 13.

first voyage and the first ship there were promises." Many of these have gone unfulfilled—an endless source of ambiguity and equivocation. More than that, "Jacobethan" travelers and settlers discovered that the various images projected of America could be contradictory. The New World turned out to be hospitable to radically different expectations. If America seemed to promise everything that men had always wanted, it also threatened to obliterate much of what they had already achieved. Critics and intellectuals throughout our past have recognized not only the gap between national aspirations and numbing realities, but also ambiguities endemic in the actual configuration of American goals.[6]

Guilt and insecurity have played a major part in keeping contradictory tendencies inherent in our style. First we wiped out the Indians whose land this was; then we emasculated the Africans brought to work the land. Few cultures in history have had to bear this kind of double collective culpability.

There are also paradoxes of freedom in this country. There seemed to be no limits to what America and Americans, beginning *de novo*, could become. Consequently, the American way is so restlessly creative as to be essentially destructive: witness our use of natural resources. Because achievement seems so accessible, Americans are competitive and competition is a major source of inner conflict. Because unlimited competition is not good for either individuals or the public interest, we seek restraints; but the restraints themselves involve irreconcilable antagonisms. Mutual exercise of complete freedom by rulers and subjects alike is impossible; but only recently, and very painfully, have we begun to learn that there must be limits placed upon democratic resistance to democratic authority.[7]

Above all other factors, however, the greatest source of

6. See MacLeish: *America Was Promises* (New York, 1939); John Morton Blum: *The Promise of America* (Baltimore, 1967), 53, 55, 161.

7. See Sidney Hook: *The Paradoxes of Freedom* (Berkeley, 1962), 3, 10, 12, 25, 39–40.

dualisms in American life has been unstable pluralism in all its manifold forms: cultural, social, sequential, and political. *E pluribus unum* is a misbegotten motto because we have *not* become one out of many. The myth of the melting pot is precisely that: a myth. Moreover, our constitutional system seems to foster fragmentation of power while our economic-technological system seems to encourage consolidation of power. Thus the imperatives of pluralism under conditions of large-scale technology commonly conflict with principles and practices of constitutional democracy.

Political factionalism in colonial America was simply the most manifest symptom of unstable pluralism, just as party coalitions in the national period have been expedients to make our political biformities functional. It is difficult to make a sharp distinction between "loyal opposition" and "government" in America because both merge imperceptibly into a system of coalitions, bargains, and compromises in which no one coalition can really be said to govern steadily, and none is definitely and persistently in opposition. This seems to be a salient feature of political culture in a pluralistic nation. Parties and personalities cannot put together a winning combination without organizing factions of different, and often contradictory, interests. Even the American conception of sovereignty is pluralistic, for federalism is the institutional embodiment of political pluralism.[8]

As immigrant groups were transformed by diverse influences in American society, they lost many of their original attributes, were re-created as something new, but still remained discrete, identifiable groups. The impact of trends and pressures for assimilation was felt in divergent ways because the groups themselves were dissimilar to begin with. Catholic peasants from southern Italy were affected differently in the same American cities and at the same time than were urbanized

8. See Robert A. Dahl: "The American Oppositions: Affirmation and Denial," in *Political Oppositions in American Democracies*, ed. Dahl (New Haven, 1966), 62; William H. Riker: *The Theory of Political Coalitions* (New Haven, 1962), 54–66.

Jewish workers and merchants from eastern Europe. It is a basic condition of unstable pluralism in this country that American society has not assimilated all immigrant groups fully or in the same degree.[9] Is it any wonder, then, that World Wars I and II were causes of conflicting loyalties for many hyphenated Americans?

It has been the impulse of our egalitarianism to make all men American and alike, but the thrust of our social order and intolerance to accentuate differences among groups. We have achieved expertise at both xenophobia and self-hate! At several stages of our history, population growth has outstripped institutional change. The result in many cases has been violence, vigilante movements, or economic unrest, all with the special coloration of unstable pluralism. Because there are significant variations in state laws regulating economic enterprise, taxation, and welfare payments, people and corporations move to tax-sheltered states and to those with the most generous welfare provisions. In this way mobility becomes a function of pluralism.

I do not argue that pluralism is a peculiarly American phenomenon. But I do believe that unstable pluralism on a scale of unprecedented proportion is especially American. The classic cosmopolitanism of great cities around the world has usually been limited to the élite portion of the population, whereas urban heterogeneity in the United States occurs most profoundly at the grass roots level. In what other country has there been such a cerebral response to conditions of cultural pluralism? America's most distinctive and original thinkers have sought to provide a rationale for diversity and tolerance. Thus William James is pre-eminently our philosopher of plu-

9. See Nathan Glazer and D. P. Moynihan: *Beyond the Melting Pot. The Negroes, Puerto Ricans, Jews, Italians, and Irish of New York City* (Cambridge, Mass., 1963), 13–14. Consider the case of Fiorello LaGuardia: his father a lapsed Roman Catholic, his mother a lukewarm Jew; an Italian-American, he was raised an Episcopalian in a predominantly Catholic environment; called by his enemies "the half-Jewish wop," his first wife was Catholic, and his second wife Lutheran. In Congress he served as a link between urban and rural Progressives.

ralism, particularly religious pluralism. John Dewey is our philosopher of educational pluralism, and Carl Becker our philosopher of historical pluralism, or relativism.[1]

There is a sense in which the super-highway is the most appropriate American metaphor. We have vast and anonymous numbers of people rushing individually (but simultaneously) in opposite directions. In between lies a no-man's-land, usually landscaped with a barrier of shrubs and trees, so that we cannot see the road to Elsewhere, but cannot easily turn back either. Indeed, the American experience in some spheres has moved from unity to diversity (e.g., denominationalism), while in other areas it has flowed in the opposite direction, from diversity to unity (e.g., political institutions). Along both roads we have paused from time to time in order to pay substantially for the privilege of traveling these thoroughfares.

There have always been Americans aware of unresolved contradictions between creed and reality, disturbed by the performance of their system and culture. Told how much liberty they enjoy, they feel less free; told how much equality they enjoy, they feel less equal; told how much progress they enjoy, their environment seems even more out of control. Most of all, told that they should be happy, they sense a steady growth in American unhappiness. Conflicts *between* Americans have been visible for a very long time, but most of us are just beginning to perceive the conflicts *within* us individually.

It is a consequence of some concern that our ambiguities often appear to the wider world as malicious hypocrisies. As when we vacillate, for example, between our missionary impulse and our isolationist instinct. From time to time we recognize that the needs of national security and the furtherance of national ideals may both be served by our vigorous but restrained participation in world affairs. At other times these two desiderata tug in opposite directions. However much we desperately want to be understood, we are too often misunderstood.

1. See James: *The Varieties of Religious Experience* (New York, 1902); Dewey: *Democracy and Education* (New York, 1916); Becker: *Everyman His Own Historian* (New York, 1935).

Because of our ambivalent ambiance, we are frequently indecisive. "I cannot be a crusader," remarked Ralph McGill, "because I have been cursed all my life with the ability to see both sides." [2] Our experience with polarities provides us with the potential for flexibility and diversity; yet too often it chills us into sheer inaction, or into contradictory appraisals of our own designs and historical development. Often we are willing to split the difference and seek consensus. "It is this intolerable paradox," James Reston writes, "of being caught between the unimaginable achievements of men when they cooperate for common goals, and their spectacular failures when they divide on how to achieve the simple decencies of life, that creates the present atmosphere of division and confusion." [3]

Because of our pluralist inheritance of biformities, we are also given to forms of inadvertent overcompensation. Take for example our longstanding vacillation between nature and civilization. After generations of abuse and neglect, we are beginning in sizable numbers to appreciate the spiritual value and aesthetic beauty of the American wilderness. Yet this very increase in appreciation may ultimately prove to be its undoing, for we are beginning to love our national forests and wonders right out of existence, so crowded have they become with campers and their litter.

I suppose it seems to many just now that the United States has become "successfully unhealthy." Oddly enough, I am fairly sanguine about the future; for I have come to believe that America historically has achieved the ultimate stability of an arch (think of the Natural Bridge in Virginia, beloved by Jefferson): those very forces which are logically calculated to drag stones to the ground actually provide props of support—derived from a principle in which thrust and counter-thrust become means of counterpoise. [4]

2. *The New York Times*, Feb. 5, 1969, 28.
3. *Ibid.*, Aug. 3, 1969, E10.
4. Political scientists contend persuasively that the more complex an institution or system is, the more likely it is to achieve stability. Simple forms of government are more likely to degenerate; the "mixed state"

We should recognize, as Hawthorne did, the innocence as well as the evil in our natures. We should understand, as William James did, that Americanism is a volatile mixture of hopeful good and curable bad. We must maintain, as Carl Becker pleaded, a balance between freedom and responsibility. For freedom unrestrained by responsibility becomes mere license, while responsibility unchecked by freedom becomes arbitrary power. We must pursue, as we have at our best, the politics of "utopian pragmatism."

We have reached a moment in time when the national condition seems neither lifeless nor deathless. It's like the barren but sensuous serenity of the natural world in late autumn, before Thanksgiving, containing the promise of rebirth and the potential for resurrection. On bare branches whose leaves have fallen, buds bulge visibly in preparation for spring. Along the roadside, goldenrod stands sere and grizzled, and the leafless milkweed with its goosehead pods strews fluff and floss to every breeze, thereby seeding the countryside with frail fertility. The litter of autumn becomes the mulch, and then the humus, for roots and tender seeds. So it was, so it has been, and so it will be with the growth of American Civilization.

---

is more given to endurance. Both Plato and Aristotle suggested that the most practical polity would combine democracy and oligarchy. Perhaps, then, there are considerable advantages in our "democratic élitism."

Bibliographical
Suggestions

Index

❦ · ❦

BIBLIOGRAPHICAL
SUGGESTIONS

A BIBLIOGRAPHICAL ESSAY appropriate to this volume almost
seems an all or nothing proposition: either recompose the *Harvard
Guide to American History* with suitable glosses; or else abandon
the project entirely and ask readers to accept the Word on faith
and footnotes alone. Well, ever faithful to the spirit of my inquiry,
I shall compromise by offering some highly selective suggestions
for further reading. They are organized according to the chapter
structure of the book itself, and are almost entirely *supplementary*
to the footnote citations. I confine myself, moreover, largely to
secondary sources readily available; to works I found especially
stimulating; to materials illustrative of my central themes; and to
extra evidence on certain matters dealt with in greater depth than
could conveniently be contained in the footnotes (e.g., the outbreak
of paradoxology in Stuart England).

Chapter 1—The Old World and the New, *Pari Passu*

For the study of national style through perspectives of personality and culture, see H. C. Duijker and N. H. Frijda: *National
Character and National Stereotypes. Trend Report Prepared for
the International Union of Scientific Psychology* (Amsterdam,
1960). A good bibliography on the subject of American character
specifically appears in Michael McGiffert, ed.: *The Character of
Americans. A Book of Readings* (Homewood, Ill., 1964), 361–77.
I found valuable insights in Henry Nash Smith: "Can American
Studies Develop a Method?" in *Studies in American Culture.*

Dominant Ideas and Images, ed. J. J. Kwiat and Mary C. Turpie (Minneapolis, 1960), 3–15; in David E. Stannard: "American Historians and the Idea of National Character," *American Quarterly*, XXIII (1971), 202–20; and in Clifton E. Hart: "The Minor Premise of American Nationalist Thought" (unpublished Ph.D. dissertation, University of Iowa, 1962), ch. 1 ("The Establishment of the Antithesis Assumption") and ch. 6 ("The New Polarity").

Intellectuals are commonly torn by contradictory tendencies; and American historians are very much a part of the pattern. C. Vann Woodward comments upon countervailing forces in American historiography in "Clio with Soul," *Journal of American History*, LVI (1969), 16; and Staughton Lynd does so from a more radical perspective in "Historical Past and Existential Present," *The Dissenting Academy*, ed. Theodore Roszak (New York, 1968), 94, 108. In *Virgin Land. The American West as Symbol and Myth* (New York, 1957), 240–1, 299, Henry Nash Smith discussed dualisms in Frederick Jackson Turner's work. Sidney Mead does the same for "Prof. [William W.] Sweet's *Religion and Culture in America*," in *Church History*, XXII (1953), 33–49. Two historians have written about ambiguities within the work of Perry Miller—Gene Wise: "Implicit Irony in Recent American Historiography: Perry Miller's *New England Mind*," *Journal of the History of Ideas*, XXIX (1968), 579–600; and David A. Hollinger: "Perry Miller and Philosophical History," *History and Theory*, VII (1968), 189–202. Daniel Boorstin, whose work stresses seamlessness rather than seaminess in the American experience, is discussed insightfully by John P. Diggins in "Consciousness and Ideology in American History: The Burden of Daniel J. Boorstin," *American Historical Review*, LXXVI (1971), 99–118, and "The Perils of Naturalism: Some Reflections on Daniel J. Boorstin's Approach to American History," *American Quarterly*, XXIII (1971), 153–80.

Alexis de Tocqueville's *Democracy in America* is still the finest book with which to begin any inquiry into the meaning of American civilization—the book I would want to have on a remote island if I could choose only one. The best edition now available is J. P. Mayer and Max Lerner, eds.: *Democracy in America* (New York, 1966); see especially xxv–xxvi of the Introduction. Several scholars have noticed significant paradoxes in Tocqueville's perception of American civilization; see Cushing Strout: "Tocqueville's Duality: Describing America and Thinking of Europe," *American Quarterly*, XXI (1969), 87–99, and Marvin Meyers: *The Jacksonian*

Persuasion: Politics and Belief (2nd ed., New York, 1960), 33–56.

Chapter 2—The Quest for Legitimacy in Colonial America

Paul Bastid and others have written an important collection of fourteen essays concerning the principle, phenomenology, philosophy, and typology of legitimacy: *"L'Idée de Légitimité,"* in *Annales de Philosophie Politique*, VII (Paris, 1967). There is an interesting discussion and critique by Bertrand de Jouvenel: *Sovereignty; An Inquiry into the Political Good* (Chicago, 1957). I gained clarification from four general books on the American context: Roland Young: *American Law and Politics. The Creation of Public Order* (New York, 1967), especially 150–6; Francis R. Aumann: *The Changing American Legal System: Some Selected Phases* (Columbus, Ohio, 1940), especially Part I; John Dickinson: *Administrative Justice and the Supremacy of Law in the United States* (Cambridge, Mass., 1927); and Edward S. Corwin: *The "Higher Law" Background of American Constitutional Law* (1928–9; Ithaca, 1955).

For specific applications to the period of early American history, I would suggest the following. Chester E. Eisinger: "The Puritans' Justification for Taking the Land," *Essex Institute Historical Collections*, LXXXIV (1948), 131–43; Stanley N. Katz: "The Politics of Law in Colonial America: Controversies Over Chancery Courts and Equity Law in the Eighteenth Century," *Perspectives in American History*, V (1971), 257–84; Kirk G. Alliman: "The Incorporation of Massachusetts Congregational Churches, 1692–1833: The Preservation of Religious Autonomy" (unpublished Ph.D. dissertation, University of Iowa, 1970), which "examines the development of ecclesiastical corporations as a means of discharging the temporal responsibilities and defining the legal existence of eighteenth century Massachusetts Standing Order churches"; R. A. Humphreys: "The Rule of Law and the American Revolution," in Humphreys: *Tradition and Revolt in Latin America and Other Essays* (New York, 1969), 77–91; Richard Hofstadter: *The Idea of a Party System. The Rise of Legitimate Opposition in the United States, 1780–1840* (Berkeley, 1969), especially ch. 5; Robert K. Faulkner: *The Jurisprudence of John Marshall* (Princeton, 1968); and W. B. Hamilton: "The Transmission of English Law to the Frontier of America," *South Atlantic Quarterly*, LXVII (1968), 243–64.

Chapter 3—Invertebrate America: The Problem of Unstable
    Pluralism

Social scientists, especially in recent years, have begun to ex-
plore pluralism from various perspectives. In addition to those es-
says cited on p. 59 (note) above, I would also recommend Kung
Chuan Hsiao: *Political Pluralism. A Study in Contemporay Political
Theory* (London, 1927); Andrew S. McFarland: *Power and
Leadership in Pluralist Systems* (Stanford, 1969); William E.
Connolly, comp.: *The Bias of Pluralism* (New York, 1969);
William McCord: *The Springtime of Freedom. Evolution of De-
veloping Societies* (New York, 1965); and Charles Wagley and
Marvin Harris: *Minorities in the New World. Six Case Studies*
(New York, 1958). Samuel P. Huntington's *Political Order in
Changing Societies* (New Haven, 1968) provides a powerful inter-
pretive synthesis of a wide range of empirical and theoretical
scholarship. Despite serious inconsistencies and some questionable
historical assertions, it is a book of great insight and works at a
significant level of generalization. For Huntington's discussion of
liberal conservatism in America, see 98, 129, 132–3.

For pluralism and instability in the colonial context, see David
E. Ingersoll: "Machiavelli and Madison: Perspectives on Political
Stability," *Political Science Quarterly*, LXXXV (1970), 259–80;
Dietmar Rothermund: *The Layman's Progress. Religious and Po-
litical Experience in Colonial Pennsylvania, 1740–1770* (Phila-
delphia, 1961), especially ch. 7, "The Interaction of Groups";
H. Richard Niebuhr: *The Social Sources of Denominationalism*
(New York, 1929), chs. 6–7; and Franklin H. Littell: *From State
Church to Pluralism. A Protestant Interpretation of Religion in
American History* (New York, 1962).

For contemporary consequences of unstable pluralism in American life, there are several extraordinarily trenchant books. Edward Shils's *The Torment of Secrecy. The Background and
Consequences of American Security Policies* (London, 1956), a
wise and profound work, is far broader in scope than its title indicates (for pluralism and dualisms, see especially 153–75, 225–
30). Other useful and related books are by Stewart G. and Mildred
W. Cole: *Minorities and the American Promise. The Conflict of
Principle and Practice* (New York, 1954); Henry S. Kariel: *The
Decline of American Pluralism* (Stanford, 1961), especially 179–
87 ("The Conflict Within Pluralism"); and Robert A. Dahl:
Pluralist Democracy in the United States: Conflict and Consent
(Chicago, 1967).

Chapter 4—Biformity: A Frame of Reference

For philosophical reflections upon irony and polarity, see Søren Kierkegaard: *The Concept of Irony, with Constant Reference to Socrates* (1841: London, 1966), especially Part II; Paul Roubiczek: *Thinking in Opposites. An Investigation of the Nature of Man as Revealed by the Nature of Thinking* (London, 1952); Louis W. Norris: *Polarity: A Philosophy of Tensions Among Values* (Chicago, 1956); and W. V. Quine: "Paradox," *Scientific American*, CCVI (April 1962), 84–96.

For approaches to ambiguity in aesthetics and literary criticism, see Charles Augustin Sainte-Beuve: "A Critic's Account of His Own Critical Method," in *Library of the World's Best Literature*, ed. Charles D. Warner (New York, 1896), XXII, 12,666; William Empson: *Seven Types of Ambiguity* (London, 1930); E. H. Gombrich: *Art and Illusion. A Study in the Psychology of Pictorial Representation* (New York, 1960), ch. 8, "Ambiguities of the Third Dimension"; Nikolaus Pevsner: *The Englishness of English Art* (London, 1956).

Psychological perspectives are provided by C. K. Ogden: *Opposition. A Linguistic and Psychological Analysis* (London, 1932); Gregory Bateson: "Morale and National Character," in *Civilian Morale*, ed. Goodwin Watson (New York, 1942), 71–91; June L. Tapp and Fred Krinsky, eds.: *Ambivalent America. A Psycho–Political Dialogue* (Beverly Hills, 1971); and most profoundly by Erik H. Erikson: *Childhood and Society* (2nd ed., New York, 1963), ch. 8, "Reflections on the American Identity."

Various commentators, travelers, political scientists, and literary critics have discussed contradictory tendencies in American civilization. I drew together eighteen of their efforts in *The Contrapuntal Civilization. Essays Toward a New Understanding of the American Experience* (New York, 1971). Among general works, I find the following particularly insightful: James Fullarton Muirhead: *The Land of Contrasts. A Briton's View of His American Kin* (Boston, 1898), especially ch. 2; Ralph Barton Perry: *Characteristically American* (New York, 1949), especially ch. 1; Ronald Segal: *The Americans: A Conflict of Creed and Reality* (New York, 1969), which seems to be written primarily for non-Americans; and Helene S. Zahler: *The American Paradox* (New York, 1964), a work of sociological history which is well written but somewhat simplistic.

Among historical essays, I learned especially from Alpheus T. Mason: "*The Federalist*—A Split Personality," *American His-*

torical Review, LVII (1952), 625–43; Merle E. Curti: *American Paradox: The Conflict of Thought and Action* (New Brunswick, 1956); Merrill D. Peterson: *The Jefferson Image in the American Mind* (New York, 1960); Eric F. Goldman: "Democratic Bifocalism," in *Romanticism in America. Papers Contributed to a Symposium*, ed. George Boas (Baltimore, 1940), 1–11; and Arthur P. Dudden: "Nostalgia and the American," *Journal of the History of Ideas*, XXII (1961), 515–30.

Chapter 5—Conflict, Crisis, and Change: The Context of English Colonization

The English obsession with paradoxology between about 1600 and 1660 may be traced through the following representative samples. Thomas Scott: *Fowre Paradoxes: Of Arte, of Lawe, of Warre, of Service* (London, 1602); John Donne: *Paradoxes and Problemes, With Two Characters and an Essay of Valour* (London, 1633); Herbert Palmer: *Memorials of Godlines & Christianity. Part II. Containing 1. The Character of a Christian in Paradoxes and Seeming Contradictions* (London, 1645); Ralph Venning: *Orthodox Paradoxes, Theoreticall and Experimental* (London, 1647); John Hall: *Paradoxes* (London, 1650); Robert Heath: *Paradoxical Assertions and Philosophical Problems* (London, 1659); and Arthur O. Lovejoy: "Milton and the Paradox of the Fortunate Fall," in Lovejoy: *Essays in the History of Ideas* (Baltimore, 1948), 277–95.

Some of the tensions in English political and religious thought of this period may be traced in George L. Mosse: *The Holy Pretence: A Study in Christianity and Reason of State from William Perkins to John Winthrop* (Oxford, 1957); John F. H. New: "Cromwell and the Paradoxes of Puritanism," *Journal of British Studies*, V (1965), 53–9; and Thomas Wood: *English Casuistical Divinity During the Seventeenth Century* (London, 1952).

The Elizabethan mind on the eve of colonization is lucidly sketched in a brief book by E. M. W. Tillyard: *The Elizabethan World Picture* (London, 1943). A neglected work of value by John D. Brite: "The Attitude of European States Toward Emigration to the American Colonies and the United States, 1607–1820" (unpublished Ph.D. dissertation, University of Chicago, 1937) contains an extraordinary compilation of information without much interpretive focus. Brite's work is especially rich in German, Austrian, and Swiss materials.

Chapter 6—Contradictory Tendencies in Colonial America

In "The New England Colonists' English Image, 1550–1714" (unpublished Ph.D. dissertation, University of California at Berkeley, 1970), David H. Corkran traces the shifting nature of early American ambivalence about the mother country. Two recent books about Moravian life in the colonies tell a great deal about the impact of transplantation upon European communities and sects: Gillian L. Gollin: *Moravians in Two Worlds: A Study of Changing Communities* (New York, 1967), a comparison of Herrnhut in Saxony with Bethlehem, Pennsylvania, 1730's to 1840's; and William J. Murtagh: *Moravian Architecture and Town Planning: Bethlehem, Pennsylvania, and Other Eighteenth-century American Settlements* (Chapel Hill, 1967).

Henry Steele Commager's collected essays, *Freedom and Order. A Commentary on the American Political Scene* (New York, 1966), include several pieces pertinent to my frame of reference, especially 149–70, 246–54, 279–85. In *Toward Lexington. The Role of the British Army in the Coming of the American Revolution* (Princeton, 1965), John Shy treats the military history of colonial America in terms of its unresolved ambiguities and contradictions, and argues that "failure to resolve these issues by force brought about the disruption of the first British empire." For a revealing look at the mid-eighteenth-century American mind responding explicitly to problems of legitimacy and unstable pluralism, see William Livingston, *et al.: The Independent Reflector* [1752–3], ed. Milton M. Klein (Cambridge, Mass., 1963).

In "The Anglican Middle Way in Early Eighteenth-Century America: Anglican Religious Thought in the American Colonies, 1702–1750" (unpublished Ph.D. dissertation, University of Wisconsin, 1965), Gerald J. Goodwin discerns a growing emphasis upon "practical moralism," and the same author treats "The Myth of 'Arminian-Calvinism' in Eighteenth-Century New England," in *The New England Quarterly*, XLI (1968), 213–37. David Pierce examines tensions between new piety and old belief, between "restraint" and "enlargement," in "Jonathan Edwards and the 'New Sense' of Glory," *ibid.*, 82–95. In "A Biography of Charles Chauncy (1705–1787)" (unpublished Ph.D. dissertation, Stanford, 1967), Edward M. Griffin views his subject as being both hardhearted and sentimental, rational and passionate, liberal yet a staunch Puritan.

I learned much about ambiguous social values in the colonies

from Jack P. Greene: "Search for Identity. An Interpretation of
the Meaning of Selected Patterns of Social Response in Eighteenth-
Century America," *Journal of Social History*, III (1970), 189–
220; Frederick B. Tolles: " 'Of the Best Sort But Plain': The
Quaker Esthetic," *American Quarterly*, XI (1959), 484–502; and
C. C. Pearson and J. Edwin Hendricks: *Liquor and Anti-Liquor
in Virginia, 1619–1919* (Durham, 1967); and about ambiguities
in colonial historical thought from Sacvan Bercovitch: "Puritan
New England Rhetoric and the Jewish Problem," *Early American
Literature*, V (1970), 63–73.

For biformities in the American Enlightenment, see Henry
F. May: "The Problem of the American Enlightenment," *New
Literary History*, I (1970), 201–14; Adrienne Koch: "Pragmatic
Wisdom and the American Enlightenment," *William and Mary
Quarterly*, 3d series, XVIII (1961), 313–29; Richard M. Gum-
mere: "The Reverend Hugh Jones: A Spiritual Pragmatist," in
Gummere: *Seven Wise Men of Colonial America* (Cambridge,
Mass., 1967); Gerald Stourzh: *Benjamin Franklin and American
Foreign Policy* (Chicago, 1954), especially 30–2, "The Dual
Character of Franklin's Political Thought"; and Conrad Wright:
The Liberal Christians. Essays on American Unitarian History
(Boston, 1970), ch. 1 on "Supernatural Rationalism."

Epilogism to Part Two—Some Comparisons

I have been greatly influenced by the marvelous speculative
essays of Professor Richard Morse, written over the past decade.
See, for example, "Crosscurrents in New World History," in *Politics of Change in Latin America*, ed. Joseph Maier and R. W.
Weatherhead (New York, 1964), 45–65; and "Some Themes of
Brazilian History," *South Atlantic Quarterly*, LXI (1962),
159–82. See also the eclectic and fanciful work of Hugh B. Fox:
"Latin America and the United States—A Study of Origins," *Mid-
west Quarterly*, IX (1968), 285–96; and the emphasis upon tensions in José Honório Rodrigues: *The Brazilians. Their Character
and Aspirations* (Austin, 1967).

For implicit contrasts between English thought and that of
her colonists in the eighteenth century, see Martin Price: *To the
Palace of Wisdom. Studies in Order and Energy from Dryden to
Blake* (New York, 1964); John Dunn: "The Politics of Locke in
England and America in the Eighteenth Century," in *John Locke:
Problems and Perspectives*, ed. John W. Yolton (Cambridge,
1969), 45–80; Robert R. Palmer: "The Great Inversion: America
and Europe in the Eighteenth-Century Revolution," in *Ideas in*

History. Essays Presented to Louis Gottschalk by His Former Students, ed. Richard Herr (Durham, 1965), 3–19.

For explicit comparisons between English and American institutions, see the very original work of John M. Murrin: "Anglicizing an American Colony. The Transformation of Provincial Massachusetts" (unpublished Ph.D. dissertation, Yale, 1966); E. R. Norman: *The Conscience of the State in North America* (Cambridge, 1968); Leonard W. Levy: *Origins of the Fifth Amendment. The Right Against Self-Incrimination* (New York, 1968); and Marvin K. Singleton: "New Light on the Chancery Side of Virginia's Evolution to Statehood," *Journal of American Studies*, II (1968), 149–60.

Chapter 7—Ambiguities of the American Revolution

Tensions and ambiguities in Anglo-American allegiances are discussed by Max Savelle in "Nationalism and Other Loyalties in the American Revolution," *American Historical Review*, LXVII (1962), 901–23; and John W. Blassingame in "American Nationalism and Other Loyalties in the Southern Colonies, 1763–1775," *Journal of Southern History*, XXXIV (1968), 50–75. Jesse Lemisch looks at contradictions in the political thought of revolutionary leaders in "The American Revolution Seen from the Bottom Up," in *Towards a New Past. Dissenting Essays in American History*, ed. Barton J. Bernstein (New York, 1968), 14–15, 38–9.

Anomalies and compromises within particular leaders emerge in John W. Ellsworth: "John Adams: The American Revolution as a Change of Heart," *Huntington Library Quarterly*, XXVIII (1965), 293–300; Timothy H. Breen: "John Adams' Fight Against Innovation in the New England Constitution, 1776," *New England Quarterly*, XL (1967), 501–20; John C. Miller: *Alexander Hamilton. Portrait in Paradox* (New York, 1959); William Cohen: "Thomas Jefferson and the Problem of Slavery," *Journal of American History*, LVI (1969), 503–26; and Sidney E. Mead: "Neither Church Nor State: Reflections on James Madison's 'Line of Separation,'" *Journal of Church and State*, X (1968), 349–64.

Clinton Rossiter found in the Revolution the beginnings of a native tradition of "ordered liberty"; see *Seedtime of the Republic. The Origin of the American Tradition of Political Liberty* (New York, 1953). In *The Upper House in Revolutionary America, 1763–1788* (Madison, 1967), Jackson Turner Main indicates that both political thought and past experience guided the colonists in remodeling their governments. That same emphasis upon pragmatic idealism provides the central theme in Bernard Bailyn's "Political Experience and Enlightenment Ideas in Eighteenth-Century America," *American Historical Review*, LXVII (1962), 339–51. I have benefited enormously from Gordon S. Wood's *The Creation of the American Republic, 1776–1787* (Chapel Hill, 1969).

Other studies of thought and culture in this period which emphasize ambiguities, dualisms, and compromise are Arthur O. Lovejoy: "The Theory of Human Nature in the American Constitution and the Method of Counterpoise," in Lovejoy: *Reflections on Human Nature* (Baltimore, 1961), 37–65; Robert W. Shoemaker: " 'Democracy' and 'Republic' as Understood in Late Eighteenth-Century America," *American Speech*, XLI (1966), 83–95; David Tyack: "Forming the National Character: Paradox in the Educational Thought of the Revolutionary Generation," *Harvard Education Review*, XXXVI (1966), 29–41; Elayne A. Rapping: "Theory and Experience in Crèvecoeur's America," *American Quarterly*, XIX (1967), 707–18; James C. Mohr: "Calculated Disillusionment: Crèvecoeur's Letters Reconsidered," *South Atlantic Quarterly*, LXIX (1970), 354–63; and Roger Burlingame, "The Paradox of 1812," in Burlingame: *The American Conscience* (New York, 1957), 231–46.

Chapter 8—Encrustations of Space and Time, circa 1825–1925

Richard Hofstadter's *The American Political Tradition and the Men Who Made It* (New York, 1948) sets conservative political behavior and thought (emphasizing the sanctity of private property) within the framework of a liberal tradition that is both democratic and progressive. Hofstadter wryly indicated contradictory tendencies within his biographees: Jefferson, "the aristocrat as democrat," a "practical visionary"; Jackson as a "pioneer aristocrat"; Lincoln's "responsible opportunism"; Theodore Roosevelt, "the conservative as progressive"; Woodrow Wilson, "the conservative as liberal," a self-styled "conservative progressive"; Hoover as a philosopher of collective individualism.

There is a recurrent intertwining of conservative motives, libertarian rhetoric, and ambiguous methods traced by Rowland Berthoff in *An Unsettled People: Social Order and Disorder in American History* (New York, 1971), especially 262, 272, 301, 341, 345, 356–7, and 426–8. Other general works which treat paradoxes in nineteenth-century development include Rush Welter: *Popular Education and Democratic Thought in America* (New

York, 1962); Leland D. Baldwin: *The Meaning of America: Essays Toward an Understanding of the American Spirit* (Pittsburgh, 1955), which emphasizes the contradiction between our ideal of thrift and our wasteful practices; and Marshall Fishwick: *The Hero, American Style* (New York, 1969), especially 117–33 on "smooth rough-necks" like Buffalo Bill.

The American studies approach through history and literature has produced a cluster of excellent essays touching upon contradictory tendencies in American culture between the Revolution and the Civil War. See in particular Fred Somkin: *Unquiet Eagle. Memory and Desire in the Idea of American Freedom, 1815–1860* (Ithaca, 1967); William R. Taylor: *Cavalier and Yankee. The Old South and American National Character* (New York, 1961); and Michael D. Fellman: "The Unbounded Frame: Freedom and Community in Nineteenth-Century American Utopianism" (unpublished Ph.D. dissertation, Northwestern University, 1969).

For the Jacksonian period, see Michael A. Lebowitz: "The Jacksonians: Paradox Lost?" in *Towards a New Past. Dissenting Essays in American History*, ed. Barton J. Bernstein (New York, 1968), 65–89; Rex S. Burns: "The Yeoman Mechanic: 'Venturous Conservative,'" *Rocky Mountain Social Science Journal*, IV (1967), 8–21; William H. Goetzmann: "The Mountain Man as Jacksonian Man," *American Quarterly*, XV (1963), 402–15; Barbara Welter: "The Merchant's Daughter: A Tale from Life," *New England Quarterly*, XLII (1969), 3–22, concerning New England ambivalence about the man of commerce—scorning his pursuit of money while regarding prosperity as a sign of divine favor; and William W. Freehling: "Spoilsmen and Interests in the Thought and Career of John C. Calhoun," *Journal of American History*, LII (1965), 25–42.

For incongruities in American responses to racial problems, see especially George M. Fredrickson: *The Black Image in the White Mind. The Debate on Afro-American Character and Destiny, 1817–1914* (New York, 1971), particularly his stress upon "*herrenvolk*" (master race) democracy. Also C. Vann Woodward: *American Counterpoint: Slavery and Racism in the North-South Dialogue* (Boston, 1971); William H. and Jane H. Pease: "Antislavery Ambivalence: Immediatism, Expediency, Race," *American Quarterly*, XVII (1965), 682–95; David M. Potter: "John Brown and the Paradox of Leadership Among American Negroes," in *The South and the Sectional Conflict* (Baton Rouge, 1968), 201–18; Theodore Draper: "The Father of American Black Nationalism [Martin R. Delany]," *New York Review of Books*, XIV (March 12,

1970), 33–41; and Lawrence J. Friedman: *The White Savage: Racial Fantasies in the Postbellum South* (Englewood Cliffs, 1970).

Dualisms in the Civil War era, problems of instability, ambiguities about militarism and the war, and polarities in American political thought are examined in John Higham: *From Boundlessness to Consolidation: The Transformation of American Culture, 1848–1860* (Ann Arbor, 1969); Marcus Cunliffe: *Soldiers and Civilians. The Martial Spirit in America, 1775–1865* (Boston, 1968); George M. Fredrickson: *The Inner Civil War. Northern Intellectuals and the Crisis of the Union* (New York, 1965); Paul W. Gates: "The Homestead Law in an Incongruous Land System," *American Historical Review*, XLI (1936), 652–81; and Robert G. McCloskey: *American Conservatism in the Age of Enterprise, 1865–1910* (Cambridge, Mass., 1951).

For the development of civil religion in American life, see Robert N. Bellah: "Civil Religion in America," in *Religion in America*, ed. William G. McLoughlin (Boston, 1968), 3–23; Sidney E. Mead: "The 'Nation with the Soul of a Church,'" *Church History*, XXXVI (1967), 262–83; Ernest Lee Tuveson: *Redeemer Nation. The Idea of America's Millennial Role* (Chicago, 1968); and T. Scott Miyakawa: *Protestants and Pioneers. Individualism and Conformity on the American Frontier* (Chicago, 1964).

Tensions and anomalies within various reform movements are analyzed in Daniel Walden, ed.: *American Reform. The Ambiguous Legacy* (Yellow Springs, Ohio, 1967); Philip Gleason: *The Conservative Reformers. German-American Catholics and the Social Order* (Notre Dame, 1968); Michael B. Katz: *The Irony of Early School Reform: Educational Innovation in Mid-Nineteenth Century Massachusetts* (Cambridge, Mass., 1968); Daniel M. Fox: *The Discovery of Abundance. Simon N. Patten and the Transformation of Social Theory* (Ithaca, 1967); Hace S. Tishler: *Self-Reliance and Social Security, 1870–1917* (Port Washington, 1971); and David W. Noble: *The Paradox of Progressive Thought* (Minneapolis, 1958).

In *As a City Upon a Hill. The Town in American History* (New York, 1966), Page Smith contends that the small town has been politically conservative yet fairly egalitarian in its social structure and practices. Robert M. Fogelson: *The Fragmented Metropolis. Los Angeles, 1850–1930* (Cambridge, Mass., 1967) stresses the ambivalence of Californians toward urbanization; and rural-urban tensions are prominent in G. Edward White: *The Eastern Establishment and the Western Experience. The West of*

Frederic Remington, Theodore Roosevelt, and Owen Wister (New Haven, 1968); and Milton Plesur, ed.: *The 1920's. Problems and Paradoxes* (Boston, 1969).

There are a number of fascinating studies of literature and American thought in the nineteenth century which concentrate on dialectical impulses, notably R. W. B. Lewis: *The American Adam. Innocence, Tragedy, and Tradition in the Nineteenth Century* (Chicago, 1955); A. N. Kaul: *The American Vision. Actual and Ideal Society in Nineteenth-Century Fiction* (New Haven, 1963); David W. Noble: *The Eternal Adam and the New World Garden. The Central Myth in the American Novel Since 1830* (New York, 1968); Leo Marx: *The Machine in the Garden. Technology and the Pastoral Ideal in America* (New York, 1964); Philip Rahv: "Paleface and Redskin," in Rahv: *Image and Idea* (Norfolk, Conn., 1949), 1–5; Charles C. Walcutt: *American Literary Naturalism. A Divided Stream* (Minneapolis, 1956); and Harold Bloom: "Bacchus and Merlin: The Dialectic of Romantic Poetry in America," *The Southern Review*, VII (1971), 140–75.

Themes of dualism and ambiguity in particular American authors are prominent in Joel Porte: "Emerson, Thoreau, and the Double Consciousness," *New England Quarterly*, XLI (1968), 40–50; Gloria C. Erlich: "Deadly Innocence: Hawthorne's Dark Women," *ibid.*, 163–79; Herman Melville: *Pierre; or, The Ambiguities*, ed. Henry A. Murray (1852; New York, 1949); William K. Spofford: "Melville's Ambiguities: A Re-evaluation of 'The Town-Ho's Story,'" *American Literature*, XLI (1969), 264–9; Edward Wagenknecht: *John Greenleaf Whittier: A Portrait in Paradox* (New York, 1967); Edmund Wilson: "The Ambiguity of Henry James," in *The Question of Henry James*, ed. F. W. Dupee (New York, 1945), 160–90; Ellen D. Leyburn: *Strange Alloy. The Relation of Comedy to Tragedy in the Fiction of Henry James* (Chapel Hill, 1968); and Jean F. Blackall: *Jamesian Ambiguity and the Sacred Fount* (Ithaca, 1965).

In *American Painting of the Nineteenth Century. Realism, Idealism, and the American Experience* (New York, 1969), Barbara Novak defines persuasively a new genre of American landscape painting, revolving around "luminism," which combined a conceptualism based partially on Emersonian transcendental thought with scrupulous observation of visual facts. At the opening of the new National Portrait Gallery in Washington in 1968, the museum staff produced a splendid exhibition and catalog entitled *This New Man. A Discourse in Portraits*, ed. J. Benjamin Townsend. Among the subjects on display were Joseph Brant, "Noble Savage"; William Cullen Bryant, "City Editor and Country

Poet"; Henry Clay, "The Intemperate Moderator"; John Dewey, "Practical Cogitator"; and John D. Rockefeller, "Benevolent Monopolist."

Chapter 9—The Contrapuntal Civilization

Political institutions and ideas in modern America have been examined with attention to their contradictory tendencies by J. William Fulbright: *The Arrogance of Power* (New York, 1966), 245–58 ("The Two Americas"); Sidney Hook: *The Paradoxes of Freedom* (Berkeley, 1962); Robert G. McCloskey, "The American Ideology," in *Continuing Crisis in American Politics*, ed. Marian D. Irish (Englewood Cliffs, 1963), 10–25; John H. Bunzel: *Anti-Politics in America. Reflections on the Anti-Political Temper and Its Distortions of the Democratic Process* (New York, 1967); Arnold S. Kaufman: *The Radical Liberal. New Man in American Politics* (New York, 1968); Robert H. Finch and R. C. Cornvelle: *The New Conservative-Liberal Manifesto* (San Diego, 1968); and Brooks Hays: *Hotbed of Tranquility. My Life in Five Worlds* (New York, 1968), a profoundly American autobiography. Hays describes a card game in which one of the players looks up and says sharply: "Now play the cards fair, Reuben! I know what I dealt you."

The ways in which Americans view other peoples, and vice versa, are related to national style in Gabriel A. Almond: *The American People and Foreign Policy* (New York, 1960), ch. 3; Louis L. Gerson: *The Hyphenate in Recent American Politics and Diplomacy* (Lawrence, 1964); Joseph P. Lyford, ed.: *The Agreeable Autocracies. A Series of Conversations on American Institutions* (New York, 1961); and Joseph M. Franz, ed.: *As Others See Us. The United States Through Foreign Eyes* (Princeton, 1959).

Paradoxical aspects of the contemporary economy are treated in Kenneth E. Boulding, "America's Economy: The Qualified Uproarious Success," in *America Now*, ed. John G. Kirk (New York, 1968), 143–61; Richard S. Morrison: *The Paradox of Capitalism. A Discussion of Certain of the Inner Contradictions of Our System of Free Capitalism and How They May Be Resolved* (New York, 1964); Lauren Soth: *An Embarrassment of Plenty* (New York, 1965); Samm Sinclair Baker: *The Permissible Lie. The Inside Truth About Advertising* (Cleveland, 1968); and Sidney Lens: *Poverty. America's Enduring Paradox* (New York, 1969).

Incongruities in American social life are looked at by W. Lloyd Warner: *American Life. Dream and Reality* (Chicago, 1953);

Hendrik Ruitenbeek: *The Individual and the Crowd: A Study of Identity in America* (New York, 1964); Robin M. Williams, Jr.: *Strangers Next Door. Ethnic Relations in American Communities* (Englewood Cliffs, 1964); Patricia C. Sexton: *The Feminized Male. Classrooms, White Collars and the Decline of Manliness* (New York, 1969); Harry S. Broudy: *Paradox and Promise. Essays on American Life and Education* (Englewood Cliffs, 1961); and Gregory P. Stone: "American Sports: Play and Dis-Play," *Chicago Review*, IX (1955), 83–100.

Writers concerned with the American south have been especially inclined to comment upon anomalous tendencies there. See C. Vann Woodward: "The Irony of Southern History," in Woodward: *The Burden of Southern History* (Baton Rouge, 1960), 167–91; Allen Guttmann: "The Paradox of Southern Liberalism," in Guttmann: *The Conservative Tradition in America* (New York, 1967), 32–46; Frank Vandiver, ed.: *The Idea of the South* (Chicago, 1964); and T. Harry Williams: *Romance and Realism in Southern Politics* (Athens, 1961).

Dilemmas of dissidence and dissent are explored by Christopher Lasch: *The New Radicalism in America, 1889–1963: The Intellectual as a Social Type* (New York, 1965), ch. 9, "The Anti-Intellectualism of the Intellectuals"; Lasch: *The Agony of the American Left* (New York, 1969); Gershon Legman: *Love and Death. A Study in Censorship* (New York, 1949); Nathan Glazer: "America's Race Paradox. The Gap Between Social Progress and Political Despair," *Encounter*, XXXI (1968), 9–18; and Eugene D. Genovese: "The Influence of the Black Power Movement on Historical Scholarship," *Daedalus*, IC (1970), 473–94.

Turning finally to modern American literature, I find that the characters of Conrad Richter's historical novels are persistently practical idealists. Sayward Luckett in *The Trees* (New York, 1940) and Henner Frey in *The Free Man* (New York, 1943) use the most expedient means in achieving idealistic ends. *The Crucible* (New York, 1959) by Arthur Miller dramatizes brilliantly the agony of a semi-innocent man who must confess falsely if he wants to live, but who finally gains the courage to insist upon his innocence and be hanged.

John Steinbeck's "Paradox and Dream" appears in his pictorial essay *America and Americans* (New York, 1966), 29–34. Norman Mailer, with his usual mixture of guile and gall, has identified himself as "The White Negro" in *Advertisements for Myself* (New York, 1959), 337–58; and as a "Left Conservative" in *The Armies of the Night: History as a Novel, The Novel as History* (New York,

1968), especially 67–8, 125, 168. John Barth has been trying to write for "printed voice"; see *Lost in the Funhouse. Fiction for Print, Tape, Live Voice* (New York, 1968).

One can only hope that America has not and will not become what William Faulkner feared in *Go Down, Moses:* a "gilded pustule." Be not gilded, nor gelded, nor gulled.

INDEX

A

Michael Kammen was born in Rochester, New York, in 1936. He was graduated from The George Washington University in 1958 and received his A.M. (1959) and Ph.D. (1964) from Harvard University, where he was an instructor in history, 1964–5. He has taught at Cornell University since 1965, becoming professor in 1969, and was a Fellow of the Humanities Center at Johns Hopkins University, 1968–9. The National Endowment for the Humanities has selected him as a Senior Fellow for 1972–3. He is the author of *A Rope of Sand: The Colonial Agents, British Politics, and the American Revolution* (1968) and *Empire & Interest: The American Colonies and the Politics of Mercantilism* (1970), editor of *Politics and Society in Colonial America: Democracy or Deference?* (1967), *The Contrapuntal Civilization: Essays Toward a New Understanding of the American Experience* (1971), and *The History of the Province of New-York* by William Smith, Jr. (1972), and co-editor of *The Glorious Revolution: Documents on the Colonial Crisis of 1689* (1964).

VINTAGE HISTORY—AMERICAN

VINTAGE CRITICISM,
LITERATURE, MUSIC, AND ART

VINTAGE BIOGRAPHY AND AUTOBIOGRAPHY

VINTAGE BELLES-LETTRES